Russian

Phrasebook & Dictionary

D1319672

Acknowledgments

Product Editor Bruce Evans

Language Writers Catherine Eldridge, James Jenkin, Grant Taylor

Cover Image Researcher Naomi Parker

Thanks

James Hardy, Valentina Kremenchutskaya, Campbell McKenzie, Angela Tinson, Tony Wheeler, Juan Winata

Published by Lonely Planet Global Limited

CRN 554153

7th Edition – September 2018

ISBN 978 1 78657 463 3

Text © Lonely Planet 2018

Cover Image State Historical Museum, Moscow. Damir Karan/ Getty ©

Printed in China   10 9 8 7 6 5 4 3 2 1

Contact lonelyplanet.com/contact

MIX
Paper from
responsible sources
FSC® C021741

HOW TO USE THIS BOOK

Look out for the following icons throughout the book:

'Shortcut' Phrase
Easy to remember alternative to the full phrase

Q&A Pair
'Question-and-answer' pair – we suggest a response to the question asked

Look For
Phrases you may see on signs, menus etc

Listen For
Phrases you may hear from officials, locals etc

Language Tip
An insight into the foreign language

Culture Tip
An insight into the local culture

How to read the phrases:
- Coloured words and phrases throughout the book are phonetic guides to help you pronounce the foreign language.
- Lists of phrases with tinted background are options you can choose to complete the phrase above them.

These abbreviations will help you choose the right words and phrases in this book:

a	adjective	**lit**	literal	**pol**	polite
adv	adverb	**m**	masculine	**sg**	singular
f	feminine	**n**	neuter	**v**	verb
inf	informal	**pl**	plural		

Contents

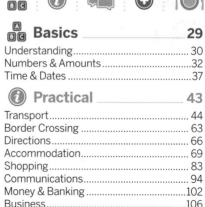

PAGE 209

📖 Menu Decoder
Dishes and ingredients explained –
order with confidence and try new foods.

PAGE 217

📖 Two-Way Dictionary
Quick reference vocabulary guide –
3500 words to help you communicate.

INTRO

Russian

русский *rus·ki*

Who Speaks Russian?

WIDELY UNDERSTOOD

ARMENIA · AZERBAIJAN
BELARUS · ESTONIA
GEORGIA · KAZAKHSTAN
KYRGYZSTAN · LATVIA
LITHUANIA · MOLDOVA
TAJIKISTAN
TURKMENISTAN
UKRAINE
UZBEKISTAN

OFFICIAL LANGUAGE

RUSSIA

Why Bother

Admirers of Russian literature claim that the 'Slavic soul' of writers such as Chekhov or Tolstoy can't be fully appreciated in translation. For the less ambitious, the language will bring you closer to deciphering the 'riddle wrapped in a mystery inside an enigma' that is Russia.

Distinctive Sounds

Rolled r and guttural kh (as in the name Bach).

Russian Script

Russian uses Cyrillic script, developed from Ancient Greek

150 MILLION
speak Russian as their
first language

120 MILLION
speak Russian as their
second language

letters in the 9th century to translate the Bible into Old Church Slavonic. Several Cyrillic letters are the same as those in the Roman alphabet. Note, however, that some Cyrillic letters are used for a different sound: Cyrillic 'B' is the Roman 'V', 'H' is used for 'N', 'P' for 'R' and 'C' for 'S'.

Russian Lexicon

Russian boasts a rich lexicon and highly colourful expressions. This linguistic flamboyance has thankfully resisted the influence of dour communist style and the 'socrealist' literature of the 20th century. For example, if something is impossible to pronounce, just say *Язык сломаешь!* yi·*zihk* sla·ma·*yish* (literally 'You'll break your tongue!').

False Friends

Warning: some Russian words look like English words but have a different meaning altogether, eg *магазин* ma·ga·*zin* is a shop, not a magazine (which is *журнал* zhur·*nal* in Russian).

Language Family

Russian belongs to the East Slavic group of Slavonic languages. Close relatives include Belarusian and Ukrainian.

Must-Know Grammar

Russian words can have a number of different endings, depending on their role in the sentence. There's also a polite and informal word for 'you' (*вы* vih and *ты* tih respectively).

Donations to English

Several – you may recognise *apparatchik, sputnik, steppe, tundra, tsar, vodka* ...

5 Phrases to Learn Before You Go

1 **Is this Moscow or local time?**
Это московское или местное время?
e·ta ma·*skof*·ska·ye i·li *myes*·na·ye *vryem*·ya

Russia has 11 time zones but the entire country's rail and air networks run on Moscow time. Ask if you're not certain what time zone your transport is running on.

2 **I live in Moscow, I won't pay that much.**
Я живу в Москве, я не буду платить так много.
ya zhih·*vu* v mask·*vye* ya nye *bu*·du pla·*tit'* tak *mno*·ga

Taxi drivers and market sellers sometimes try to charge foreigners more, so you may want to bargain in Russian.

3 **Are you serving?**
Вы обслуживаете? vih aps·*lu*·zhih·va·it·ye

It may be hard to attract the attention of workers in the service industry – if you want to get served, use this polite expression.

4 **I don't drink alcohol.**
Я не пью спиртного.
ya nye pyu spirt·*no*·va

Refusing a drink from generous locals can be very difficult, so if you're really not in the mood you'll need a firm, clear excuse.

5 **May I have an official receipt, please?**
Дайте мне официальную расписку, пожалуйста.
deyt·ye mnye a·fi·tsi·*yal'*·nu·yu ras·*pis*·ku pa·*zhal*·sta

Russian authorities might expect an unofficial payment to expedite their service, so always ask for an official receipt.

10 Phrases to Sound Like a Local

What's new?	**Что нового?**	shto *no*·va·va
Sure!	**Конечно!**	kan·*yesh*·na
Great!	**Отлично!**	at·*lich*·na
Maybe.	**Может быть.**	*mo*·zhiht biht'
No way!	**Вы шутите!**	vih *shu*·tit·ye
Just a minute.	**Минутку.**	mi·*nut*·ku
Just joking.	**Я шучу.**	ya shu·*chu*
No problem!	**Ничего!**	ni·chi·*vo*
Fine.	**Нормально.**	nar·*mal'*·na
It's a nightmare!	**Кошмар!**	kash·*mar*

ABOUT RUSSIAN

Pronunciation

Many Russian sounds are also found in English, and the less familiar ones aren't difficult to master. Use the coloured pronunciation guides to become familiar with them, then read from the Cyrillic alphabet when you feel more confident.

Despite the Russian Federation's vast expanse and the age of the language itself, there are remarkably few variations in Russian pronunciation and vocabulary – for much of the last century only the teaching of the 'literary' language has been permitted. This phrasebook is written in standard Russian as it's spoken around Moscow, and you're sure to be understood by Russian speakers everywhere.

Vowel Sounds

Russian vowels are relatively simple to pronounce:

SYMBOL	ENGLISH EQUIVALENT	RUSSIAN EXAMPLE	TRANSLITERATION
a	path	да	da
ai	aisle	май	mai
e	ten	это	e·ta
ey	they	бассейн	bas·yeyn
i	ski	мир	mir
ih	any	мыло	mih·la
o	more	дом	dom
oy	boy	сырой	sih·roy
u	put	ужин	u·zhihn

Consonant Sounds

Most consonants are similar to English sounds, so they won't cause you too much difficulty. The apostrophe is used in our pronunciation guides (eg in *бедность byed*·nast') to show that the consonant before it is pronounced with a soft y sound.

SYMBOL	ENGLISH EQUIVALENT	RUSSIAN EXAMPLE	TRANSLITERATION
b	bit	брат	brat
ch	chip	чай	chai
d	day	вода	va·*da*
f	fun	кофе	*ko*·fi
g	goat	город	*go*·rat
k	king	сок	sok
kh	Bach	смех	smyekh
l	lump	лифт	lift
m	my	место	*mye*·sta
n	not	нога	na·*ga*
p	put	письмо	pis·*mo*
r	rib (but rolled)	река	ri·*ka*
s	sit	снег	snyek
sh	shop	душа	du·*sha*
t	ton	так	tak
ts	hits	отец	at·*yets*
v	vet	врач	vrach
y	toy	мой	moy
z	zoo	звук	zvuk
zh	pleasure	жизнь	zhihzn'
'	like a soft y	власть	vlast'

Word Stress

Russian stress is free (it can fall on any syllable) and mobile (it can change in different forms of the same word). Each word has only one stressed syllable, which you'll need to learn as you go. In the meantime, follow our pronunciation guides which have the stressed syllable marked in italics.

Intonation

You can change a statement into a question by simply changing your intonation, or the way you raise or lower your voice in a sentence.

In a statement (like the first example below), keep your voice level and drop it in the last word, as in English.

In a yes/no question (in the second example) keep your voice level, but then raise your tone in the last word and drop it again right at the end.

This is our hotel.	Это наша гостиница. e·ta *na*·sha gas·*ti*·nit·sa
Is this our hotel?	Это наша гостиница? e·ta *na*·sha gas·*ti*·nit·sa

Reading & Writing

Russian uses a variant on the Cyrillic script, which was devised in the 9th century by the Greek missionary St Cyril. He used a modified Greek alphabet to translate the Bible into a language called Old Church Slavonic.

The current Russian alphabet has developed from this writing system. It consists of 31 letters and two signs – hard and soft. As the table on the next page shows, the alphabet includes the letter *Ё ё* yo (which is used in dictionaries and grammars for non-native speakers) but in Russia it's usually written as *E e*. For spelling purposes (eg when you spell your name to book into a hotel), the pronunciation of each letter is also provided. The order shown in the alphabet table has been used in the **menu decoder** and **russian–english dictionary**.

The 'soft' sign ь and the 'hard' sign ъ don't have sounds of their own, but show in writing whether the consonant before them is pronounced 'soft' (with a slight y sound after it) or 'hard' (as it's written). The hard sign isn't included in our pronunciation guides as it's very rarely used.

Just as letters in Latin script look different if they're in roman font (a) or in italics *(a)*, so too do some lower-case Cyrillic letters. To eyes accustomed to English script, recognising these letters in the two different written forms can be a challenge. Pay attention to the following pairs of Cyrillic letters – listed in roman/italic font – when reading menus, schedules and signs: г/*г*, д/*д*, и/*и*, й/*й*, т/*т*.

Just like in the English alphabet, the pronunciation of some vowels and consonants in the Cyrillic alphabet can vary from the standard sound. Even so, if you read a Cyrillic word phonetically you should be understood, and as you listen to Russians speaking you'll pick up on the sound variations.

~ **RUSSIAN ALPHABET** ~

А а	a	**К к**	ka	**Х х**	kha
Б б	be	**Л л**	el	**Ц ц**	tse
В в	ve	**М м**	em	**Ч ч**	che
Г г	ge	**Н н**	en	**Ш ш**	sha
Д д	de	**О о**	o	**Щ щ**	shcha
Е е	ye	**П п**	pe	**Ъ ъ**	*tvyor*·dih znak
Ё ё	yo	**Р р**	er	**Ы ы**	ih
Ж ж	zhe	**С с**	es	**Ь ь**	*myakh*·ki znak
З з	ze	**Т т**	te	**Э э**	e
И и	i	**У у**	u	**Ю ю**	yu
Й й	i·*krat*·ka·ye	**Ф ф**	ef	**Я я**	ya

ABOUT RUSSIAN

Grammar

This chapter is designed to explain the main grammatical structures you need in order to make your own sentences. Look under each heading – listed in alphabetical order – for information on functions which these grammatical categories express in a sentence. For example, demonstratives are used for giving instructions, so you'll need them to tell the taxi driver where your hotel is, etc. A glossary of grammatical terms is included at the end of the chapter to help you.

Adjectives & Adverbs

Describing People/Things • Doing Things

Adjectives normally come before the noun, and they change their gender, number and case endings to agree with the nouns they describe. In our **dictionary** and any others you may use, adjectives are given in the masculine form (generally ending in *-ый* -ih). This ending changes to *-ая* -a·ya to describe a feminine noun, *-ое* -a·ye for neuter nouns, and *-ые* -ih·ye for plural ones. We've used *красивый* kra·si·vih (beautiful) in the examples below. See also **case**, **gender** and **plurals**.

This is a beautiful city.	Это красивый город. (lit: this beautiful city-**m-nom**) e·ta kra·si·vih go·rat
This is a beautiful river.	Это красивая река. (lit: this beautiful river-**f-nom**) e·ta kra·si·va·ya ri·ka

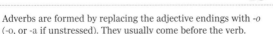
Adverbs are formed by replacing the adjective endings with *-o* (-о, or -а if unstressed). They usually come before the verb.

He played beautifully.   Он прекрасно играл.
(lit: he beautifully played)
on pri·*kras*·na i·*gral*

You can use this *-o* form to make simple sentences.

It's cold.   Холодно. (lit: cold-o)
kho·lad·na

That's interesting.   Интересно. (lit: interesting-o)
in·tir·*yes*·na

Articles

Naming People/Things

Russian doesn't have an equivalent for 'the' or 'a' – *турист* tu·*rist* means 'the tourist' or 'a tourist', depending on context.

Be

Doing Things • Negating

The Russian verb 'be' isn't used in the present tense (ie 'am', 'is' and 'are').

I'm a tourist.   Я турист.
(lit: I-**nom** tourist-**nom**)
ya tu·*rist*

To make a sentence negative, just use the word *не* nye (not).

I'm not a tourist.   Я не турист.
(lit: I-**nom** not tourist-**nom**)
ya nye tu·*rist*

See also **verbs** for more information on past and future tenses.

Case

Doing Things • Giving Instructions • Indicating Location • Naming People/Things • Possessing

Russian uses cases to indicate a noun or pronoun's role and its relationship to other words in a sentence. Russian has six cases (indicated by word endings), as shown below. The word lists in this book and in the **dictionary** and **menu decoder** provide words in the nominative case – this will always be understood, even when it isn't completely correct within a sentence.

~ CASES ~

NOMINATIVE nom – shows the subject of a sentence	
The guide has paid.	Гид уже заплатил. (lit: guide-**nom** already paid) git u·zhe za·pla·til
ACCUSATIVE acc – shows the direct object of a sentence	
Did you see the play?	Вы посмотрели пьесу? (lit: you-**sg-pol-nom** saw play-**acc**) vih pas·mat·rye·li pye·su
GENITIVE gen – shows possession ('of')	
The price of the room is too high.	Цена номера слишком высокая. (lit: price-**nom** room-**gen** too high) tse·na no·mi·ra slish·kam vih·so·ka·ya
DATIVE dat – shows the indirect object of a sentence	
I gave my passport to the policeman.	Я дал паспорт милиционеру. (lit: I-**nom** gave passport-**acc** policeman-**dat**) ya dal pas·part mi·lit·sih·an·ye·ru
INSTRUMENTAL inst – shows how something is done	
You need to write with a pen.	Нужно писать ручкой. (lit: must write pen-**inst**) nuzh·na pi·sat' ruch·kay
PREPOSITIONAL prep – used after на na (on), в v (in) and o a (about)	
The timetable is in the bag.	Расписание в сумке. (lit: timetable-**nom** in bag-**prep**) ras·pi·sa·ni·ye f sum·kye

The most common case endings for nouns are presented below. You'll see that masculine and neuter nouns share most endings. For plural words, use the nominative plural ending (see **plurals**) and you'll be understood.

~ CASE ENDINGS ~

	m example паспорт (passport)	f example машина (car)	n example блюдо (dish)
nom	ends in a consonant	-a -a	-o -o/a*
	паспорт *pas*·part	машина ma·*shih*·na	блюдо *blyu*·da
acc	ends in a consonant	-y -u	-o -o/a*
	паспорт *pas*·part	машину ma·*shih*·nu	блюдо *blyu*·da
gen	-a -a	-ы -ih	-a -a
	паспорта *pas*·par·ta	машины ma·*shih*·nih	блюда *blyu*·da
dat	-y -u	-e -ye	-y -u
	паспорту *pas*·par·tu	машине ma·*shih*·ye	блюду *blyu*·du
inst	-ом -om/-am*	-ой -oy/-ay*	-ом -om/-am*
	паспортом *pas*·par·tam	машиной ma·*shih*·nay	блюдом *blyu*·dam
prep	-e -ye	-e -ye	-e -ye
	паспорте *pas*·part·ye	машине ma·*shihn*·ye	блюде *blyud*·ye

* Indicates alternative pronunciation of an ending (eg -o -o/-a) depending on the stress of the word it's attached to.

Note that the genitive case is not only used to show possession, but also with amounts, prices and most quantifiers (such as 'much' or 'many').

A hundred roubles. Сто рублей.
(lit: hundred roubles-**gen**)
sto rub·*lyey*

I haven't got much money.	У меня мало денег. (lit: at me-**gen** little money-**gen**) u min·*ya* ma·la dyen·ik

Keep in mind too that, except for the three prepositions listed in the table on page 16, all other prepositions are not followed by the prepositional case. As in the next example, *c* s (with) is followed by the instrumental case. See also **prepositions**.

I'm here with my husband.	Я здесь с мужем. (lit: I-**nom** here with husband-**inst**) ya zdyes' s *mu*·zhem

Demonstratives

Giving Instructions • Indicating Location • Pointing Things Out

The Russian word *это e*·ta means 'this/that is' and 'these/those are', and is followed by the nominative case (see **case**).

This is my husband.	Это мой муж. (lit: this-is my husband-**nom**) *e*·ta moy mush
Those are your things.	Это ваши вещи. (lit: those-are your things-**nom**) *e*·ta *va*·shih *vye*·shi

Gender

Naming People/Things

Russian nouns have gender – masculine **m**, feminine **f** or neuter **n**. You need to learn the grammatical gender for each noun as you go, but you can generally recognise it by the noun's ending – masculine nouns end in a consonant, feminine in -*a* -a, and neuter in -*o* -o. You need to know gender to mark case and to form adjectives and past tense verbs. The nouns in this book's word lists, the **dictionary** and **menu decoder** all have their gender marked as required.

passport	паспорт m	*pas*·part
visa	виза f	*vi*·za
consulate	консульство n	*kon*·sulst·va

See also **adjectives & adverbs**, **case** and **verbs**.

Negatives

Negating

Negative sentences are formed by adding the word *не* nye (not) before the verb:

| I read Russian. | Я читаю порусски.
(lit: I-nom read Russian)
ya chi·*ta*·yu pa·*rus*·ki |
| I don't read Russian. | Я не читаю порусски.
(lit: I-nom not read Russian)
ya nye chi·*ta*·yu pa·*rus*·ki |

Nouns

Naming People/Things

Russian nouns have many forms – various endings are used to show their role in a sentence. See **case**, **gender** and **plurals**.

Personal Pronouns

Doing Things • Giving Instructions • Naming People/Things • Possessing

Personal pronouns ('I', 'you', etc) change according to case to indicate the person's role in a sentence (eg whether the person is a subject or an object). In the table below, we've only shown the nominative case of the pronouns to keep it simple. These forms won't always be correct in every sentence, but you'll be understood.

I want to eat.	Я хочу есть. (lit: I-nom want eat) *ya kha·chu yest'*
Give me a map.	Дайте мне карту. (lit: give me-dat map-acc) *day·tye mnye kar·tu*

~ PERSONAL PRONOUNS ~

I	я	ya	**we**	мы	mih
you sg inf	ты	tih	**you** pl inf&pol	вы	vih
you sg pol	вы	vih			
he	он	on	**they**	они	a·ni
she	она	a·na			
it	оно	a·no			

Note that Russian has a polite and an informal word for 'you' – see the box **polite & informal** (p140) for more information.

Plurals

Naming People/Things

Russian generally uses the ending *-ы* -ih to show plurals – it won't always be correct, but you should be understood fine. Just add *-ы* to a word ending in a consonant, and use it to replace the final *-a* -a on feminine nouns. One exception: for neuter nouns simply replace the final *-o* -o/-a with *-a* -a (this may not always change the pronunciation). See also **gender**.

	~ SINGULAR ~		~ PLURAL ~	
m	**tourist**	турист tu·*rist*	**tourists**	туристы tu·*ris*·tih
f	**apartment**	квартира kvar·*ti*·ra	**apartments**	квартиры kvar·*ti*·rih
n	**dish**	блюдо *blyu*·da	**dishes**	блюда *blyu*·da

Possession

Naming People/Things • Possessing

To say someone 'has' something, say *y ... есть ...* u ... yest' ...
(lit: at someone-**gen** there-is something-**nom**).

Do you have a menu? У вас есть меню?
(lit: at you-**gen** there-is
menu-**nom**)
u vas yest' min·*yu*

You can also use possessive adjectives (the equivalents of 'my',
'your', etc) to talk about ownership. The words *его* yi·*vo* (his),
её yi·*yo* (her) and *их* ikh (their) don't change, but the trans-
lations of 'my' and 'your' take different endings to match the
gender and case of the noun they describe. See also **case**,
gender and **plurals**.

~ POSSESSIVE ADJECTIVES ~

	m	f	n	pl
my	мой moy	моя ma·*ya*	моё ma·*yo*	мои ma·*yi*
your sg pol & pl	ваш vash	ваша va·*sha*	ваше va·*she*	ваши va·*shih*

Here's my visa. Вот моя виза.
(lit: here my visa-**nom**)
vot ma·*ya vi*·za

Is this your passport?	Это ваш паспорт? (lit: this your-**pl** passport-**nom**) *e*·ta vash *pas*·part

Prepositions

Indicating Location • Pointing Things Out

Russian uses prepositions – small words like *в* v (in/at) and *на* na (on) – to express where something is. After any preposition, add *-e* -ye to the noun:

bus	автобус (lit: bus-**nom**)	af·*to*·bus
in the bus	в автобусе (lit: in bus-**prep**)	v af·*to*·bus·ye

The table below shows some useful prepositions and the case of the noun they're attached to. See also **case**.

~ PREPOSITIONS ~

			noun case
about	о	o	prep
in/at (place)	в	v	prep
near	рядом с	*rya*·dam s	inst
on/at (event)	на	na	prep
to	до	do	gen
via	через	*che*·ris	acc
with	с	s	inst

Questions

Asking Questions

You can change a statement into a yes/no question simply by making your voice rise and fall sharply towards the end of a sentence. To make it really clear that you're asking a question, you can also add the word *да* da (yes) at the end. See also the information on intonation in **pronunciation** (p12).

This is my room.	Это мой номер. (lit: this my room-**nom**) *e*·ta moy *no*·mir
Is this my room?	Это мой номер? (lit: this my room-**nom**) *e*·ta moy *no*·mir
This is my room, isn't it?	Это мой номер, да? (lit: this my room-**nom** yes) *e*·ta moy *no*·mir da

To ask about specific information, just add one of the question words from the table below to the start of a sentence.

Where are you studying Russian?	Где вы изучаете русский язык? (lit: where you-**sg-pol-nom** study Russian language-**acc**) gdye vih i·zu·*cha*·i·tye *rus*·ki yi·*zihk*

~ QUESTION WORDS ~

How?	Как?	kak
How many/much?	Сколько?	*skol'*·ka
What?	Что?	shto
When?	Когда?	kag·*da*
Where?	Где?	gdye
Where to?	Куда?	ku·*da*
Who?	Кто?	kto
Why?	Почему?	pa·chi·*mu*

Verbs

Doing Things • Giving Instructions

Russian has three tenses – past, present, and future. Tenses are formed by taking the infinitive (or 'dictionary form') of the verb, dropping the *-ать* -at' or *-ить* -it' endings, and adding the appropriate tense ending. For an English verb, the dictionary usually gives two Russian infinitives – the entry for 'read' will give *читать* chi·*tat'* and *прочитать* pra·chi·*tat'*. The first form shows the 'imperfective aspect', and is used for habitual or continuing actions (ie when it's not important if the action is completed or not). It can be used both in the present and the past tense.

I often read in Russian.	Я часто читаю порусски. (lit: I-**nom** often read-**imp** Russian) ya *chas*·ta chi·*ta*·yu pa·*rus*·ki
Yesterday I did some reading.	Я вчера читала. (lit: I-**nom** yesterday read-**imp**) ya f·chi·*ra* chi·*ta*·la

The second form shows the 'perfective aspect', and is used to emphasise the result of an action. This stresses that a single event is finished, and the main use is for completed past actions.

I finished reading the book yesterday.	Я вчера прочитала книгу. (lit: I-**nom** yesterday read-**perf** book-**acc**) ya f·chi·*ra* pra·chi·*ta*·la *kni*·gu

The table opposite shows the present tense endings for perfective and imperfective verbs ending in *-ать* -at' or *-ить* -it'. Both kinds of verb use the same set of endings.

~ PRESENT TENSE ENDINGS ~

	verb ending	читать (read)	**verb ending**	говорить (speak)
I	-ю / -yu	читаю chi·ta·yu	-ю / -yu	говорю ga·var·yu
you sg inf	-ешь / -yish'	читаешь chi·ta·yish'	-ишь / -ish'	говоришь ga·va·rish'
you sg pol	-ете / -yit·ye	читаете chi·ta·yit·ye	-ите / -it·ye	говорите ga·va·rit·ye
he/she	-ет / -yit	читает chi·ta·yit	-ит / -it	говорит ga·va·rit
we	-ем / -yim	читаем chi·ta·yim	-им / -im	говорим ga·va·rim
you pl	-ете / -yit·ye	читаете chi·ta·yit·ye	-ите / -it·ye	говорите ga·va·rit·ye
they	-ют / -yut	читают chi·ta·yut	-ят / -yat	говорят ga·var·yat

Do you speak English?   Вы говорите по-английски?
(lit: you-sg-pol-nom speak English)
vih ga·va·ri·tye pa·an·gli·ski

Past tense endings depend on the gender and number of the subject doing the action. For most perfective and imperfective verbs, drop the final -*ть* -t' and add the endings in the table below. We've used the example *купить* ku·pit (buy).

~ PAST TENSE ENDINGS ~

m sg	f sg	n sg	pl • you sg pol
-л -l	-ла -la	-ло -lo	-ли -li

He bought a ticket.   Он купил билет.
(lit: he-nom bought ticket-acc)
on ku·pil bil·yet

Did you buy a ticket?	Вы купили билет? pol (lit: you-**nom-sg-pol** bought ticket-**acc**) vih ku·*pi*·li bil·*yet*

Grammatically, perfective and imperfective verbs take different forms in the future tense. An easy way to sidestep this complexity is to say a sentence in the present tense, and add a 'future time marker' (eg 'tomorrow') to it, just like in English. You can find these in the **dictionary**.

I'm working tomorrow.	Я работаю завтра. (lit: I-**nom** work tomorrow) ya ra·*bo*·ta·yu *zaf*·tra

Word Order

Asking Questions • Doing Things • Giving Instructions • Making a Statement • Negating

Russian is often said to have free word order, as the case endings in words show who is doing what, regardless of where each word appears in the sentence. Normally, however, Russian word order is subject–verb–object, like in English. Note that pronoun objects like 'her' or 'it' come before verbs.

I love beer.	Я люблю пиво. (lit: I-**nom** love beer-**acc**) ya lyub·*lyu* pi·va
I love you.	Я вас люблю. (lit: I-**nom** you-**sg-pol-acc** love-**pres**) ya vas lyub·*lyu*

Russians also start a sentence with background information, and build up to crucial new information – like a punchline in a joke.

There's no toilet on the bus!

В автобусе нет туалета!
(lit: in bus-**prep** no toilet-**gen**)
v af·*to*·bus·ye nyet tu·al·*ye*·ta

For more information on word order, also see **adjectives & adverbs**, **negating** and **questions**.

~ GLOSSARY ~

accusative (case)	type of *case marking* used for the *direct object* – 'the cosmonaut opened **the airlock**'
adjective	a word that describes something – 'she floated out into **deep** space'
adverb	a word saying how an action is done – 'she breathed **deeply** and started her spacewalk'
article	the words 'a', 'an' and 'the'
aspect	Russian verbs have two aspects – *perfective* and *imperfective*
case (marking)	word ending which tells us the role of a thing or person in the sentence
dative (case)	type of *case marking* for the *indirect object* – 'she drifted back towards **the space station**'
gender	Russian nouns and pronouns are defined as masculine, feminine or neuter
genitive (case)	type of *case marking* showing possession – '**the space station's** door loomed before her'
imperfective (aspect)	*verb aspect* showing an incomplete action – 'she **was waiting** for airlock clearance'
infinitive	the dictionary form of the *verb* – 'the door began to **open** ...'
instrumental (case)	type of *case marking* which shows how something is done – 'and she pulled herself up **with the handrails**'
nominative (case)	type of *case marking* which shows the *subject* of the sentence – '**the crew** in the spaceship cheered wildly'
noun	a thing, person or idea – '**the spaceship** rocked'
number	whether a word is singular or plural – 'several **meteorites** had hit the shuttle's **tail**'

continued on p28

continued from p27

object (direct)	the thing or person in the sentence that has the action directed to it – 'the science officer checked **the instrument panel**'
object (indirect)	the recipient of an action – 'the commander sent an order **to the people** in the tail'
perfective (aspect)	*verb aspect* showing a complete action – 'they **fixed** the damage and **reported** back'
possessive pronoun	a word that means 'mine', 'yours', etc
preposition	a word like 'under' in '**under** the control panel'
prepositional (case)	type of *case marking* used after the prepositions на na (on), в v (in) and о a (about)
personal pronoun	a word that means 'I', 'you', etc
quantifiers	a word like 'some', 'all' or 'many'
subject	the thing or person in the sentence that does the action – '**the commander** transmitted a message to ground control'
tense	indicates when an action happens – eg 'breathed' is past tense in 'the whole crew **breathed** a sigh of relief'
verb	the word that tells you what action happened – 'the mission could safely **continue**'

Basics

Understanding

BASICS UNDERSTANDING

KEY PHRASES

Do you speak English?	Вы говорите по-английски?	vih ga·va·*rit*·ye pa·an·*gli*·ski
I don't understand.	Не понимаю.	nye pa·ni·*ma*·yu
What does ... mean?	Что обозначает слово ...?	shto a·baz·na·*cha*·it *slo*·va ...

Q Do you speak (English)?	Вы говорите (по-английски)? vih ga·va·*rit*·ye (pa·an·*gli*·ski)
Q Does anyone speak (English)?	Кто-нибудь говорит (по-английски)? *kto*·ni·bud' ga·va·rit (pa·an·*gli*·ski)
A I speak (English).	Я говорю (по-английски). ya ga·var·*yu* (pa·an·*gli*·ski)
A I don't speak (Russian).	Я не говорю (по-русски). ya nye ga·var·*yu* (pa·*ru*·ski)
A I speak a little.	Я немного говорю. ya nim·*no*·ga ga·var·*yu*
Q Do you understand?	Вы понимаете? vih pa·ni·*ma*·it·ye
A I (don't) understand.	Я (не) понимаю. ya (nye) pa·ni·*ma*·yu
Pardon?	Простите? pras·*tit*·ye
Let's speak (Russian).	Давайте поговорим (по-русски). da·*veyt*·ye pa·ga·va·rim (pa·*ru*·ski)

LANGUAGE TIP

False Friends

Beware of *ложные друзья* lozh·nih·ye druz·ya (false friends) – words which sound like English words but have a different meaning altogether. Using them in the wrong context could confuse, or amuse, the locals.

интеллигентный m	in·ti·lig·yent·nih	cultured
not 'intelligent', which is *умный* um·nih		
машина f	ma·shih·na	car
not 'machine', which is usually *станок* sta·nok		
фамилия f	fa·mi·li·ya	surname
not 'family', which is *семья* sim·ya		

What does ... mean?	Что обозначает слово ...? shto a·baz·na·cha·it slo·va ...
How do you say ... in Russian?	Как будет ... по-русски? kak bu·dit ... pa·ru·ski
How do you pronounce this?	Как это произносится? kak e·ta pra·iz·no·sit·sa
How do you write ...?	Как пишется ...? kak pi·shiht ...
Could you please repeat that?	Повторите, пожалуйста. paf·ta·rit·ye pa·zhal·sta
Could you please write it down?	Запишите, пожалуйста. za·pi·shiht·ye pa·zhal·sta
Could you please speak more slowly?	Говорите помедленее, пожалуйста. ga·va·rit·ye pa·mid·lin·ye·ye pa·zhal·sta

✂	**Slowly, please!**	Помедленее, пожалуйста.	pa·mid·lin·ye·ye pa·zhal·sta

Numbers & Amounts

KEY PHRASES

How much/many?	Сколько?	*skol'*·ka
a little	немножко	nim·*nosh*·ka
a few	немного	nim·*no*·ga
a lot/many	много	*mno*·ga

Cardinal Numbers

The numbers 'one' and 'two' are the only ones which take different forms for masculine, feminine and neuter words. Numbers also change form to reflect their case (see **grammar**, p16) but we've only included the nominative case here.

If you're counting in sequence (one, two, three ...) note that you use the word *раз* ras for 'one'.

1	один/одна/ одно m/f/n	a·*din*/ad·*na*/ ad·*no*
2	два/две m&n/f	dva/dvye
3	три	tri
4	четыре	chi·*tih*·ri
5	пять	pyat'
6	шесть	shest'
7	семь	syem'
8	восемь	*vo*·sim'
9	девять	*dye*·vit'
10	десять	*dye*·sit'
11	одиннадцать	a·*di*·nat·sat'
12	двенадцать	dvi·*nat*·sat'

13	тринадцать	tri·*nat*·sat'
14	четырнадцать	chi·*tihr*·nat·sat'
15	пятнадцать	pit·*nat*·sat'
16	шестнадцать	shihst·*nat*·sat'
17	семнадцать	sim·*nat*·sat'
18	восемнадцать	va·sim·*nat*·sat'
19	девятнадцать	di·vit·*nat*·sat'
20	двадцать	*dvat*·sat'
21	двадцать один	*dvat*·sat' a·*din*
22	двадцать два	*dvat*·sat' dva
30	тридцать	*trit*·sat'
40	сорок	*so*·rak
50	пятьдесят	pi·dis·*yat*
60	шестдесят	shihs·dis·*yat*
70	семьдесят	*syem*'·di·sit
80	восемьдесят	*vo*·sim'·di·sit
90	девяносто	di·vi·*no*·sta
100	сто	sto
132	сто тридцать два	sto *trit*·sat' dva
200	двести	*dvye*·sti
300	триста	*tri*·sta
400	четыреста	chi·*tih*·ri·sta
500	пятьсот	pit'·*sot*
600	шестьсот	shihst'·*sot*
700	семьсот	sim'·*sot*
800	восемьсот	va·sim'·*sot*
900	девятьсот	di·vit'·*sot*
1000	тысяча	*tih*·si·cha
1,000,000	миллион	mi·li·*on*

Ordinal Numbers

Ordinal numbers from 'first' to 'ninth' are irregular, so we've listed them here. To form numbers from 'tenth' onward, drop the ь (shown in the pronunciation guide by the apostrophe ') from the end of the cardinal number and add -ый -ih. For example, *двадцать* dvat·sat' (twenty) becomes *двадцатый* dvat·*sa*·tih (twentieth).

1st	первый	*pyer*·vih
2nd	второй	fta·*roy*
3rd	третий	*trye*·tih
4th	четвёртый	chit·*vyor*·tih
5th	пятый	*pya*·tih
6th	шестой	shih·*stoy*
7th	седьмой	sid'·*moy*
8th	восьмой	vas'·*moy*
9th	девятый	div·*ya*·tih
10th	десятый	dis·*ya*·tih

 Counting in a Shop

If you're asking for a certain number of something in a shop, you need to use a word meaning 'thing' – *штука* shtu·ka – after the number. It changes form depending on the number before it, as shown below.

One, please.	Одну штуку, пожалуйста. ad·*nu* shtu·ku pa·*zhal*·sta
Two/Three/Four, please.	Две/Три/Четыре штуки, пожалуйста. dvye/tri/chi·*tih*·ri shtu·ki pa·*zhal*·sta
Five, please.	Пять штук, пожалуйста. pyat' shtuk pa·*zhal*·sta

BASICS NUMBERS & AMOUNTS

LOOK FOR

It's useful to know how to read Cyrillic dates and abbreviations when you're checking out buildings, artworks and monuments. Centuries are written in Roman numerals.

год (г.)/лет	got/lyet	year
век (в.)	vyek	century
начало	na·*cha*·la	beginning
середина	si·ri·*di*·na	middle
конец	kan·*yets*	end
нашей эры (н.э.)	*na*·shey e·rih	AD (lit: our era)
до нашей эры (до н.э.)	da *na*·shey e·rih	BC (lit: before our era)
десятый век нашей эры	dis·*ya*·tih vyek *na*·shey e·rih	10th century AD

Decimals & Fractions

Russian decimals use a *запятая* za·pi·*ta*·ya (comma) instead of a dot: '2,5' means 'two and a half'. Saying decimals is quite complicated, and the easiest solution is to read out the numbers and the comma in the order you see them. For example, *два запятая пять* dva za·pi·*ta*·ya pyat' (lit: two comma five) will get you by just fine.

a quarter	четверть	*chet*·virt'
a third	треть	tryet'
a half	половина	pa·la·*vi*·na
three-quarters	три четверти	tri *chet*·vir·ti
all	весь pl	vyes'
none	никаких pl	ni·ka·*kikh*

Amounts

How much/many?	Сколько? *skol'*·ka

CULTURE TIP

Russian Currency
The currency of Russia is the *рубль* rubl' (rouble) which is divided into 100 *копейка* kap·*yey*·ka (kopecks). Abbreviations for the rouble are *py* or *p*. Coins come in denominations of one, five, 10 and 50 kopecks, and one, two, five and 10 roubles. Banknotes are available for 50, 100, 500, 1000 and 5000 roubles.

The slang term for '50 roubles' is *полтинник* pal·*ti*·nik (lit: half) while *сотник* *sot*·nik means '100 roubles'.

Please give me ...	Дайте, пожалуйста ...
	deyt·ye pa·*zhal*·sta ...

a few	немного	nim·*no*·ga
less	меньше	*myen*'·she
(just) a little	(только)	(*tol*'·ka)
	немножко	nim·*nosh*·ka
a lot/many	много	*mno*·ga
more	больше	*bol*'·she
some	несколько	*nye*·skal'·ka

For more useful amounts, see **self-catering** (p203).

Time & Dates

KEY PHRASES

What time is it?	Который час?	ka·to·rih chas
At what time ...?	В котором часу ...?	f ka·to·ram chi·su ...
What date?	Какого числа?	ka·ko·va chis·la

Telling the Time

The Russian word *час* chas (hour) also means 'o'clock'. It becomes *часа* chi·sa for two, three and four o'clock, and *часов* chi·sof for five o'clock and later hours. In speech, the Russians use the 12-hour clock, but you'll see 24-hour time written in schedules and timetables.

Q	**What time is it?**	Который час? ka·to·rih chas
A	**It's one o'clock.**	Час. chas
A	**It's (two/three/four) o'clock.**	(Два/Три/Четыре) часа. (dva/tri/chi·tih·ri) chi·sa
A	**It's (10) o'clock.**	(Десять) часов. (dye·sit') chi·sof

Saying the minutes before or after the hour is a bit more complicated. The easiest way is to say the hour plus the minutes, eg 'ten fifteen'. If the minutes are less than 10, say *ноль* nol' (zero) in the middle.

| A | **Five past (10).** | (Десять) ноль пять.
(lit: ten zero five)
(dye·sit') nol' pyat' |
| A | **Quarter past (10).** | (Десять) пятнадцать.
(lit: ten fifteen)
(dye·sit') pit·nat·sat' |

A Half past (10).	(Десять) тридцать. (lit: ten thirty) (dye·sit') trit·sat'
A Twenty to (11).	(Десять) сорок. (lit: ten forty) (dye·sit') so·rak
in the morning (5am–12pm)	утра ut·ra
in the afternoon (12pm–5pm)	дня dnya
in the evening (5pm–12am)	вечера vye·chi·ra
Q At what time ...?	В котором часу ...? f ka·to·ram chi·su ...
A At (10).	В (десять) часов. v (dye·sit') chi·sof
A At (7.57pm).	В (семь пятьдесят семь вечера). (lit: at seven fifty seven in-the-evening) f (syem' pi·dis·yat syem' vye·chi·ra)

The Calendar

Monday	понедельник m	pa·ni·dyel'·nik
Tuesday	вторник m	ftor·nik
Wednesday	среда f	sri·da
Thursday	четверг m	chit·vyerk
Friday	пятница f	pyat·nit·sa
Saturday	суббота f	su·bo·ta
Sunday	воскресенье n	vas·kris·yen'·ye

January	январь m	yin·var'
February	февраль m	fiv·ral'
March	март m	mart
April	апрель m	ap·ryel'
May	май m	mey
June	июнь m	i·yun'
July	июль m	i·yul'
August	август m	av·gust
September	сентябрь m	sint·yabr'
October	октябрь m	akt·yabr'
November	ноябрь m	na·yabr'
December	декабрь m	di·kabr'
Q What date is it today?	Какое сегодня число?	ka·ko·ye si·vod·nya chis·lo
A It's 1 May.	Первое мая. (lit: first May)	pyer·va·ye ma·ya
On what date?	Какого числа?	ka·ko·va chis·la
spring	весна f	vis·na
summer	лето n	lye·ta
autumn/fall	осень f	o·sin'
winter	зима f	zi·ma

Present

now	сейчас	si·chas
today	сегодня	si·vod·nya
tonight	сегодня вечером	si·vod·nya vye·chi·ram
this morning	сегодня утром	si·vod·nya ut·ram
this afternoon	сегодня днём	si·vod·nya dnyom

CULTURE TIP

Russian Holidays

| **New Year (1 January)** | Новый год | *no*·vih got |

Russia's most important secular holiday – friends and family gather for a sumptuous feast on New Year's Eve, and turn on Radio Moscow to hear the Kremlin bells sound at midnight. Everyone toasts with champagne, wishing each other *С Новым годом!* s *no*·vihm *go*·dam (Happy New Year!). The *дед-мороз* dyet·ma·*ros* (Grandfather Frost, ie Santa Claus), brings presents to all good children.

| **Defender of the Motherland Day (23 February)** | День Защитника Родины | dyen' za·*shit*·ni·ka *ro*·di·nih |

A day of great significance to Russian men, as most have served in the army. It's a de facto 'men's day', when women buy gifts like aftershave for the men in their lives.

| **Women's Day (8 March)** | Восьмое марта | vas'·*mo*·ye *mar*·ta |

Also called 'Mother's Day', this celebration calls for men to give flowers to women, and boys to give a present to their female teachers. Some men may cook dinner for the family to make up for the times in the year when they didn't and they feel that maybe they should have.

| **Orthodox Easter (March/April)** | Пасха | *pas*·kha |

Easter is of far greater significance than Christmas to Orthodox Christians. Families gather for lavish celebrations on the Saturday evening. Just before midnight the priest opens the church doors and announces *Христос воскресе!* khris·*tos* vas·*kryes*·ye (Christ is risen!). The congregation responds *Воистину воскресе!* va·*yi*·sti·nu vas·*kryes*·ye (He is truly risen!). The priest leads a procession around the church three times in a symbolic search for Christ's body.

| **Victory Day (9 May)** | День Победы | dyen' pab·ye·dih |

A day of military parades and veterans gathering commemorating victory over the Nazis in WWII, remembered by Russians as the *Великая Отечественная война* vi·*li*·ka·ya at·*ye*·chist·vi·na·ya vey·*na* (Great Patriotic War). Over 20 million people in the former USSR were killed.

this week	на этой неделе	na e·tey nid·yel·ye
this month	в этом месяце	v e·tam *mye*·sit·se
this year	в этом году	v e·tam ga·*du*

Past

day before yesterday	позавчера	pa·zaf·chi·*ra*
(three days) ago	(три дня) назад	(tri dnya) na·*zat*
since (May)	с (мая)	s (*ma*·ya)
yesterday morning	вчера утром	fchi·*ra* ut·ram
yesterday afternoon	вчера днём	fchi·*ra* dnyom
yesterday evening	вчера вечером	fchi·*ra* vye·chi·ram
last night	вчера вечером	fchi·*ra* vye·chi·ram
last week	на прошлой неделе	na *prosh*·ley nid·yel·ye
last month	в прошлом месяце	f *prosh*·lam *mye*·sit·se
last year	в прошлом году	f *prosh*·lam ga·*du*

Future

day after tomorrow	послезавтра	pos·li·*zaf*·tra
in (six days)	через (шесть дней)	*che*·ris (shest' dnyey)
until (June)	до (июня)	da (i·*yun*·ya)
tomorrow morning	завтра утром	*zaf*·tra ut·ram
tomorrow afternoon	завтра днём	*zaf*·tra dnyom
tomorrow evening	завтра вечером	*zaf*·tra *vye*·chi·ram
next week	на следующей неделе	na *slye*·du·yu·shi nid·*yel*·ye
next month	в следующем месяце	f *slye*·du·yu·shim *mye*·sit·se
next year	в следующем году	f *slye*·du·yu·shim ga·*du*

During the Day

after lunch	после обеда	*pos*·lye ab·*ye*·da
dawn	рассвет m	ras·*vyet*
day	день m	dyen'
evening	вечер m	*vye*·chir
midday	полдень m	*pol*·din'
midnight	полночь f	*pol*·nach'
morning	утро n	*ut*·ra
night	ночь f	noch'
sunrise	восход солнца m	vas·*khot* sont·sa
sunset	заход солнца m	za·*khot* sont·sa

Practical

Transport

KEY PHRASES

When's the next bus?	Когда будет следующий автобус?	kag·*da* bu·dit *slye*·du·yu·shi af·*to*·bus
A ticket to ...	Билет на ...	bil·*yet* na ...
Can you tell me when we get to ...?	Скажите, пожалуйста, когда мы подъедем к ...	ska·*zhiht*·ye pa·*zhal*·sta kag·*da* mih pad·*ye*·dim k ...
Please take me to this address.	До этого адреса не довезёте?	da e·ta·va *a*·dri·sa nye da·viz·*yot*·ye
I'd like to hire a car.	Я бы хотел/ хотела взять машину. m/f	ya bih khat·*yel*/ khat·*ye*·la vzyat' ma·*shih*·nu

Getting Around

Which ... goes to (Minsk)?	Какой ... идёт в (Минск)? ka·*koy* ... id·*yot* v (minsk)
Does this ... go to (Moscow)?	Этот ... идёт в (Москву)? e·tat ... id·*yot* v (mask·*vu*)

boat	параход	pa·ra·*khot*
bus	автобус	af·*to*·bus
plane	самолёт	sa·mal·*yot*
train	поезд	*po*·yist

What time does it leave?	Когда он отправляется? kag·da on at·prav·lya·it·sa
When's the first/last (train)?	Когда будет первый/последний (поезд)? kag·da bu·dit pyer·vih/pas·lyed·ni (po·yist)
When's the next (bus)?	Когда будет следующий (автобус)? kag·da bu·dit slye·du·yu·shi (af·to·bus)
How long does it take to get to (Volgograd)?	Сколько времени нужно ехать до (Волгограда)? skol'·ka vrye·mi·ni nuzh·na ye·khat' da (vol·ga·gra·da)
How long will it be delayed?	На сколько он опаздывает? na skol'·ka on a·paz·dih·va·yet
Is this seat occupied?	Это место занято? e·ta mye·sta za·ni·ta
That's my seat.	Это моё место. e·ta ma·yo mye·sta
Please tell me when we get to (Kursk).	Скажите, пожалуйста, когда мы подъедем к (Курску). ska·zhiht·ye pa·zhal·sta kag·da mih pad·ye·dim k (kurs·ku)
Please stop here.	Остановитесь здесь, пожалуйста! a·sta·na·vi·tis' zdyes' pa·zhal·sta
Can we get there by public transport?	Можно ездить туда на общественном транспорте? mozh·na yez·dit' tu·da na ab·shyest·vyen·nam trans·port·ye

| I'd prefer to walk there. | Я предпочитаю идти туда пешком. |
| | ya prit·pa·chi·ta·yu id·ti tu·da pish·kom |

Tickets

| Where do I buy a ticket? | Где можно купить билет? |
| | gdye mozh·na ku·pit' bil·yet |

| A ... ticket (to Novgorod). | Билет ... (на Новгород). |
| | bil·yet ... (na nov·ga·rat) |

1st-class	в первом классе	f pyer·vam klas·ye
2nd-class	во втором классе	va fta·rom klas·ye
child's	для детей	dlya dit·yey
one-way	в один конец	v a·din kan·yets
return	в оба конца	v o·ba kant·sa
student	для студентов	dlya stud·yen·taf

| (Ten) roubles' worth of tickets, please. | Билетов на (десять) рублей, пожалуйста! |
| | bil·ye·taf na (dye·sit') rub·lyey pa·zhal·sta |

| Can I have a monthly ticket, please? | Единый билет, пожалуйста. |
| | yi·di·nih bil·yet pa·zhal·sta |

| How long does the trip take? | Сколько времени уйдёт на эту поездку? |
| | skol'·ka vrye·mi·ni uyd·yot na e·tu pa·yest·ku |

| Is it a direct route? | Это прямой рейс? |
| | e·ta pri·moy ryeys |

| What time is check in? | Во сколько начинается регистрация? |
| | va skol'·ka na·chi·na·yet·sa ri·gi·strat·si·ya |

Buying a Ticket

When is the next ...?

Когда будет следующий ...?
kag·da bu·dit slye·du·yu·shi ...

 boat
параход
pa·ra·khot

 bus
автобус
af·to·bus

 train
поезд
po·yist

One ... ticket, please.

Один билет ..., пожалуйста.
a·din bil·yet ... pa·zhal·sta

one-way
в один конец
v a·din kan·yets

return
в оба конца
v o·ba kant·sa

I'd like a/an ... seat.

Я бы хотел/хотела ... m/f
ya bih khat·yel/khat·ye·la ...

aisle
боковое
место
ba·ka·vo·ye
mye·sta

window
место у
окна
mye·sta u
ak·na

Which platform does it depart from?

С какой платформы он отправляется?
s ka·koy plat·for·mih on at·prav·lya·it·sa

48

PRACTICAL **TRANSPORT**

I'd like a/an ... seat.

Я бы хотел/хотела ... **m/f**
ya bih khat·*yel*/khat·*ye*·la ...

aisle	боковое место	ba·ka·*vo*·ye *mye*·sta
nonsmoking	место в отделении для некурящих	*mye*·sta v a·dil·*ye*·ni·i dlya ni·kur·*ya*·shikh
smoking	место в отделении для курящих	*mye*·sta v a·dil·*ye*·ni·i dlya kur·*ya*·shikh
window	место у окна	*mye*·sta u ak·*na*

Is there (a) ...?

Есть ...?
yest' ...

air-conditioning	кондиционер	kan·dit·sih·an·*yer*
blanket	плед	plyet
heating	отопление	a·tap·*lye*·ni·ye
sick bag	гигиенический пакет	gi·gi·ye·*ni*·chi·ski pak·*yet*
toilet	туалет	tu·al·*yet*

I'd like to cancel my ticket, please.

Я бы хотел/хотела отменить билет, пожалуйста. **m/f**
ya bih khat·*yel*/khat·*ye*·la at·mi·*nit'* bil·*yet* pa·*zhal*·sta

I'd like to change my ticket, please.

Я бы хотел/хотела поменять билет, пожалуйста. **m/f**
ya bih khat·*yel*/khat·*ye*·la pa·min·*yat'* bil·*yet* pa·*zhal*·sta

LISTEN FOR

Внимание!	vni·*ma*·ni·ye	
	Attention!	
Билеты!	bil·*ye*·tih	
	Tickets!	
Предъявите паспорт!	prid·yi·*vit*·ye pas·part	
	Passports, please!	
Все места проданы.	fsye mi·*sta* pro·da·nih	
	It's full.	

билетная касса f	bil·*yet*·na·ya *ka*·sa	ticket office
забастовка f	za·ba·*stof*·ka	strike
кассовый	*ka*·sa·vih	ticket machine
автомат m	af·ta·*mat*	
книжка талонов f	*knish*·ka ta·*lo*·naf	book of tickets
опаздывает	a·*paz*·dih·va·yet	delayed
отменили	at·mi·*ni*·li	cancelled
проводник m	pra·*vad*·nik	conductor
расписание n	ras·pi·*sa*·ni·ye	timetable
то/это	to/*e*·ta	that/this one

I'd like to confirm my ticket, please.	Я бы хотел/хотела подтвердить билет, пожалуйста. **m/f** ya bih khat·*yel*/khat·*ye*·la pat·vir·*dit'* bil·*yet* pa·*zhal*·sta
Please punch my ticket.	Закомпостируйте, пожалуйста. za·kam·pa·*sti*·ruy·tye pa·*zhal*·sta
Can I have a token?	Жетон, пожалуйста. zhih·*ton* pa·*zhal*·sta

PRACTICAL TRANSPORT

Luggage

Where's a/the ...?	Где ...?	gdye ...

baggage claim	выдача багажа	*vih*·da·cha ba·ga·*zha*
left-luggage office	багажное отделение	ba·*gazh*·na·ye o·dil·*ye*·ni·ye
luggage locker	камера-автомат	*ka*·mi·ra·af·ta·*mat*
trolley	тележка	til·*yesh*·ka

My luggage has been damaged.	Мой багаж повредили.	moy ba·*gash* pa·vri·*di*·li
My luggage has been lost.	Мой багаж пропал.	moy ba·*gash* pra·*pal*
My luggage has been stolen.	Мой багаж украли.	moy ba·*gash* u·*kra*·li
That's (not) mine.	Это (не) моё.	*e*·ta (nye) ma·*yo*
Can I have some coins/tokens?	Дайте, пожалуйста, монет/жетонов.	*deyt*·ye pa·*zhal*·sta man·*yet*/zhih·*to*·naf

 LISTEN FOR

доплатить	da·pla·*tit'*	pay extra v
жетон m	zhih·*ton*	token
перевес багажа m	pi·riv·*yes* ba·ga·*zha*	excess baggage
ручная кладь f	ruch·*na*·ya klat'	carry-on baggage

🔊 LISTEN FOR

пересадка f	pi·ri·*sat*·ka	transfer
посадочный	pa·*sa*·dach·nih	boarding pass
талон m	ta·*lon*	
транзит m	tran·*zit*	transit

Plane

Which gate for (Omsk)?	Какой выход на посадку до (Омска)? ka·*koy vih*·khat na pa·*sat*·ku da (*om*·ska)
Where's (the) ...?	Где ...? gdye ...

arrivals hall	зал прибытий	zal pri·*bih*·ti·ye
departures hall	зал отправлений	zal at·prav·*lye*·ni
duty-free shop	товары без пошлины	ta·*va*·rih byes *posh*·li·nih
gate (number three)	выход на посадку (номер три)	*vih*·khat na pa·*sat*·ku (*no*·mir tri)

Bus, Trolleybus & Coach

How often do buses come?	Как часто ходят автобусы? kak *cha*·sta *kho*·dit af·*to*·bu·sih
Does it go to (Novgorod)?	Этот автобус идёт в (Новгород)? e·tat af·*to*·bus id·*yot* v (*nov*·ga·rat)

PRACTICAL TRANSPORT

Public Transport
Russia has an extensive transport system which runs frequently. Unfortunately, passengers are often *битком набит* bit·*kom* na·*bit* (pounded to a rissole). Feel free to say *Не толкать!* nye tal·*kat'* (Don't push!).

What's the next stop?	Какая следующая остановка? ka·*ka*·ya *slye*·du·yu·sha·ya a·sta·*nof*·ka
city a	городской m ga·rat·*skoy*
intercity a	междугородный m mizh·du·ga·*rod*·nih
local a	местный m *myes*·nih
minibus (fixed-route taxi)	маршрутка f marsh·*rut*·ka
trolleybus	троллейбус m tral·*yey*·bus

For bus and trolleybus numbers, see **numbers & amounts** (p32).

Train & Metro

What station is this?	Какая эта станция? ka·*ka*·ya e·ta *stant*·sih·ya
What's the next station?	Какая следующая станция? ka·*ka*·ya *slye*·du·yu·sha·ya *stant*·sih·ya
Which line goes to (Spartak)?	Какая линия идёт в (Спартак)? ka·*ka*·ya *li*·ni·ya id·*yot* f (spar·*tak*)

Does it stop at (Solntsevo)?	Поезд останавливается в (Солнцево)? *po*·yist a·sta·*nav*·li·va·yit·sa v (*sont*·si·va)
Do I need to change?	Мне нужно делать пересадку? mnye *nuzh*·na *dye*·lat' pi·ri·*sat*·ku
Which platform is for the Trans-Siberian Railway?	Транссибирский с какой платформы? trans·si·*bir*·ski s ka·*koy* plat·*for*·mih
How long do we stop here?	Сколько времени поезд стоит на этой станции? *skol*'·ka *vrye*·mi·ni *po*·ist sta·*it* na e·tay *stant*·si

Когда он отправляется?
kag·*da* on at·prav·*lya*·it·sa
What time does it leave?

How long does the train take to (Domodedovo)?	Сколько времени идёт электричка до (Домодедово)? *skol'·ka vrye·mi·ni id·yot el·ik·trich·ka da (da·mad·ye·da·va)*
Can you please open/close the window?	Откройте/Закройте, пожалуйста, окно. *at·kroyt·ye/za·kroyt·ye pa·zhal·sta ak·no*
The toilet is locked.	Туалет заперт. *tu·al·yet za·pirt*
Is it ...?	Это ...? *e·ta ...*

direct	прямой поезд	*pri·moy po·yist*
express	экспресс	*iks·pryes*
intercity	пассажирский поезд	*pa·sa·zhihr·ski po·yist*
local (suburban)	электричка	*e·lik·trich·ka*

Where's the ... carriage?	Где ...? *gdye ...*

1st-class (sleeper)	спальный вагон	*spal'·nih va·gon*
2nd-class (sleeper)	купейный вагон	*ku·pey·nih va·gon*
3rd-class	плацкартный вагон	*plats·kart·nih va·gon*
4th-class	общий вагон	*op·shi va·gon*
dining	вагон-ресторан	*va·gon·ri·sta·ran*

Boat

Is there a hydrofoil to (St Petersburg)?	Есть ракета до (Санкт-Петербурга)? yest' rak·ye·ta da (sankt·pi·tir·bur·ga)
I want to book a cruise along the (Volga).	Я бы хотел/хотела заказать круиз по (Волге). m/f ya bih khat·yel/khat·ye·la za·ka·zat' kru·is pa (vol·gye)
Are there life jackets?	Есть спасательные жилеты? yest' spa·sa·til'·nih·ye zhihl·ye·tih
I feel seasick.	Меня тошнит. min·ya tash·nit
boat	пароход m pa·ra·khot
cabin	каюта f ka·yu·ta
(car) deck	(автомобильная) палуба f (af·ta·ma·bil'·na·ya) pa·lu·ba
ferry	паром m pa·rom
hydrofoil	ракета f rak·ye·ta
lifeboat	спасательная лодка f spa·sa·til'·na·ya lot·ka
steamboat	пароход m pa·ra·khot
terminal	речной вокзал m rich·noy vag·zal
yacht	яхта f yakh·ta

CULTURE TIP — **Private Taxi**

If you're travelling with a *частник* chas·nik (private driver), sound confident and ask *Как мы будем ехать?* kak mih *bu*·dim *ye*·khat' (How are we getting there?). They may *think* you know where you're going, and feel less inclined to take advantage of your ignorance if so inclined ...

Taxi

I'd like a taxi at (9am).	Мне нужно такси в (девять часов утра). mnye *nuzh*·na tak·*si* v (*dye*·vit' chi·*sof* u·*tra*)
I'd like a taxi now/ tomorrow.	Мне нужно такси сейчас/ завтра. mnye *nuzh*·na tak·*si* si·*chas*/ *zaf*·tra
Where's the taxi rank?	Где стоянка такси? gdye sta·*yan*·ka tak·*si*
Is this taxi available?	Свободен? sva·*bo*·din
Please put the meter on.	Включите счётчик, пожалуйста! fklyu·*chit*·ye *shot*·chik pa·*zhal*·sta
How much is it to (Abramtsevo)?	Сколько стоит доехать до (Абрамцево)? *skol*'·ka *sto*·it da·*ye*·khat' da (ab·*ram*·tsih·va)
Please take me to (this address).	До (этого адреса) не довезёте? da (*e*·ta·va *a*·dri·sa) nye da·viz·*yot*·ye

✂ To ...   До ...   da ...

I'll give you (50) roubles.	Я вам дам (пятьдесят) рублей. ya vam dam (pi·dis·*yat*) rub·*lyey*
I want to get out!	Я хочу выйти! ya kha·*chu* vih·ti
Please ...	..., пожалуйста. ... pa·*zhal*·sta

slow down	Не так быстро	ni tak *bih*·stra
step on it	Газуйте	ga·*zuyt*·ye
stop here	Остановитесь здесь	a·sta·na·*vit*·yes' zdyes'
wait here	Подождите здесь	pa·dazh·*dit*·ye zdyes'

For other useful phrases, see **directions** (p66).

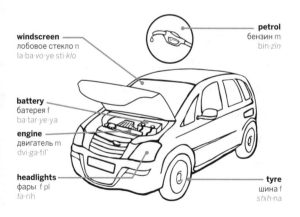

petrol
бензин m
bin·*zin*

windscreen
лобовое стекло n
la·ba·vo·ye sti·*klo*

battery
батарея f
ba·tar·ye·ya

engine
двигатель m
dvi·ga·til'

headlights
фары f pl
fa·rih

tyre
шина f
shih·na

Car & Motorbike

I'd like to hire a car.	Я бы хотел/хотела взять машину. m/f ya bih khat·*yel*/khat·*ye*·la vzyat' ma·*shih*·nu
I'd like to hire a 4WD.	Я бы хотел/хотела взять машину с полным приводом на прокат. m/f ya bih khat·*yel*/khat·*ye*·la vzyat' ma·*shih*·nu s *pol*·nihm pri·*vo*·dam na pra·*kat*
I'd like to hire a motorbike.	Я бы хотел/хотела взять мотоцикл в прокат. m/f ya bih khat·*yel*/khat·*ye*·la vzyat' ma·tat·*sihkl* f pra·*kat*
with air-conditioning	с кондиционером s kan·dit·sih·an·ye·ram
with a driver	с шофёром s shaf·*yo*·ram

🔍 LOOK FOR

бензин номер 93 m	bin·*zin no*·mir di·vi·*no*·sta tri regular
бензин номер 98 m	bin·*zin no*·mir di·vi·*no*·sta *vo*·sim' premium
дизельное топливо n	*di*·zil'·na·ye *to*·pli·va diesel
октановое число n	ak·*ta*·na·va·ye chis·*lo* octane level
очищенный бензин m	a·*chi*·shi·nih bin·*zin* unleaded
СУГ m	es·u·*ge* LPG

🔊 LISTEN FOR

бесплатно	bis·*plat*·na	free
водительские права n pl	va·*di*·til'·ski·ye pra·*va*	drivers licence
километров m pl	ki·*lam*·ye·traf	kilometres
стояночный счётчик m	sta·*ya*·nach·nih *shot*·chik	parking meter

How much for daily/ weekly hire?	Сколько стоит однодневный/ недельный прокат? *skol'*·ka *sto*·it ad·nad·*nyev*·nih/ nid·*yel'*·nih pra·*kat*
Does that include insurance?	Сюда входит страховка? syu·*da* fkho·dit stra·*khof*·ka
Do you have a road map?	У вас есть карта дорог? u vas yest' *kar*·ta da·*rok*
Do you have a guide to the road rules (in English)?	Есть правила уличного движения (на английском)? yest' *pra*·vi·la u·lich·na·va dvi·*zhe*·ni·ya (na an·*gli*·skam)
What's the speed limit?	Какое ограничение скорости? ka·ko·ye a·gra·ni·*che*·ni·ye sko·ra·sti
Is this the road to (Kursk)?	Эта дорога ведёт в (Курск)? e·ta da·*ro*·ga vid·*yot* f (kursk)
Where's a petrol/gas station?	Где заправка? gdye za·*praf*·ka
Is it self-service?	Здесь самообслуживание? zdyes' sa·ma·aps·*lu*·zhih·van·i·ye
Please fill it up.	Заполните бак, пожалуйста. za·*pol*·nit·ye bak pa·*zhal*·sta

🔍 LOOK FOR

БЕРЕГИСЬ (ТРАМВАЯ)!	bi·ri·gis' (tram·va·ya)	Look Out For (Trams)
ВНИМАНИЕ	vni·ma·ni·ye	Caution
ВПЕРЕДИ ВЕДУТСЯ РАБОТЫ	fpi·ri·di vi·dut·sa ra·bo·tih	Roadworks In Progress
ВЪЕЗД	vyest	Entrance
ВЫЕЗД	vih·yest	Exit
ГАИ	ge·a·el	Police
ОБЪЕЗД	ab·yest	Detour
ОДНОСТОРОННЕЕ ДВИЖЕНИЕ	ad·na·sta·ro·ni·ye dvi·zhe·ni·ye	One-Way
ОПАСНО	a·pas·na	Danger
ПРОЕЗД ЗАПРЕЩЕН	pra·yest za·pri·shon	No Entry
СТОП	stop	Stop
СТОЯНКА ЗАПРЕЩЕНА	sta·yan·ka za·pri·shi·na	No Parking
УСТУПИ ДОРОГУ	u·stu·pi do·ra·gu	Give Way

I'd like (15) litres.	(Пятнадцать) литров, пожалуйста. (pit·nat·sat') li·traf pa·zhal·sta
Please check the oil/ water.	Проверьте, пожалуйста, масло/воду. prav·yert·ye pa·zhal·sta mas·la/vo·du
Please check the tyre pressure.	Проверьте, пожалуйста, давление колёс. prav·yert·ye pa·zhal·sta dav·lye·ni·ye kal·yos

(How long) Can I park here?	(Сколько) Здесь можно стоять? (*skol'*·ka) zdyes' *mozh*·na sta·*yat'*
Do I have to pay?	Нужно платить? *nuzh*·na pla·*tit'*
I need a mechanic.	Мне нужен автомеханик. mnye *nu*·zhihn af·ta·mi·*kha*·nik
I've had an accident.	Я потерпел/потерпела аварию. **m/f** ya pa·tir·*pyel*/pa·tir·*pye*·la a·*va*·ri·yu
The car has broken down (at Kursk).	Машина сломалась (в Курске). ma·*shih*·na sla·*ma*·las' (v *kur*·skye)

Bicycle

I'd like to buy a bicycle.	Я бы хотел/хотела купить велосипед. **m/f** ya bih khat·*yel*/khat·*ye*·la ku·*pit'* vi·la·sip·*yet*
I'd like to hire a bicycle.	Я бы хотел/хотела взять велосипед на прокат. **m/f** ya bih khat·*yel*/khat·*ye*·la vzyat' vi·la·sip·*yet* na pra·*kat*
I'd like a mountain bike.	Я бы хотел/хотела горный велосипед. **m/f** ya bih khat·*yel*/khat·*ye*·la *gor*·nih vi·la·sip·*yet*
I'd like a racing bike.	Я бы хотел/хотела спортивный велосипед. **m/f** ya bih khat·*yel*/khat·*ye*·la spar·*tiv*·nih vi·la·sip·*yet*

PRACTICAL TRANSPORT

CULTURE TIP **Superstitions**
If you whistle indoors or in an enclosed space like a car, it's believed that *денег не будет dye*·nik ni *bu*·dit' (you won't have money).

I'd like a second-hand bike.	Я бы хотел/хотела подержанный велосипед. **m/f** ya bih khat·*yel*/khat·*ye*·la pad·*yer*·zha·nih vi·la·sip·*yet*
How much is it per day/ hour?	Сколько стоит прокат в сутки/час? *skol'*·ka *sto*·it pra·*kat* f *sut*·ki/chas
Do I need a helmet?	Нужно носить шлем? *nuzh*·na na·*sit'* shlyem
Can we get there by bicycle?	Можно ездить туда на велосипеде? *mozh*·na yez·*dit'* tu·*da* na vi·la·si·*pye*·dye
Are there bicycle paths?	Велодорожки есть? vi·la·da·*rosh*·ki yest'
Is there a bicycle-path map?	Есть карта велодорожек? yest' *kar*·ta vi·la·da·*ro*·zhek
I have a puncture.	У меня лопнула шина. u min·*ya lop*·nu·la *shih*·na
Where can I get my bicycle repaired?	Где можно починить велосипед? gdye *mozh*·na pa·chi·*nit'* vi·la·sip·*yet*

Border Crossing

KEY PHRASES

I'm here for ... days.	Я здесь ... дней.	ya zdyes' ... dnyey
I'm staying at ...	Я останавливаюсь в ...	ya as·ta·*nav*·li·va·yus' v ...
I have nothing to declare.	Мне нечего декларировать.	mnye *nye*·chi·va di·kla·*ri*·ra·vat'

Border Crossing

I'm here to study.	Я здесь учусь. ya zdyes' u·*chus'*
I'm here on business.	Я здесь по бизнесу. ya zdyes' pa *biz*·ni·su
I'm here on holiday.	Я здесь в отпуске. ya zdyes' v *ot*·pus·kye
I'm here for (10) days.	Я здесь (десять) дней. ya zdyes' (*dye*·sit') dnyey
I'm here for (three) weeks.	Я здесь (три) недели. ya zdyes' (tri) nid·*ye*·li
I'm here for (two) months.	Я здесь (два) месяца. ya zdyes' (dva) *mye*·sit·sa
I'm going to ...	Я еду в ... ya *ye*·du v ...
I'm going to (Lithuania) through (Belarus).	Я еду в (Литву) через (Беларусь). ya *ye*·du v (lit·*vu*) *che*·riz (bi·la·*rus'*)

PRACTICAL BORDER CROSSING

I'm staying at ...	Я останавливаюсь в ... ya as·ta·*nav*·li·va·yus' v ...
Do you have this form in English?	У вас есть этот бланк на английском языке? u vas yest' e·tat blank na an·*gli*·skam yi·zihk·ye
Do I need a visa?	Нужна ли виза? nuzh·*na* li *vi*·za
Where can I have my visa registered?	Где регистрировать визу? gdye re·gist·*ri*·ra·vat' *vi*·zu
The children are on this passport.	Дети вписаны в паспорт. *dye*·ti fpi·*sa*·nih f *pas*·part

LISTEN FOR

билет m	bil·*yet*	ticket
группа f	*gru*·pa	group
иммиграционная карточка f	i·mi·grat·sih·o·na·ya *kar*·tach·ka	immigration card
одинодна m/f	a·*din*/ad·na	alone
регистрация виз f	ri·gist·*rat*·si·ya vis	visa registration
семья f	sim·*ya*	family
таможенная декларация f	ta·*mo*·zhih·na·ya di·kla·*rat*·si·ya	customs declaration form
Откуда вы прилетели?		Where have you flown from? at·*ku*·da vih pri·lit·*ye*·li
На сколько вы приехали?		How long are you here for? na *skol*'·ka vih pri·*ye*·kha·li
Наличные есть?		Are you carrying cash? na·*lich*·nih·ye yest'
Ждите здесь!		Wait here! *zhdih*·tye zdyes'

🔍 LOOK FOR

ИММИГРАЦИЯ	i·mi·*grat*·si·ya	Immigration
КАРАНТИН	ka·ran·*tin*	Quarantine
ПАСПОРТНЫЙ КОНТРОЛЬ	*pas*·part·nih kan·*trol'*	Passport Control
ТАМОЖЕННЫЙ КОНТРОЛЬ	ta·*mo*·zhih·nih kan·*trol'*	Customs
ТОВАРЫ БЕЗ ПОШЛИНЫ	ta·va·rih bis *posh*·li·nih	Duty-Free

At Customs

I have nothing to declare.	Мне нечего декларировать. mnye *nye*·chi·va di·kla·*ri*·ra·vat'
I have something to declare.	Мне нужно что-то задекларировать. mnye *nuzh*·na *shto*·ta za·di·kla·*ri*·ra·vat'
Do I have to declare this?	Это нужно декларировать? e·ta *nuzh*·na di·kla·*ri*·ra·vat'
Everything is for personal use.	У меня только вещи личного пользования. u min·ya tol'·ka *vye*·shi *lish*·na·va pol'·za·va·ni·ya
That's (not) mine.	Это (не) моё. e·ta (nye) ma·yo
I didn't know I had to declare it.	Я не знал/знала, что это нужно декларировать. m/f ya ni znal/*zna*·la shta e·ta *nuzh*·na di·kla·*ri*·ra·vat'

For phrases on payments and receipts, see **money & banking** (p102).

Directions

KEY PHRASES

Where's ...?	Где ...?	gdye ...
What's the address?	Какой адрес?	ka·*koy* a·dris
Is it far?	Далеко?	da·li·*ko*

Where's a/the ... (around here)?	Где (здесь) ...? gdye (zdyes') ...
How do I get there?	Как туда попасть? kak tu·*da* pa·*past'*
Do you know the way?	Вы знаете дорогу? vih *zna*·yi·tye da·*ro*·gu
Is it nearby?	Близко? *blis*·ka
Is it far away?	Далеко? da·li·*ko*
What's the address?	Какой адрес? ka·*koy* a·dris
Can you show me (on the map)?	Покажите мне, пожалуйста (на карте). pa·ka·*zhih*·tye mnye pa·*zhal*·sta (na *kart*·ye)
Which street/suburb is this?	Что это за улица/ район? shto *e*·ta za *u*·li·tsa/ ra·*yon*
Which village is this?	Что это за деревня? shto *e*·ta za dir·*yev*·nya

on foot	пешком	pish·*kom*
by bus	автобусом	af·*to*·bu·sam
by taxi	на такси	na tak·*si*
by train	электричкой	e·lik·*trich*·key
Turn (at the) ...	Поверните ...	pa·vir·*nit*·ye ...

corner	за угол	*za*·u·gal
left	налево	nal·*ye*·va
right	направо	na·*pra*·va
traffic lights	на светофоре	na svi·ta·*for*·ye

🔊 LISTEN FOR

Близко.	*blis*·ka	It's close.
Далеко.	da·li·*ko*	It's far.
За ...	za ...	It's behind ...
Здесь.	zdyes'	It's here.
На углу.	na u·*glu*	It's on the corner.
Напротив ...	na·*pro*·tif ...	It's opposite ...
Около ...	*o*·ka·la ...	It's near ...
Перед ...	*pye*·rit ...	It's in front of ...
Прямо.	*prya*·ma	It's straight ahead.
Рядом с ...	*rya*·dam s ...	It's next to ...
С той стороны.	s toy sta·ra·*nih*	It's on that side.
С этой стороны.	s e·toy sta·ra·*nih*	It's on this side.
Там.	tam	It's there.

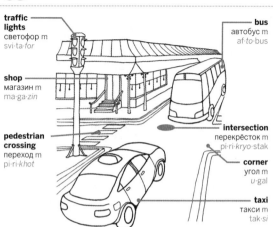

traffic lights
светофор m
svi·ta·*for*

shop
магазин m
ma·ga·*zin*

pedestrian crossing
переход m
pi·ri·*khot*

bus
автобус m
af·*to*·bus

intersection
перекрёсток m
pi·ri·*kryo*·stak

corner
угол m
u·gal

taxi
такси m
tak·*si*

🔍 LOOK FOR

бульвар (бул.) m	bul'·*var*	boulevard
город (г.) m	*go*·rat	city
дом (д.) m	dom	housing complex
дорога (дор.) f	da·*ro*·ga	road
деревня (дер.) f	dir·*yev*·nya	village
квартира (кв.) f	kvar·*ti*·ra	apartment
корпус (корп.) m	*kor*·pus	building (in a complex)
переулок (пер.) m	pi·ri·*u*·lak	lane
площадь (пл.) f	*plo*·shit'	square
проспект (пр.) m	prasp·*yekt*	avenue
район (р./р-н) m	ra·*yon*	suburb
улица (ул.) f	*u*·lit·sa	street

Accommodation

KEY PHRASES

Where's a hotel?	Где гостиница?	gdye ga·sti·nit·sa
Do you have a double room?	У вас есть номер с двуспальней кроватью?	u vas yest' no·mir z dvu·spaln·yey kra·vat·yu
How much is it per night?	Сколько стоит за ночь?	skol'·ka sto·it za noch'
Is breakfast included?	Цена включает завтрак?	tse·na fklyu·cha·yit zaf·trak
What time is checkout?	Когда нужно освободить номер?	kag·da nuzh·na as·va·ba·dit' no·mir

Finding Accommodation

Where's a ...?	Где ...? gdye ...	
boarding house	пансионат	pan·si·a·nat
campsite	кемпинг	kyem·ping
hotel	гостиница	ga·sti·nit·sa
hut	сторожка	sta·rosh·ka
motel	мотель	mat·yel'
room (for rent)	комната (для съёма)	kom·na·ta (dlya syo·ma)
tourbase	турбаза	tur·ba·za
youth hostel	общежитие	ap·shi·zhih·ti·ye

Can you recommend somewhere ...?	Вы можете порекомендовать что-нибудь ...? vih *mo*·zhiht·ye pa·ri·ka·min·da·*vat'* *shto*·ni·bud' ...

cheap	дешёвое	di·*sho*·va·ye
luxurious	роскошное	ras·*kosh*·na·ye
nearby	близко отсюда	*blis*·ka at·*syu*·da
romantic	романтичное	ra·man·*tich*·na·ye

Where can I find a room in a private flat?	Где можно снять комнату в частной квартире? gdye *mozh*·na snyat' *kom*·na·tu f *chas*·nay kvar·*tir*·ye

For phrases on how to get there, see **directions** (p66).

Booking Ahead & Checking In

I'd like to book a room, please.	Я бы хотел/хотела забронировать номер. m/f ya bih khat·*yel*/khat·*ye*·la za·bra·*ni*·ra·vat' *no*·mir

✂	**Are there rooms?**	Есть ли свободные номера?	yest' li svo·*bod*·ni·ye *no*·mi·ra

I have a reservation.	Я заказал/заказала номер. m/f ya za·ka·*zal*/za·ka·*za*·la *no*·mir

Overnight only.	Только сутки. *tol'*·ka *sut*·ki

Finding a Room

Do you have a ... room?

У вас есть ...?   *u vas yest'* ...

 double
номер с двуспальней кроватью
no·mir z dvu·spaln·yey kra·vat·yu

 single
одноместный номер
ad·nam·yes·nih no·mir

How much is it per ...?

Сколько стоит ...?   *skol'·ka sto·it* ...

 night
за ночь
za noch'

 person
на одного человека
na ad·no·vo che·la·vye·ka

Is breakfast included?

Цена включает завтрак?
tse·na fklyu·cha·yit zaf·trak

Can I see the room?

Можно посмотреть?
mozh·na pas·mat·ryet'

I'll take it.
Я беру.
ya bi·ru

I won't take it.
Я не возьму.
ya nye vaz'·mu

For (three) nights.	(Трое) суток. *(tro·ye) su·tak*
From (5 July) to (8 July).	С (пятого июля) по (восьмое июля). *s (pya·ta·va i·yul·ya) pa (vas'·mo·ye i·yul·ya)*
Do you have a single room?	У вас есть одноместный номер? *u vas yest' ad·nam·yes·nih no·mir*
Do you have a double room?	У вас есть номер с двуспальней кроватью? *u vas yest' no·mir z dvu·spaln·yey kra·vat·yu*
Do you have a twin room?	У вас есть двухместный номер? *u vas yest' dvukh·myes·nih no·mir*
How much is it per night/ week?	Сколько стоит за ночь/ неделю? *skol'·ka sto·it za noch'/ nid·yel·yu*
How much is it per person?	Сколько стоит на одного человека? *skol'·ka sto·it na ad·no·vo che·la·vye·ka*
How much is it for two people?	Сколько стоит за двоих? *skol'·ka sto·it za dva·ikh*
Is breakfast included?	Цена включает завтрак? *tse·na fklyu·cha·yit zaf·trak*
Can I see it?	Можно посмотреть? *mozh·na pas·mat·ryet'*
The price is very high.	Цена очень высокая. *tsih·na o·chin' vih·so·ka·ya*
Are there other rooms?	У вас есть другие номера? *u vas yest' dru·gi·ye na·mi·ra*

LISTEN FOR

всё занято	fsyo *zan*·yi·ta	full
ключ m	klyuch	key
регистрация f	ri·gi·*strat*·sih·ya	reception
Сколько суток?	*skol'*·ka *su*·tak	How many nights?
Сколько человек?	*skol'*·ka chi·*lav*·*yek*	How many people?

I'll take it.	Я беру. ya bi·*ru*
Do I need to pay a deposit/upfront?	Нужно платить аванс/вперёд? *nuzh*·na pla·*tit'* a·*vans*/fpir·*yot*

For methods of payment, see **money & banking** (p102).

Requests & Queries

When/Where is breakfast served?	Когда/Где завтрак? kag·*da*/gdye *zaf*·trak
Please wake me at (seven).	Позвоните мне, пожалуйста, в (семь) часов. paz·va·*nit'*·ye mnye pa·*zhal*·sta v (syem') chi·*sof*
Is hot water available all day?	Горячая вода бывает целый день? gar·*ya*·chi·ya va·*da* bih·*va*·yit *tse*·lih dyen'
Can I use the kitchen?	Можно воспользоваться кухней? *mozh*·na vas·*pol'*·za·vat'·sa *kukh*·nyey
Can I use the laundry?	Можно воспользоваться прачечной? *mozh*·na vas·*pol'*·za·vat'·sa *pra*·chich·nay

Can I use the telephone?	Можно воспользоваться телефоном? *mozh·na vas·pol'·za·vat'·sa ti·li·fo·nam*
Do you have a/an ...?	У вас есть ...? *u vas yest' ...*

elevator/lift	лифт	lift
laundry service	прачечная	*pra·chich·na·ya*
message board	доска объявлений	*da·ska ob·yiv·lye·ni*
safe	сейф	*syeyf*
satellite TV	спутниковое телевидение	*sput·ni·ka·va·ye ti·li·vi·di·ni·ye*
swimming pool	бассейн	*bas·yeyn*

Can I change money here?	Здесь можно поменять деньги? *zdyes' mozh·na pa·min·yat' dyen'·gi*
Can I join a tour here?	Здесь можно присоединиться к экскурсии? *zdyes' mozh·na pri·sa·yi·di·nit'·sa k iks·kur·si*
Could I have (a/an) ..., please?	Дайте, пожалуйста ... *dayt·ye pa·zhal·sta ...*

(extra) blanket	(ещё) одеяло	*(yi·sho) a·di·ya·la*
bulb	лампочку	*lam·pach·ku*
receipt	квитанцию	*kvi·tant·sih·yu*
my key	ключ от моего номера	*klyuch at ma·yi·vo no·mi·ra*

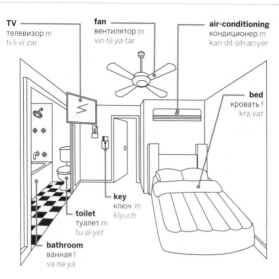

TV
телевизор m
ti·li·vi·zar

fan
вентилятор m
vin·til·ya·tar

air-conditioning
кондиционер m
kan·dit·sih·an·yer

bed
кровать f
kra·vat

key
ключ m
klyuch

toilet
туалет m
tu·al·yet

bathroom
ванная f
va·na·ya

Is there a message for me?	Мне передавали? mnye pi·ri·da·va·li
Can I leave a message for someone?	Вы можете передать кому-то? vih mo·zhiht·ye pi·ri·dat' ka·mu·ta
I'm locked out of my room.	Я забыл/забыла ключ в номере. **m/f** ya za·bihl/za·bih·la klyuch v no·mir·ye
There's no need to change my sheets.	Не надо менять постельное бельё. ne na·da min·yat' pas·tyel'·na·ye bil'·yo

Complaints

It's too ...		В комнате очень ... f *kom*·nat·ye *o*·chin' ...
bright/light	ярко	*yar*·ka
cold	холодно	*kho*·lad·na
dark	темно	tim·*no*
noisy	шумно	*shum*·na
small	тесно	*tyes*·na

The air-conditioning doesn't work.	Кондиционер не работает. kan·dit·sih·an·*yer* nye ra·*bo*·ta·yit
The heater doesn't work.	Отопление не работает. a·tap·*lye*·ni·ye nye ra·*bo*·ta·yit
The toilet doesn't work.	Туалет не работает. tu·al·*yet* nye ra·*bo*·ta·yit
This (pillow) isn't clean.	Эта (подушка) грязная. *e*·ta (pa·*dush*·ka) *gryaz*·na·ya
There's no (hot water).	Нет (горячей воды). nyet (gar·*ya*·chey va·*dih*)
I/We can't sleep because of (the renovations).	(Ремонт) мешает мне/нам спать. (ri·*mont*) mi·*sha*·yet mnye/nam spat'

Answering the Door

Who is it?	Кто там? kto tam
Just a moment!	Одну минуту! ad·*nu* mi·*nu*·tu
Come in!	Заходите! za·kha·*dit*·ye

CULTURE TIP

Hotel Assistance

Each floor of a Russian hotel is supervised by a *дежурная* di·*zhur*·na·ya (floor lady). You can rely on her for help with *горячая вода* gar·*ya*·cha·ya va·*da* (hot water) and *стирка* stir·ka (laundry).

I'm not decent!	Я переодеваюсь! ya pi·ri·a·di·va·yus'
Come back later, please.	Приходите попозже, пожалуйста. pri·kha·*dit*·ye pa·*po*·zhe pa·*zhal*·sta

Checking Out

What time is checkout?	Когда нужно освободить номер? kag·*da* nuzh·na as·va·ba·*dit'* *no*·mir
Can you call a taxi for me (for 11 o'clock)?	Мне нужно такси (на одиннадцать часов). mnye *nuzh*·na tak·*si* (na a·*di*·nat·sat' chi·*sof*)
I'm leaving now.	Я сейчас уезжаю. ya si·*chas* u·yi·*zha*·yu
We're leaving now.	Мы сейчас уезжаем. mih si·*chas* u·yi·*zha*·im
Can I leave my bags here?	Здесь можно оставлять багаж? zdyes' *mozh*·na a·stav·*lyat'* ba·*gash*
Could I have my deposit, please?	Дайте, пожалуйста мой аванс. *dayt*·ye pa·*zhal*·sta moy a·*vans*

78

🔍 LOOK FOR

ВАННАЯ	va·na·ya	Bathroom
МЕСТ НЕТ	myest nyet	No Vacancy
СВОБОДНЫЕ МЕСТА	sva·bod·nih·ye mi·sta	Vacancy

Could I have my passport, please?	Дайте, пожалуйста мой паспорт. dayt·ye pa·zhal·sta moy pas·part
Could I have my valuables, please?	Дайте, пожалуйста мои ценности. dayt·ye pa·zhal·sta ma·i tse·nas·ti
There's a mistake in the bill/check.	Меня обсчитали. min·ya ap·shi·ta·li
I'll be back in (three) days.	Я вернусь через (три) дня. ya vir·nus' che·ris (tri) dnya
I'll be back on (Monday).	Я вернусь в (понедельник). ya vir·nus' f (pa·nid·yel'·nik)
I had a great stay, thank you.	Спасибо, я отлично провёл/провела время. m/f spa·si·ba ya at·lich·na prav·yol/pra·vi·la vryem·ya

Camping

Who's in charge here?	Кто здесь заведующий? kto zdyes' zav·ye·du·yu·shi
Can I camp here?	Можно устроить стоянку здесь? mozh·na u·stro·it' sta·yan·ku zdyes'

Can I park next to my tent?	Можно поставить машину рядом с палаткой? *mozh*·na pa·*sta*·vit' ma·*shih*·nu *rya*·dam s pa·*lat*·kay
How much is it per ...?	Сколько стоит за ...? *skol'*·ka *sto*·it za ...

caravan	автофургон	af·ta·fur·*gon*
person	одного	ad·na·*vo*
	человека	chi·lav·*ye*·ka
tent	палатку	pa·*lat*·ku
vehicle	машину	ma·*shi*·nu

Есть ли свободные номера?
yest' li svo·*bod*·ni·ye *no*·mi·ra
Are there rooms?

🔍 LOOK FOR

НЕ ДЛЯ ПИТЬЯ	nye dlya pi·*tya* Not For Drinking
ПИТЬЕВАЯ ВОДА	pi·ti·*va*·ya va·*da* Drinking Water
ПРАВИЛА ВНУТРЕННЕГО РАСПОРЯДКА	*pra*·vi·la *vnu*·tri·ni·va ras·par·*yat*·ka Site Regulations
РАЗЖИГАТЬ КОСТРЫ ЗАПРЕЩАЕТСЯ	ra·zhih·*gat'* kast·*rih* za·pri·*sha*·it·sa No Campfires
СТОЯНКА ТУРИСТОВ ЗАПРЕЩЕНА	sta·*yan*·ka tu·*ri*·staf za·pri·*shi*·na No Camping

Do you have (a) ...? Здесь есть ...?
zdyes' yest' ...

electricity	электричество	e·lik·*tri*·chist·va
laundry	прачечная	*pra*·chich·na·ya
shower facilities	душ	dush
site	место	*mye*·sta
tents for hire	палатки напрокат	pa·*lat*·ki na·pra·*kat*

Is the water drinkable? Эту воду можно пить?
e·tu *vo*·du *mozh*·na pit'

Is it coin-operated? Это монетно?
e·ta man·*yet*·na

Could I borrow ...? Можно взять взаймы ...?
mozh·na vzyat' vzay·*mih* ...

LISTEN FOR

дыра f	dih·*ra*	a dive
наводнено крысами	na·vad·ni·*no* *krih*·sa·mi	rat-infested
настоящая находка f	na·sta·*ya*·shi·ya na·*khot*·ka	a real find
прелестно	pril·*yes*·na	charming
удобно	u·*dob*·na	comfortable

PRACTICAL ACCOMMODATION

Renting

Do you have a/an ... for rent?	У вас сдаётся ...? u vas zda·*yot*·sa ...

apartment	квартира	kvar·*ti*·ra
holiday house	дача	*da*·cha
house	дом	dom
room	комната	*kom*·na·ta
traditional country house	изба	*iz*·ba

car space	место для машины n *mye*·sta dlya ma·*shih*·nih
furniture	мебель f *mye*·bil'
security door	бронированные двери f pl bra·ni·*ro*·va·nih·ye *dvye*·ri

Staying with Locals

Can I stay at your place?	Можно пожить у вас? *mozh*·na pa·*zhiht'* u vas

CULTURE TIP

Visiting Etiquette
When visiting Russian people at home, it's customary to take a small gift. There are no strict rules – a bottle of wine or vodka, a box of chocolates or flowers are fine. If it's winter, a gift of fruit shows that you've made an effort. Children will appreciate small gifts such as chocolate bars.

Many thanks for your hospitality.	Огромное спасибо за ваше гостеприимство. a·*grom*·na·ye spa·*si*·ba za va·shih ga·sti·pri·*imst*·va
I have my own mattress.	У меня есть матрац. u min·*ya* yest' ma·*trats*
I have my own sleeping bag.	У меня есть спальный мешок. u min·*ya* yest' spal'·nih mi·*shok*
Is there anything I can do to help?	Разрешите вам помочь! raz·ri·*shiht*·ye vam pa·*moch*'
Let me ...	Разрешите мне ... raz·ri·*shiht*·ye mnye ...

buy the groceries	сделать покупки	*zdye*·lat' pa·*kup*·ki
clear the table	убрать со стола	u·*brat*' sa sta·*la*
do the dishes	помыть посуду	pa·*miht*' pa·*su*·du
set the table	накрыть на стол	na·*kriht*' na·stal
take out the rubbish	вынести мусор	*vih*·ni·sti *mu*·sar

To compliment your hosts' cooking, see **eating out** (p191).

Shopping

KEY PHRASES

I'd like to buy ...	Я бы хотел/хотела купить ... m/f	ya bih khat·*yel*'/khat·ye·la ku·*pit*'...
Can I look at it?	Покажите, пожалуйста.	pa·ka·*zhiht*·ye pa·*zhal*·sta
Can I try it on?	Можно это примерить?	*mozh*·na e·ta prim·ye·*rit*'
How much is it?	Сколько стоит?	*skol*'·ka *sto*·it
That's too expensive.	Это очень дорого.	e·ta o·*chin*' *do*·ra·ga

Looking For ...

Where's a (supermarket)?	Где (универсам)? gdye (u·ni·vir·*sam*)
Where can I buy locally produced goods/souvenirs?	Где можно покупать продукты/сувениры в местном масштабе? gdye *mozh*·na pa·ku·*pat*' pra·*duk*·tih/su·vi·*ni*·rih v *myest*·nam mash·*ta*·bye

For more items and shopping locations, see the **dictionary**.

Making a Purchase

I'm just looking.	Я просто смотрю. ya *pros*·ta smat·*ryu*
Could you help me?	Будьте добры. *but*·ye da·*brih*

I'd like to buy ...	Я бы хотел/хотела купить ... **m/f** ya bih khat·*yel*'/khat·*ye*·la ku·*pit*' ...
Can I look at it?	Покажите, пожалуйста. pa·ka·*zhiht*·ye pa·*zhal*·sta
Is this the latest model?	Это последняя модель? e·ta pas·*lyed*·nya·ya mad·*yel*'
How much is it?	Сколько стоит? *skol*'·ka *sto*·it

✂ **How much?**	Сколько?	*skol*'·ka

Please write down the price.	Запишите, пожалуйста, цену. za·pi·*shiht*·ye pa·*zhal*·sta *tse*·nu
Do you have any others?	У вас есть другие? u vas yest' dru·*gi*·ye
I'll take it.	Возьму. vaz'·*mu*
That's just what I want.	Это как раз. e·ta kak ras
Do I pay here?	Вам платить? vam pla·*tit*'
Please write me out a docket.	Выпишите, пожалуйста. *vih*·pi·shiht·ye pa·*zhal*·sta

---

CULTURE TIP

Three-Queue System

Be prepared for the 'three-queue system' in older shops. When you choose an item, ask the shop assistant for a docket: *Выпишите, пожалуйста vih*·pi·shiht·ye pa·*zhal*·sta (Please write it out). Take the docket to a *касса ka*·sa (cashier), pay and have it stamped. Go to the counter with the docket and collect your purchase.

◀)) LISTEN FOR

Вам помочь?	vam pa·*moch'*	Can I help you?
Что вы хотите?	shto vih kha·*tit*·ye	What would you like?
Что ещё?	shto yi·*sho*	Anything else?
У нас нету.	u nas *nye*·tu	No, we don't have any.
Платите в кассу.	pla·*tit*·ye f *ka*·su	Pay at the cashier.

Who's last in the queue?	Кто последний? kto pas·*lyed*·ni
Do you accept credit/debit cards?	Вы принимаете оплату кредитной/дебитной карточкой? vih pri·ni·*ma*·it·ye a·*pla*·tu kri·*dit*·ney/*dye*·bit·ney *kar*·tach·key
Do you accept travellers cheques?	Вы принимаете оплату дорожным чеком? vih pri·ni·*ma*·it·ye a·*pla*·tu da·*rozh*·nihm *che*·kam
Could I have (a) ..., please?	Дайте ..., пожалуйста. *deyt*·ye ... pa·*zhal*·sta

bag	пакет	pak·*yet*
receipt	квитанцию	kvi·*tant*·sih·yu
some change	мелкими монетами	*myel*·ki·mi man·ye·ta·mi
smaller notes	мелкими купюрами	*myel*·ki·mi kup·*yu*·ra·mi

✂	Receipt, please.	Квитанцию, пожалуйста.	kvi·*tant*·sih·yu pa·*zhal*·sta

I don't need a bag, thanks.	Пакет не нужен. *pak·yet* nye *nu·zhihn*
Could I have it wrapped?	Заверните, пожалуйста. *za·vir·nit·ye pa·zhal·sta*
Does it have a guarantee?	Есть гарантия? *yest' ga·ran·ti·ya*
It's faulty.	Это браковано. *e·ta z bra·ko·va·na*
Can you repair this?	Вы можете это починить? *vih mo·zhiht·ye e·ta pa·chi·nit'*
When will it be ready?	Когда будет готово? *kag·da bu·dit ga·to·va*
I'd like a refund.	Будьте добры, я бы хотел/хотела получить обратно деньги. m/f *but·ye da·brih ya bih khat·yel/khat·ye·la pa·lu·chit' ab·rat·na dyen'·gi*
I'd like my change.	Будьте добры, я бы хотел/хотела сдачу. m/f *but·ye da·brih ya bih khat·yel/khat·ye·la zda·chu*
I'd like to return this.	Будьте добры, я бы хотел/хотела это возвратить. m/f *but·ye da·brih ya bih khat·yel/khat·ye·la e·ta vaz·vra·tit'*

Bargaining

That's too expensive.	Это очень дорого. *e·ta o·chin' do·ra·ga*
Can you lower the price?	Вы можете снизить цену? *vih mo·zhiht·ye sni·zit' tse·nu*

Making a Purchase

 I'd like to buy ...
Я бы хотел/хотела купить ... m/f
ya bih khat·*yel'*/khat·ye·la ku·*pit'* ...

 How much is it?
Сколько стоит?
skol'·ka *sto*·it

-------------------- OR --------------------

 Please write down the price.
Запишите, пожалуйста, цену.
za·pi·*shiht*·ye pa·*zhal*·sta *tse*·nu

 Do you accept credit cards?
Вы принимаете оплату кредитной карточкой?
vih pri·ni·*ma*·it·ye a·*pla*·tu kri·*dit*·ney *kar*·tach·key

 Could I have a ..., please?
Дайте ..., пожалуйста.
deyt·ye ... pa·*zhal*·sta

 receipt
квитанцию
kvi·*tan*·tsih·yu

 bag
пакет
pak·*yet*

PRACTICAL SHOPPING

🔊 LISTEN FOR

выгодная покупка f	*vih*·gad·na·ya pa·*kup*·ka	bargain
густо	*gu*·sta	easy-to-get
дефицит m	di·fit·*siht*	shortage
очередь f	o·chi·rit'	queue
очередь по списку f	o·chi·rit' pa *spis*·ku	waiting list
распродажа f	ras·pra·*da*·zha	sale
сплошная обдираловка f	splash·*na*·ya ab·di·*ra*·laf·ka	absolute rip-off

Do you have something cheaper?	Есть подешевле? yest' pa·di·*shev*·li
I'll give you (100) roubles.	Я вам дам (сто) рублей. ya vam dam (sto) rub·*lyey*

Books & Reading

Is there an English-language bookshop/section?	Есть магазин/секция английской книги? yest' ma·ga·*zin*/*syekt*·sih·ya an·*gli*·skey *kni*·gi
Can you recommend a book for me?	Вы можете порекомендовать мне книгу? vih *mo*·zhiht·ye pa·ri·ka·min·da·*vat*' mnye *kni*·gu
Do you have a novel by ...?	У вас есть роман ...? u vas yest' ra·*man* ...
Do you have an entertainment guide?	У вас есть список местных развлечений? u vas yest' *spi*·sak *myes*·nihkh raz·vli·*che*·ni

I'd like a dictionary.	Я бы хотел/хотела словарь. **m/f** ya bih khat·*yel*/khat·ye·la sla·*var'*
I'd like a newspaper (in English).	Я бы хотел/хотела газету (на английском). **m/f** ya bih khat·*yel*/khat·ye·la gaz·*ye*·tu (na an·*gli*·skam)

Clothes

My size is (40).	Мой размер (сорок). moy raz·*myer* (so·rak)
Can I try it on?	Можно это примерить? *mozh*·na e·ta prim·*ye*·rit'

Это очень дорого.
e·ta *o*·chin' *do*·ra·ga
That's too expensive.

CULTURE TIP

Shop Etiquette
Russians will often attract the attention of shop assistants with the words *Девушка!* dye·vush·ka (lit: girl) and *Бабушка!* ba·bush·ka (lit: grandmother). A more respectful version is *Вы обслуживаете?* vih aps·lu·zhih·va·it·ye (Are you serving?).

| It doesn't fit. | Это не подходит.
e·ta nye pat·kho·dit |
| How do I look in this? | Как выгляжу в этом?
kak vih·gli·zhu v e·tam |

For different types of clothing, see the **dictionary**, and for sizes, see **numbers & amounts** (p32).

Music & DVD

| I'd like a ... | Я бы хотел/хотела ... m/f
ya bih khat·yel/khat·ye·la ... |

blank tape	чистую	chis·tu·yu
	кассету	kas·ye·tu
CD	компакт-диск	kam·pakt·disk
DVD	DVD	di·vi·di
video	видеокассету	vi·di·o·kas·ye·tu

I'm looking for something by ...	Я ищу что-нибудь ... ya ish·yu shto·ni·bud' ...
What's his/her best recording?	Какая его/её самая лучшая запись? ka·ka·ya yi·vo/yi·yo sa·ma·ya luch·sha·ya za·pis'
Can I listen to this?	Можно послушать? mozh·na pas·lu·shat'

Will this work on any DVD player?	Это сработает на любом DVD-плейере?
	e·ta sra·bo·ta·yit na lyu·bom di·vi·di·plyey·ir·ye

Video & Photography

I need ... film for this camera.	Мне нужна ... плёнка на этоу камеру.
	mnye nuzh·na ... plyon·ka na e·tu kam·ye·ru

B&W	чёрно-белая	chor·nab·ye·la·ya
colour	цветная	tsvet·na·ya
slide	слайд-овая	slaid·a·va·ya
(high) speed	(высоко-) чувствительная	(vih·sa·ko·) chus·vi·til'·na·ya

Can you ...?	Вы можете ...?
	vih mo·zhiht·ye ...

develop digital photos	проявить цифровые снимки	pra·yi·vit' tsihf·ra·vih·ye snim·ki
develop/load this film	проявить/ вложить эту плёнку	pra·yi·vit'/ vla·zhiht' e·tu plyon·ku
recharge the battery for my digital camera	перезарядить батарейку на мою цифровую камеру	pi·ri·za·ri·dit' ba·tar·yey·ku na ma·yu tsihf·ra·vu·yu kam·ye·ru
transfer photos from my camera to CD	перебросить снимки с камеры на компакт-диск	pi·ri·bro·sit' snim·ki s kam·ye·rih na kam·pakt·disk

🔍 LOOK FOR

ЖЕНСКИЙ	zhen·skih	Women
ЗАКРЫТО	za·krih·ta	Closed
ЗАПРЕЩЕНО	za·pri·shi·no	Prohibited
ИНФОРМАЦИЯ	in·far·mat·sih·ya	Information
МУЖСКОЙ	mush·skoy	Men
НЕ КУРИТЬ	nye ku·rit'	No Smoking
НЕ ФОТО-ГРАФИРОВАТЬ	nye fa·ta·gra·fi·ra·vat'	No Photography
ОТКРЫТО	at·krih·ta	Open
ТУАЛЕТ	tu·al·yet	Toilet

Do you have batteries for this camera?	У вас есть батарейки на этоу видеокамеру? u vas yest' ba·tar·yey·ki na e·tu vi·di·o·kam·ye·ru
Do you have memory cards for this camera?	У вас есть карты памяти на этоу видеокамеру? u vas yest' kar·tih pam·ya·ti na e·tu vi·di·o·kam·ye·ru
I need a cable to connect my camera to a computer.	Мне нужен кэйбл, чтобы соединить камеру с компьютером. mnye nu·zhin keybl shto·bih sa·yi·di·nit' kam·ye·ru s kamp·yu·ti·ram
I need a cable to recharge this battery.	Мне нужен кэйбл, чтобы перезарядить батарейку. mnye nu·zhin keybl shto·bih pi·ri·za·ri·dit' ba·tar·yey·ku
I need a video cassette for this camera.	Мне нужна видео-кассета на этоу камеру. mnye nuzh·na vi·di·o·kas·ye·ta na e·tu kam·ye·ru

> **CULTURE TIP**
> **Counterfeits**
> Some shops and banks only take crisp new notes for fear of counterfeits. If you offer them a rumpled banknote they may think it's a *фальшивка* fal'·*shihf*·ka (fake) and say *Нет рублей!* nyet rub·*lyey* (No roubles!).

Is this for a (PAL/NTSC) system?	Это на систему (PAL/NTSC)? e·ta na sist·*ye*·mu (pel/en·ti·es·*si*)
I need a passport photo taken.	Мне нужно фотографироваться на визу. mnye *nuzh*·na fa·ta·gra·*fi*·ra·vat'·sa na *vi*·zu

Souvenirs

badge	значок m zna·*chok*
chess set	шахматы f pl *shakh*·mat·ih
fur hat	меховая шапка f mi·kha·*va*·ya *shap*·ka
icon	икона f i·*ko*·na
peasant doll	матрёшка f mat·*ryosh*·ka
Soviet posters	советские плакаты m pl sav·*yet*·ski·ye pla·*ka*·tih
stamps	марки f pl *mar*·ki
toy	игрушка f i·*grush*·ka

Communications

KEY PHRASES

Where's the local internet cafe?	Где здесь интернет-кафе?	gdye zdyes' in·ter·*net*·ka·*fe*
I'd like to check my email.	Я бы хотел/ хотела проверить свой и-мэйл. **m/f**	ya bih khat·*yel*/ khat·*ye*·la prav·*ye*·rit' svoy i·*meyl*
I want to send a parcel.	Я хочу послать посылку.	ya kha·*chu* pas·*lat*' pa·*sihl*·ku
I want to make a call to ...	Я бы хотел/ хотела позвонить в ... **m/f**	ya bih khat·*yel*/ khat·*ye*·la paz·va·*nit*' v ...
I'd like a SIM card.	Я бы хотел/ хотела СИМ-карту. **m/f**	ya bih khat·*yel*/ khat·*ye*·la *sim*·kar·tu

The Internet

Where's the local internet cafe?	Где здесь интернет-кафе? gdye zdyes' in·ter·*net*·ka·*fe*
Do you have internet access here?	Есть ли у вас здесь доступ к интернету? yest' li u vas zdyes' *do*·stup k in·ter·*ne*·tu
Is there wireless internet access here?	Есть беспроводной доступ к интернету здесь? yest' bye·*spra*·va·dnoy *do*·stup k in·ter·*ne*·tu zdyes'

PRACTICAL COMMUNICATIONS

I'd like to ...	Я бы хотел/хотела ... m/f ya bih khat·yel/khat·ye·la ...	
check my email	проверить свой и-мэйл	prav·ye·rit' svoy i·meyl
download my photos	загружать мои снимки	za·gru·zhat' moy snim·ki
use a printer	воспользоваться принтером	vas·pol'·za·vat'·sa preen·te·ram
use a scanner	воспользоваться сканером	vas·pol'·za·vat'·sa skan·ye·ram
use Skype	воспользовать Skype	vas·pol'·za·vat' skaip

Can I connect my laptop here?	Можно ли здесь подключить ноутбук? mozh·no li zdyes' pad·klyu·chit' not·buk
Do you have Macs/PCs?	Есть компьютеры Макинтош/ПК? yest' kam·pyu·ti·rih ma·kin·tosh/pe·ka
Do you have a Zip drive?	Есть зип-драйв? yest' zip·dreyf
Do you have headphones (with a microphone)?	У вас есть наушники (с микрофоном)? u vas yest' na·ush·nih·ki (s mi·kra·fo·nom)
How much per ...?	Сколько стоит ...? skol'·ka sto·it ...

minute	минута	mi·nu·ta
half-hour	полчаса	pol·chi·sa
hour	час	chas
page	страница	stra·nit·sa

How do I log on?	Как подключиться? kak pat·klyu·*chit'*·sa
Please change it to the English-language setting.	Включите, пожалуйста, английский алфавит. fklyu·*chit*·ye pa·*zhal*·sta an·*gli*·ski al·*fa*·vit
Do you have English keyboards?	Есть английская клавиатура? yest' an·*gli*·ska·ya kla·vi·a·*tu*·ra
It's crashed.	Сломался. sla·*mal*·sa
I've finished.	Я закончил/ закончила. **m/f** ya za·*kon*·chil/ za·*kon*·chi·la

Mobile/Cell Phone

I'd like a ...	Я бы хотел/хотела ... **m/f** ya bih khat·*yel*/khat·*ye*·la ...

charger for my phone	зарядное устройство на телефон	zar·*yad*·na·ye ust·*royst*·va na ti·li·*fon*
mobile/cell phone for hire	взять мобильный телефон напрокат	vzyat' ma·*bil*'·nih ti·li·*fon* nap·ra·*kat*
prepaid mobile/ cell phone	предоплаченный телефон	pri·da·*pla*·chi·nih ti·li·*fon*
SIM card	СИМ-карту	*sim*·kar·tu

What are the rates?	Какие тарифы? ka·*ki*·ye ta·*ri*·fih

(Five) roubles per (30) seconds.	(pyat') rub·*lyey* za (*trit*·sat') si·*kunt* (Пять) рублей за (тридцать) секунд.

Phone

Q **What's your phone number?**	Можно ваш номер телефона? *mozh*·na vash *no*·mir ti·li·fo·na
A **My number is ...**	Мой телефон ... moy ti·li·*fon* ...
I'd like to ...	Я бы хотел/хотела ... m/f ya bih khat·*yel*/khat·*ye*·la ...

buy a (100 unit) phonecard	купить телефонную карточку (на сто единиц)	ku·*pit'* ti·li·*fo*·nu·yu *kar*·tach·ku (na sto i·*di*·nits)
buy a token	купить жетон	ku·*pit'* zhih·*ton*
call (Singapore)	позвонить (в Сингапур)	paz·va·*nit'* (v sin·ga·*por*)
make an international call	позвонить за границу	paz·va·*nit'* za gra·*nit*·su
reverse the charges	позвонить с оплатой вызываемого	paz·va·*nit'* s a·*pla*·tey vih·zih·*va*·yi·ma·va
speak for (three) minutes	поговорить (три) минуты	pa·ga·va·*rit'* (tri) mi·*nu*·tih

How much does each minute cost?	Сколько стоит минута? *skol'*·ka *sto*·it mi·*nu*·ta

PRACTICAL COMMUNICATIONS

🔊 LISTEN FOR

Вы не туда попали.	vih ni tu·*da* pa·*pa*·li	Wrong number.
Слушаю.	*slu*·sha·yu	Speaking.
Представьтесь, пожалуйста.	prit·*staf*·yes' pa·*zhal*·sta	Who's calling?
С кем вы хотите говорить?	s kyem vih kha·*tit*·ye ga·va·*rit'*	Who do you want to speak to?
Минутку.	mi·*nut*·ku	One moment.
Его/Её нету.	yi·*vo*/yi·yo *nye*·tu	He/She isn't here.

What's the code for (New Zealand)?	Какой код (Новой Зеландии)? ka·*koy* kot (*no*·vey zi·*lan*·di)
Where's the nearest pay phone?	Где ближайший телефон-автомат? gdye bli·*zhey*·shi ti·li·*fon*·af·ta·*mat*
I've been cut off.	Меня превали. min·*ya* pri·*va*·li
The connection's bad.	Плохо слышно. *plo*·kha *slihsh*·na
Hello!	Алло! al·*yo*
Can I speak to ...?	Позовите, пожалуйста, ... pa·za·*vit*·ye pa·*zhal*·sta ...
It's ...	Это ... *e*·ta ...
Please tell him/her that ... called.	Передайте, пожалуйста, что позвонил/позвонила ... pi·ri·*deyt*·ye pa·*zhal*·sta shto paz·va·*nil*/paz·va·*ni*·la ...

PRACTICAL COMMUNICATIONS

CULTURE TIP

Francophilia

When the German princess Catherine (later Catherine the Great) married into the Russian aristocracy in 1744, she brought with her a love of European pomp and a fascination for all things French. Under Catherine's influence, the Russian court made the French language and culture part of their daily lives. Speaking French was a sign of sophistication and intellect, and even today travellers to Russia will find many French words in common usage – *пляж* plyash (beach), *магазин* ma·ga·*zin* (shop), *душ* dush (shower), *тротуар* tra·tu·*ar* (footpath) and *кошмар* kash·*mar* (nightmare) are but a few of the words you may recognise. This Francophilia lasted until the October Revolution of 1917, after which time the use of 'standard' Russian was enforced nationwide.

Can I leave a message for him/her?	Вы можете передать ему/ей? vih *mo*·zhiht·ye pi·ri·*dat'* yi·*mu*/yey
I don't have a contact number.	У меня нет телефона. u min·*ya* nyet ti·li·*fo*·na
I'll call back later.	Я перезвоню попозже. ya pi·riz·van·*yu* pa·*po*·zhe
Bye!	Пока! pa·*ka*
Speak to you soon!	Созвонимся! saz·va·*nim*·sa

For telephone numbers, see **numbers & amounts** (p32).

Post Office

Where's the post office?	Где здесь почта? gdye zdyes' *poch*·ta

🔊 LISTEN FOR

внутренняя почта f	vnu·tri·ni·ya poch·ta	domestic mail
международная почта f	mizh·du·na·rod·na·ya poch·ta	international mail
почтовый индекс m	pach·to·vih in·diks	postcode
таможенная декларация f	ta·mo·zhih·na·ya di·kla·rat·sih·ya	customs declaration

I want to send a ...	Я хочу послать ... ya kha·chu pas·lat' ...	
letter	письмо	pis'·mo
parcel (small)	бандероль	ban·di·rol'
parcel (large)	посылку	pa·sihl·ku
postcard	открытку	at·kriht·ku

I want to buy an envelope.	Я хочу купить конверт. yak ha·chu ku·pit' kan·vyert
I want to buy a (10 rouble) stamp.	Я хочу купить марку (за десять рублей). yak ha·chu ku·pit' mar·ku (za dye·sit' rub·lyey)
Please send it by regular mail to (Australia).	Пошлите, пожалуйста, обычной почтой в (Австралию). pash·lit·ye pa·zhal·sta a·bihch·ney poch·tey v (af·stra·li·yu)
It contains (souvenirs).	Там (сувениры). tam (su·vi·ni·rih)

PRACTICAL COMMUNICATIONS

CULTURE TIP

Postal Addresses

Russians typically write addresses in the reverse order to English speakers – they start with the country, then the city, suburb, street, and finally the person's name. As in the example below, the abbreviation г. for город go·rat (city) appears before the name of the city, and likewise for the abbreviations for streets, buildings etc. See also the box on p68.

Россия	Russia
г. Москва 117334	Moscow City,
	117334 (Postcode)
ул. Некрасова	Nekrasov Street
д. 33, корп. 2, кв. 15	Complex 33, Building 2,
	Apartment 15
ПАВЛОВУ М.И.	M.I. Pavlov

Where's the poste restante section?	Где окно до востребования? gdye ak·*no* da vas·tri·ba·*va*·ni·ya
Is there any mail for me?	Есть почта для меня? yest' *poch*·ta dlya min·*ya*
by ... mail	... почтой ... *poch*·tay

air	авиа	*a*·vi·a
express	экспресс	iks·*pres*
registered	заказной	za·kaz·*noy*
regular	обычной	a·*bihch*·nay

Money & Banking

KEY PHRASES

How much is it?	Сколько стоит?	*skol'·ka sto·it*
What's the exchange rate?	Какой курс?	*ka·koy kurs*
Where's an ATM?	Где банкомат?	*gdye ban·ka·mat*
I'd like to change money.	Я бы хотел/ хотела поменять деньги. **m/f**	*ya bih khat·yel/ khat·ye·la pa·min·yat' dyen'·gi*
I'd like to get smaller notes.	Я бы хотел/ хотела мелкими купюрами. **m/f**	*ya bih khat·yel/ khat·ye·la myel·ki·mi kup·yu·ra·mi*

Paying the Bill

Q How much is it?	Сколько стоит? *skol'·ka sto·it*
A It's free.	Это будет бесплатно. *e·ta bu·dit bis·plat·na*
A It's (100) roubles.	Это будет (сто) рублей. *e·ta bu·dit (sto') rub·lyey*
Please write down the price.	Запишите, пожалуйста, цену. *za·pi·shiht·ye pa·zhal·sta tse·nu*

How much is it per ...?   Сколько стоит за ...?
skol'·ka *sto*·it za ...

day	день	dyen'
hour	час	chas
minute	минуту	mi·*nu*·tu
night	ночь	noch'
person	одного	ad·na·*vo*
	человека	chi·*lav*·ye·ka
vehicle	машину	ma·*shih*·nu
visit	один раз	a·*din* ras
week	неделю	nid·*yel*·yu

Do I have to pay?	Нужно платить? *nuzh*·na pla·*tit'*	
Do you accept credit/debit cards?	Вы принимаете оплату кредитной/дебитной карточкой? vih pri·ni·*ma*·it·ye a·*pla*·tu kri·*dit*·ney/*dye*·bit·ney *kar*·tach·key	
Do you accept travellers cheques?	Вы принимаете оплату дорожным чеком? vih pri·ni·*ma*·it·ye a·*pla*·tu da·*rozh*·nihm *che*·kam	

 LISTEN FOR

невозможно	ni·vaz·*mozh*·na	impossible
недостаточно	ni·da·sta·*tach*·na	insufficient funds
проблема f	prab·*lye*·ma	problem
распишитесь	ras·pi·*shiht*·yes'	to sign
удостоверение личности n	u·da·sta·vir·*ye*·ni·ye *lich*·na·sti	identification

I'd like ..., please.		Будьте добры, я бы хотел/хотела ... m/f but·ye da·brih ya bih khat·yel/khat·ye·la ...

a receipt	квитанцию	kvi·tant·sih·yu
a refund	получить обратно деньги	pa·lu·chit' a·brat·na dyen'·gi
my change	сдачу	zda·chu
some change	мелкими монетами	myel·ki·mi man·ye·ta·mi
smaller notes	мелкими купюрами	myel·ki·mi kup·yu·ra·mi

Banking

What time does the bank open/close?	Когда открывается/ закрывается банк? kag·da at·krih·va·yit·sa/ za·krih·va·yit·sa bank
Where's a foreign exchange office?	Где обмен валюты? gdye ab·myen val·yu·tih
Where's an ATM?	Где банкомат? gdye ban·ka·mat
The ATM took my card.	Банкомат съел мою карточку. ban·ka·mat syel ma·yu kar·tach·ku
I've forgotten my PIN.	Я забыл/забыла свой номер. m/f ya za·bihl/za·bih·la svoy no·mir
What's the exchange rate?	Какой курс? ka·koy kurs

PRACTICAL MONEY & BANKING

CULTURE TIP **Roubles & Dollars**

To Russians the *рубль* rubl' (rouble) is a national symbol, and their sentiments towards it are similar to the British feeling for the pound. While there's no immediate prospect of devaluation, many Russians keep savings in US dollars as the rouble has previously been devalued without warning. As Russians say:

Доллары нужно сберечь, рубли нужно потратить.	do·la·rih nuzh·na zbi·rech' ru·bli nuzh·no pa·tra·tit' Dollars are for saving, roubles are for spending.

What's the charge for that?	Сколько нужно заплатить? skol'·ka nuzh·na za·pla·tit'
Where can I ...?	Где можно ...? gdye mozh·na ...
I'd like to ...	Я бы хотел/хотела ... m/f ya bih khat·yel/khat·ye·la ...

cash a cheque	обменять чек	ab·min·yat' chek
change money	поменять деньги	pa·min·yat' dyen'·gi
get a cash advance	снять деньги по кредитной карточке	snyat' dyen'·gi pa kri·dit·ney kar·tach·kye
withdraw money	снять деньги	snyat' dyen'·gi

How much can I take out in one day?	Сколько можно взять в один день? skol'·ka mozh·na vzyat' v a·din dyen'
Has my money arrived yet?	Мои деньги уже пришли? moy dyen'·gi u·zhe prish·li
How long will it take to arrive?	Как быстро деньги придут? kak bihst·ra dyen'·gi pri·dut

Business

KEY PHRASES

I'm attending a conference.	Я на конференции.	ya na kan·fir·*yent*·sih
Where's the meeting?	Где находится собрание?	gdye na·*kho*·dit·sa sa·*bra*·ni·ye
Can I have your business card?	Можно ваша визитная карточка?	*mozh*·na va·*sha* vi·*zit*·na·ya *kar*·tach·ka

---

Where's the business centre?

Где находится бизнес-центр?
gdye na·*kho*·dit·sa *biz*·nes·tsentr

Where's the conference?

Где находится конференция?
gdye na·*kho*·dit·sa kan·fir·*yent*·sih·ya

Where's the meeting?

Где находится собрание?
gdye na·*kho*·dit·sa sa·*bra*·ni·ye

I'm attending a conference.

Я на конференции.
ya na kan·fir·*yent*·sih

I'm attending a meeting.

Я на собрании.
ya na sa·*bra*·ni

I'm attending a trade fair.

Я на торговой ярмарке.
ya na tar·*go*·vey *yar*·mark·ye

I need (a/an) ...		Я бы хотел/хотела ... **m/f** ya bih khat·*yel*/khat·*ye*·la
business cards	визитные карточки	vi·*zit*·nih·ye *kar*·tach·ki
computer	компьютер	kam·*pyu*·tir
internet connection	подключение к интернету	pat·klyu·*che*·ni·ye k in·ter·*ne*·tu
interpreter	переводчика	pi·ri·*vot*·chi·ka

Here's my ...		Вот ... vot ...
address	мой адрес	moy *a*·dris
business card	моя визитная карточка	ma·*ya* vi·*zit*·na·ya *kar*·tach·ka
email address	мой и-мейл	moy i·*meyl*
mobile/cell number	мой мобильный номер	moy ma·*bil*'·nih *no*·mir
phone number	мой номер	moy *no*·mir

Can I have yours?	Можно ваш? *mozh*·na vash
That went very well.	Всё прошло очень успешно. fsyo prash·*lo* o·chin' usp·*yesh*·na
A pleasure to do business.	Приятно иметь дело с вами. pri·*yat*·na im·*yet*' *dye*·la s *va*·mi
Thank you for your time.	Спасибо за ваше время. spa·*si*·ba za *va*·she *vryem*·ya
Shall we go for a drink/ meal?	Хотите пойти в ресторан? kha·*tit*·ye pey·*ti* v ri·sta·*ran*

PRACTICAL SIGHTSEEING

Sightseeing

KEY PHRASES

I'd like a guide.	Я бы хотел/ хотела гида. m/f	ya bih khat·*yel*/ khat·ye·la *gi*·da
Can I take a photo?	Можно сфотографировать?	*mozh*·na sfa·ta·gra·*fi*·ra·vat'
When's the museum open?	В какие часы работает музей?	f ka·*ki*·ye chi·*sih* ra·*bo*·ta·yet muz·*yey*
I'm interested in ...	Я интересуюсь ...	ya in·ti·ri·*su*·yus' ...
When's the next tour?	Когда следующая экскурсия?	kag·*da slye*·du·yu·sha·ya eks·*kur*·si·ya

I'd like to see ...	Я бы хотел/хотела посетить ... m/f ya bih khat·*yel*/khat·ye·la pa·si·*tit'* ...
I'd like a ...	Я бы хотел/хотела ... m/f ya bih khat·*yel*/khat·ye·la ...

catalogue	каталог	ka·ta·*lok*
guide	гида	*gi*·da
guidebook (in English)	путеводитель (на английском) языке	pu·ti·va·*dit*·yel' (na an·*gli*·skam) yi·zihk·*ye*
(city) map	карту (города)	*kar*·tu (*go*·ra·da)

Do you have information on ... sights?	У вас есть информация о ... достопримечательностях? u vas yest' in·far·*mat*·sih·ya a ... da·sta·pri·mi·*cha*·til'·nast·yakh

cultural	культурных	kul'·*tur*·nihkh
historical	исторических	i·sta·*ri*·chi·skikh
religious	религиозных	ri·li·gi·*oz*·nihkh
Soviet-era	советских	sav·*yet*·skikh

What's that?	Что это? shto e·ta
Who made it?	Кто это делал? kto e·ta *dye*·lal
How old is it?	Когда это построили? kag·*da* e·ta past·*tro*·i·li
Could you take a photo of me?	Сфотографируйте меня, пожалуйста. sfa·ta·gra·*fi*·ruy·tye min·*ya* pa·*zhal*·sta
Can I take a photo (of you)?	Можно сфотографировать (вас)? *mozh*·na sfa·ta·gra·*fi*·ra·vat' (vas)

Getting In

What time does it open/ close?	Когда открывается/ закрывается? kag·*da* at·krih·*va*·yit·sa/ za·krih·*va*·yit·sa
What's the admission charge?	Сколько стоит входной билет? *skol'*·ka *sto*·it fkhad·*noy* bil·*yet*

Is there a discount for ...? Есть скидка для ...?
yest' *skit*·ka dlya ...

children	детей	dit·*yey*
families	семей	sim·*yey*
groups	групп	grup
older people	пожилых	pa·zhih·*lihkh*
	людей	lyud·*yey*
students	студентов	stud·*yen*·taf

Galleries & Museums

When's the gallery/ museum open? В какие часы работает галерея/музей?
f ka·*ki*·ye chi·*sih* ra·*bo*·ta·yet ga·lir·*ye*·ya/muz·*yey*

Q **What's in the collection?** Что в коллекции?
shto f kal·*yekt*·sih

A **It's an exhibition of ...** Это выставка ...
e·ta *vih*·staf·ka ...

 LISTEN FOR

византийский стиль m	vi·zan·*tih*·ski stil' Byzantine style
графическое искусство n	gra·*fi*·chi·ska·ye is·*kust*·va graphic art
иконопись f	*i*·kan·a·pis' icon painting
искусство эпохи **Возрождения** n	is·*kust*·va e·*po*·khi vaz·vrazh·*dye*·ni·ya Renaissance art
социалистический **реализм** m	sat·sih·a·li·*sti*·chi·ski ri·a·*lizm* socialist realism

Q **What do you think of ...?**	Как вы думаете о ...?	kak vih *du*·ma·it·ye a ...
A **It reminds me of ...**	Это мне напоминает ...	e·ta mnye na·pa·mi·*na*·yet ...
A **I'm interested in ...**	Я интересуюсь ...	ya in·ti·ri·*su*·yus' ...
A **I like the works of ...**	Я люблю произведения ...	ya lyub·*lyu* pra·iz·vid·ye·ni·ya ...

Tours

When's the next tour?

Когда следующая
экскурсия?
kag·*da slye*·du·yu·sha·ya
eks·*kur*·si·ya

Можно сфотографировать?
mozh·na sfa·ta·gra·*fi*·ra·vat'

Can I take a photo?

PRACTICAL SIGHTSEEING

Can you recommend a tour?	Вы можете порекомендовать экскурсию? vih *mo*·zhiht·ye pa·ri·ka·min·da·*vat'* eks·*kur*·si·yu
Is accommodation included?	Цена включает помещение? tse·*na* fklyu·*cha*·yit pa·mi·*she*·ni·ye
Is food included?	Цена включает обед? tse·*na* fklyu·*cha*·yit ab·*yet*
Is transport included?	Цена включает транспорт? tse·*na* fklyu·*cha*·yit *tran*·spart
I'd like to hire a local guide.	Я бы хотел/хотела нанять местны гид. **m/f** ya bih kha·*tyel*/khat·*ye*·la nan·*yat'* *myest*·nih gid
How long is the tour?	Как долго продолжается экскурсия? kag *dol*·ga pra·dal·*zha*·yit·sa eks·*kur*·si·ya
What time should we be back?	Когда мы возвращаемся? kag·*da* mih vaz·vra·*sha*·yim·sa
I'm with them.	Я с ними. ya s *ni*·mi
I've lost my group.	Я потерял/потеряла свою группу. **m/f** ya pa·tir·*yal*/pa·tir·*ya*·la sva·*yu* *gru*·pu
We've seen enough (churches)!	Мы насмотрелись (церквей)! mih nas·mat·*rye*·lis' (tsihrk·*vyey*)

Senior & Disabled Travellers

KEY PHRASES

I need assistance.	Мне нужна помощь.	mnye nuzh·na po·mash
Is there wheelchair access?	Есть доступ для инвалидной коляски?	yest' do·stup dlya in·va·lid·ney kal·ya·ski
Are there toilets for people with a disability?	Есть туалет для инвалидов?	yest' tu·al·yet dlya in·va·li·daf

---

I have a disability.
Я инвалид.
ya in·va·lit

I need assistance.
Мне нужна помощь.
mnye nuzh·na po·mash

What services do you have for people with a disability?
Какие виды услуг вы оказываете инвалидам?
ka·ki·ye vi·dih us·luk vih a·ka·zih·va·yit·ye in·va·li·dam

Are there toilets for people with a disability?
Есть туалет для инвалидов?
yest' tu·al·yet dlya in·va·li·daf

Is there wheelchair access?
Есть доступ для инвалидной коляски?
yest' do·stup dlya in·va·lid·ney kal·ya·ski

How wide is the entrance?
Какова ширина входа?
ka·ka·va shih·ri·na fkho·da

Are guide dogs permitted?	Можно войти с собакой-поводырём? *mozh*·na vey·ti s sa·*ba*·key·pa·va·dihr·*yom*
How many steps are there?	Сколько здесь ступенек? *skol'*·ka zdyes' stup·*yen*·yek
Is there a lift/elevator?	Есть лифт? yest' lift
Are there rails in the bathroom?	В ванной есть перила? v *va*·ney yest' pi·*ri*·la
Could you help me cross the street safely?	Помогите мне, пожалуйста, перейти через дорогу! pa·ma·*git*·ye mnye pa·*zhal*·sta pi·*rey*·ti *che*·riz da·ro·gu
Is there somewhere I can sit down?	Можно посидеть где-нибудь? *mozh*·na pa·sid·*yet'* *gdye*·ni·but'
older person	пожилой человек m pa·zhih·*loy* chi·lav·*yek*
person with a disability	инвалид m in·va·*lit*
guide dog	собака-поводырь f sa·*ba*·ka·pa·va·*dihr'*
ramp	уклон m u·*klon*
walking frame	ходильная рама f kha·*dil'*·na·ya *ra*·ma
walking stick	трость m trost'
wheelchair	кресло для инвалидов n *kryes*·la dlya in·va·*li*·daf

Travel with Children

KEY PHRASES

Are children allowed?	Детям вход разрешён?	dyet·yam fkhot raz·ri·shon
Is there a discount for children?	Есть скидка для детей?	yest' skit·ka dlya dit·yey
Is there a baby change room?	Есть комната, оборудованная для ухода за младенцами	yest' kom·na·ta a·ba·ru·da·va·na·ya dlya u·kho·da za mlad·yent·sa·mi

Is there a ...?   Есть ...?   yest' ...

baby change room	комната, оборудованная для ухода за младенцами	kom·na·ta a·ba·ru·da·va·na·ya dlya u·kho·da za mlad·yent·sa·mi
child-minding service	служба по присмотру за детьми	sluzh·ba pa pris·mo·tru za dit'·mi
children's menu	детское меню	dyet·ska·ye min·yu
child's portion	детская порция	dyet·ska·ya port·sih·ya
discount for children	скидка для детей	skit·ka dlya dit·yey
family ticket	семейный билет	sim·yey·nih bil·yet

I need a/an ...	Я хочу ...	ya kha·*chu* ...
baby seat	детское сиденье	*dyet*·ska·ye sid·*yen*·ye
cot	детскую кроватку	*dyet*·sku·yu kra·*vat*·ku
highchair	детский стульчик	*dyet*·ski *stul'*·chik
pram/ stroller	детскую коляску	*dyet*·sku·yu kal·*yas*·ku

Do you sell ...?	Здесь продаются ...?	zdyes' pra·da·*yut*·sa ...
baby wipes	подгузники	pad·*guz*·ni·ki
disposable nappies/ diapers	одноразовые пелёнки	ad·na·*ra*·zav·nih·ye pil·*yon*·ki
painkillers for infants	болеутоляющие для младенцев	bo·li·u·tol·*ya*·yu·shi·ye dlya mlad·*yent*·sef
tissues	бумажные салфетки	bu·*mazh*·nih·ye salf·*yet*·ki

Are there any good places to take children around here?	Поблизости есть развлечения для детей? pa·*bli*·za·sti yest' raz·vli·*che*·ni·ya dlya dit·*yey*
Are children allowed?	Детям вход разрешён? *dyet*·yam fkhot raz·ri·*shon*
Is this suitable for (seven)-year-old children?	Это подходит (семи) летнему ребёнку? e·ta pat·*kho*·dit (si·mi·) *lyet*·ni·mu rib·*yon*·ku

If your child is sick, see **health** (p173).

Social

Meeting People

KEY PHRASES

My name is ...	Меня зовут ...	min·ya za·vut ...
I'm from ...	Я из ...	ya iz ...
I work in ...	Я работаю в ...	ya ra·bo·ta·yu v ...
I'm ... years old.	Мне ... лет.	mnye ... lyet
And you?	А вы/ты? pol/inf	a vih/tih

Basics

Yes.	Да. da
No.	Нет. nyet
Please.	Пожалуйста. pa·zhal·sta
Thank you (very much).	Спасибо (большое). spa·si·ba (bal'·sho·ye)
You're welcome.	Пожалуйста. pa·zhal·sta
Excuse me. (attention/apology)	Извините, пожалуйста. iz·vi·nit·ye pa·zhal·sta
Excuse me. (to get past)	Разрешите, пожалуйста. raz·ri·shiht·ye pa·zhal·sta

Greetings & Goodbyes

Russian society is generally quite affectionate. Both men and women hug, hold hands and walk around arm-in-arm. Young women kiss and hug to greet each other, while older women kiss each other on the cheek a couple of times. Shaking hands is a given between men, but a man generally doesn't extend his hand to a woman – in a business meeting, he may offer a soft handshake, but otherwise it's up to the woman to offer first. In other circumstances, men just nod hello.

Hello.	Здравствуйте.	
	zdrast·vuyt·ye	
Hi.	Привет.	
	priv·yet	
Good day/afternoon.	Добрый день.	
	do·brih dyen'	
Good evening.	Добрый вечер.	
	do·brih vye·chir	
Good morning.	Доброе утро.	
	do·bra·ye u·tra	
🅠 **How are you?**	Как дела?	
	kag dyi·la	
🅐 **Fine. And you?**	Спасибо, хорошо. А у вас?	
	spa·si·ba kha·ra·sho a u vas	
🅠 **What's your name?**	Как вас зовут?	
	kak vaz za·vut	
🅐 **My name is (Jane).**	Меня зовут (Джейн).	
	min·ya za·vut (dzheyn)	
🅐 **My name is (Jane Brown).**	Меня зовут (Джейн), а фамилия (Браун).	
	(lit: my name Jane and surname Brown)	
	min·ya za·vut (dzheyn) a fa·mi·li·ya (braun)	
I'd like to introduce you to …	Познакомьтесь, это …	
	paz·na·komt·yes' e·ta …	
✂ **This is …**	Это …	*e·ta …*

For kinship terms, see **family** (p125).

SOCIAL MEETING PEOPLE

I'm pleased to meet you.	Очень приятно.
	o·chin' pri·yat·na
See you again soon.	До скорой встречи.
	da sko·rey fstrye·chi
Goodbye.	До свидания.
	da svi·dan·ya
Bye.	Пока.
	pa·ka
Good night.	Спокойной ночи.
	spa·koy·ney no·chi

Titles & Addressing People

When you're addressing someone politely, use their first name and patronymic (not their family name). A 'patronymic' is a middle name derived from the person's father's name, and means 'son/daughter of' – Ivan's son Sergey would be called *Сергей Иванович* sir·gey i·va·no·vich (Sergey Ivanovich). There are words for 'Mr' and 'Ms/ Miss/Mrs' – *господин* ga·spa·din (lit: citizen) and *госпожа* ga·spa·zha (lit: citizeness) – but these are only used in official contexts. In informal situations, you can use your first name as in English.

Mr	господин
	ga·spa·din
Sir	сэр
	ser
Ms/Mrs/Miss	госпожа
	ga·spa·zha
Madam	мадам
	ma·dam

Making Conversation

Do you live here?	Вы здесь живёте?
	vih zdyes' zhihv·yot·ye
What a beautiful day!	Какой прекрасный день!
	ka·koy pri·kras·nih dyen'

🔊 LISTEN FOR

Как жизнь?	kag zhihzn'	How's life?
Не жалуюсь!	nye *zha*·lu·yus'	Can't complain.
Не хорошо, не плохо!	nye kha·ra·*sho* nye *plo*·kha	Not good, not bad.
Ничего нового нету!	ni·chi·*vo no*·va·va *nye*·tu	Nothing new.
Еле на ногах держусь!	*yel*·ye na na·*gakh* dyir·*zhus'*	I can barely keep going!

Nice/Awful weather, isn't it?	Какая хорошая/плохая погода! ka·*ka*·ya kha·*ro*·sha·ya/pla·*kha*·ya pa·*go*·da
Where are you going?	Далеко собираетесь? da·li·*ko* sa·bi·*ra*·yit·yes'
What are you doing?	Чем вы занимаетесь? chem vih za·ni·*ma*·yit·yes'
Do you like it here?	Вам здесь нравится? vam zdyes' *nra*·vit·sa
I love it here.	Мне здесь очень нравится! mnye zdyes' *o*·chin' *nra*·vit·sa
What's this called?	Как это называется? kak e·ta na·zih·*va*·yit·sa
That's (beautiful)!	Как (красиво)! kak (kra·*si*·va)
How long are you here for?	Как долго вы здесь будете? kag *dol*·ga vih zdyes' *bu*·dit·ye
I'm here for (five) weeks/days.	Я буду здесь (пять) недель/дней. ya *bu*·du zdyes' (pyat') nid·*yel'*/dnyey

SOCIAL MEETING PEOPLE

Q Are you here on holiday?	Вы здесь в отпуске? vih zdyes' v *ot*·pusk·ye
A I'm here for a holiday.	Я здесь в отпуске. ya zdyes' v *ot*·pusk·ye
A I'm here on business.	Я здесь по бизнесу. ya zdyes' pa *biz*·ni·su
A I'm here to study.	Я здесь учусь. ya zdyes' u·*chus*'

Nationalities

| **Q** Where are you from? | Вы откуда? vih at·*ku*·da |
| **A** I'm from Australia/ Canada. | Я из Австралии/Канады. ya iz af·*stra*·li·i/ka·*na*·dih |

For more countries, see the **dictionary**.

Age

Q How old are you?	Сколько вам лет? *skol*'·ka vam lyet
A I'm ... years old.	Мне ... лет. mnye ... lyet
Q How old is your daughter?	Сколько вашей дочке лет? *skol*'·ka va·shey *doch*·kye lyet
Q How old is your son?	Сколько вашему сыну лет? *skol*'·ka *va*·shih·mu *sih*·nu lyet
A He/She is ... years old.	Ему/Ей ... лет. ye·*mu*/yey ... lyet
I'm younger than I look.	Я выгляжу моложе своих лет. ya vih·gli·zhu ma·*lo*·zhe sva·*ikh* lyet

For your age, see **numbers & amounts** (p32).

🔊 LISTEN FOR

Здорово, мужики!	zda·*ro*·va mu·*zhih*·*ki*	Hey guys!
Здорово!	*zdo*·ra·va	Great!
Хорошо.	kha·ra·*sho*	It's OK.
Не спрашивайте!	nye *spra*·shih·veyt·ye	Don't ask!
Посмотрите!	pas·ma·*trit*·ye	Look!
Послушайте!	pas·*lu*·sheyt·ye	Listen!
Это (не) возможно.	*e*·ta (nye) vaz·*mozh*·na	It's (im)possible.

Occupations & Studies

Q What's your occupation?	Кем вы работаете? kyem vih ra·*bo*·ta·yit·ye
A I'm a/an ...	Я ... ya ...

accountant	бухгалтер	bu·*gal*·tir
chef	шеф-повар	shef·*po*·var
doctor	врач	vrach
engineer	инженер	in·zhihn·*yer*
mechanic	механик	mi·*kha*·nik
student	студент m	stud·*yent*
	студентка f	stud·*yent*·ka
teacher	учитель m	u·*chi*·til'
	учительница f	u·*chi*·til'·nit·sa

A I work in government.	Я работаю на государственной службе. ya ra·*bo*·ta·yu na ga·su·*darst*·vi·ney *sluzh*·bye

> **CULTURE TIP**
>
> **Body Language**
> Here are some distinctively Russian gestures:
> A movement like cutting your throat with your hand means 'I'm full!'.
> Flicking your throat with your index finger indicates drinking – usually 'Let's drink!' or 'He/She is drunk'.
> Nodding your head in one direction means 'Let's go!' – for a serious talk, a fight, or possibly a sexual proposition.
> A hand placed on one hip means 'So what?'.
> Tapping your forehead with your finger says you think that someone is stupid.

A I work in health.

Я работаю в здравоохранении.
ya ra·bo·ta·yu v zdra·va·a·khran·ye·ni·ye

A I work in marketing.

Я работаю в маркетинге.
ya ra·bo·ta·yu v mark·ye·ting·ye

A I'm retired.

Я на пенсии.
ya na pyen·si·i

A I'm self-employed.

Я имею свой собственный бизнес.
ya im·ye·yu svoy sopst·vi·nih biz·nis

A I'm unemployed.

Я безработный. m
ya byiz·ra·bot·nih
Я безработная. f
ya biz·ra·bot·na·ya

Q What are you studying?

Что вы изучаете?
shto vih i·zu·cha·yit·ye

A I'm studying Russian.

Я изучаю русский язык.
ya i·zu·cha·yu rus·ki yi·zihk

A I'm studying humanities.	Я изучаю гуманитарные науки. ya i·zu·*cha*·yu gu·ma·ni·*tar*·nih·ye na·*u*·ki	
A I'm studying science.	Я изучаю естественные науки. ya i·zu·*cha*·yu yist·*yest*·vi·nih·ye na·*u*·ki	

Family

Q Do you have a ...?	У вас есть ...? u vas yest' ...	
A I have a ...	У меня есть ... u min·*ya* yest' ...	

brother	брат	brat
daughter	дочка	*doch*·ka
family	семья	sim·*ya*
husband	муж	mush
partner	парень m	pa·rin'
	девушка f	*dye*·vush·ka
sister	сестра	sist·*ra*
son	сын	sihn
wife	жена	zhih·*na*

Q Are you married?	Вы женаты? (to a man) vih zhih·*na*·tih Вы замужем? (to a woman) vih *za*·mu·zhihm
A I live with someone.	Я живу с кем-то. ya zhih·*vu* s *kyem*·ta
A I'm married.	Я женат/замужем. m/f ya zhih·*nat za*·mu·zhihm

🅰	I'm separated.	Я не живу с женой/ мужем. **m/f** ya nye zhih·vu s zhih·noy/ mu·zhihm
🅰	I'm single.	Я холост/холоста. **m/f** ya kho·last/kha·la·sta

Talking with Children

In this section, phrases are in the informal *ты* tih (you) form only. If you're not sure what this means, see the box on page 140.

What's your name?	Как тебя зовут? kak tib·ya za·vut
How old are you?	Сколько тебе лет? skol'·ka tib·ye lyet
When's your birthday?	Когда твой день рождения? kag·da tvoy dyen' razhd·ye·ni·ya
Do you go to school?	Ты ходишь в школу? tih kho·dish f shko·lu
Do you like your teacher?	Тебе нравится твоя учительница? tib·ye nra·vit·sa tva·ya u·chi·til'·nit·sa
What grade are you in?	Ты в каком классе? tih f ka·kom klas·ye
Do you like school?	Тебе нравится школа? tib·ye nra·vit·sa shko·la
Do you like sport?	Тебе нравится спорт? tib·ye nra·vit·sa sport
Do you learn (English)?	Ты учишь (английский) язык? tih u·chish' (an·gli·ski) ya·zihk

LANGUAGE TIP

Conversation Dos & Don'ts
There are very few taboo topics of conversation in today's Russia. Politics is the most popular topic of all, and even on a first meeting, it's quite acceptable to ask someone in detail about their work, salary and personal life. Although Russia is a multiethnic society with citizens from many cultural backgrounds, you may come across controversial attitudes to nationality and religion.

SOCIAL MEETING PEOPLE

Talking about Children

What a beautiful child!	Какой красивый ребёнок! ka·*koy* kra·si·vih rib·*yo*·nak
How old is he/she?	Сколько ему/ей лет? *skol*'·ka yi·*mu*/yey lyet
What's his/her name?	Как его/её зовут? kak yi·*vo*/yi·*yo* za·*vut*
Does he/she go to school?	Он/Она учится? on/a·*na* u·*chit*·sa
How many children do you have?	Сколько у вас детей? *skol*'·ka u vas dit·*yey*
What type of school do your children go to?	В какую школу ходят ваши дети? f ka·*ku*·yu *shko*·lu *kho*·dit *va*·shih *dye*·ti
Where do you send your children in summer?	Куда вы летом отправляете своих детей? ku·*da* vih *lye*·tam at·prav·*lya*·yit·ye sva·*ikh* dit·*yey*

Farewells

(Tomorrow) is my last day here.	(Завтра) мой последний день. (*zaf*·tra) moy pas·*lyed*·ni dyen'

It's been great meeting you.	Было очень приятно познакомиться. *bih*·la o·chin' pri·*yat*·na paz·na·ko·mit'·sa
Keep in touch!	Не забывайте! nye za·bih·*veyt*·ye
Q **What's your ...?**	Можно ваш ...? *mozh*·na vash ...
A **Here's my address.**	Вот мой адрес. vot moy *a*·dris
A **Here's my email address.**	Вот мой и-мейл. vot moy i·*meyl*
A **Here's my phone number.**	Вот мой номер телефона. vot moy *no*·mir ti·li·*fo*·na

Well-Wishing

Russian has three ways of wishing someone good luck – *С богом!* z *bo*·gam (With God!), *Ни пуха ни пера!* ni *pu*·kha ni pi·*ra* (Neither down nor feathers!) or *Желаю успеха!* zhih·*la*·yu usp·*ye*·kha (I wish you luck!). The correct response is always *К чёрту!* k *chor*·tu (To the devil!).

Congratulations!	Поздравляю! paz·drav·*lya*·yu
All the best!	Всего хорошего! fsi·*vo* kha·ro·*shih*·va
Happy Birthday!	С днём рождения! z dnyom razh·*dye*·ni·ya
Merry Christmas!	С Рождеством Христовым! s razh·dist·*vom* khri·*sto*·vihm
Bon voyage!	Счастливого пути! shis·*li*·va·va pu·*ti*

Interests

KEY PHRASES

What do you do in your spare time?	Чем вы занимаетесь в свободное время?	chem vih za·ni·*ma*·yit·yes' f sva·*bod*·na·ye *vryem*·ya
Do you like ...?	Вам нравится ...?	vam *nra*·vit·sa ...
I (don't) like ...	Мне (не) нравится ...	mnye (nye) *nra*·vit·sa ...

Common Interests

What do you do in your spare time?	Чем вы занимаетесь в свободное время? chem vih za·ni·*ma*·yit·yes' f sva·*bod*·na·ye *vryem*·ya
Q **Do you like ...?**	Вам нравится ...? vam *nra*·vit·sa ...
A **I (don't) like ...**	Мне (не) нравится ... mnye (nye) *nra*·vit·sa ...

cooking	готовить	ga·*to*·vit'
gardening	садоводство	sa·da·*vots*·tva
photography	фотографировать	fa·ta·gra·*fi*·ra·vat'
reading	читать	chi·*tat*'
shopping	ходить по магазинам	kha·*dit*' pa ma·ga·*zi*·nam
watching TV	смотреть телевизор	smat·*ryet*' ti·li·*vi*·zar

For types of sports, see **sports** (p155) and the **dictionary**.

Music

Do you ...?	Вы ...? vih ...	
dance	танцуете	tant·*su*·it·ye
go to concerts	ходите на концерты	*kho*·dit·ye na kant·*ser*·tih
listen to music	слушаете музыку	*slu*·sha·yit·ye *mu*·zih·ku
play an instrument	играете на каком-нибудь инструменте	i·*gra*·yit·ye na ka·*kom*·ni·bud' ins·trum·*yent*·ye
sing	поёте	pa·*yot*·ye

Which bands do you like?	Какие группы вы любите? ka·*ki*·ye *gru*·pih vih *lyu*·bit·ye
Which music do you like?	Какую музыку вы любите? ka·*ku*·yu *mu*·zih·ku vih *lyu*·bit·ye
Which singers do you like?	Каких певцов вы любите? ka·*kikh* pift·*sof* vih *lyu*·bit·ye
folk songs	народные песни f pl na·*rod*·nih·ye *pyes*·ni
... music	... музыка f ... *mu*·zih·ka

classical	классическая	kla·*si*·chi·ska·ya
electronic	электронная	e·lik·*tro*·na·ya
traditional	традиционная	tra·dit·sih·o·na·ya
world	мировая	mi·ra·*va*·ya

Planning to go to a concert? See **tickets** (p46) and **going out** (p141).

CULTURE TIP

Card Games

As you travel on the Trans-Siberian Railway, the Russian passengers may introduce you to their favourite card game, *преферанс* pri·fi·*rans* (preference). It's played with the full 52-card deck less the sixes, and involves taking tricks to win points. Some call it 'bridge for children'.

Cinema & Theatre

I feel like going to ...	Мне хочется пойти на ... mnye *kho*·chit·sa pey·*ti* na ...
Do you have tickets for the ...?	Есть билеты на ...? yest' bil·*ye*·tih na ...
ballet	балет m bal·*yet*
concert	концерт m kant·*sert*
opera	опера f o·pi·ra
play	пьеса f *pye*·sa
Q How did you like the ...?	Как вам понравился ...? kak vam pan·*ra*·vil·sa ...
A I thought it was ...	По-моему, было ... pa·*mo*·i·mu *bih*·la ...

excellent	отлично	at·*lich*·na
long	слишком долго	*slish*·kam *dol*·ga
OK	нормально	nar·*mal'*·na
pretentious	претенциозно	pri·tint·sih·*oz*·na

Are there any extra tickets?	Есть лишние билеты? yest' *lish*·ni·ye bil·*ye*·tih

CULTURE TIP — Etiquette Tips

When you enter a restaurant or the theatre, leave your coat, hat and boots at the *гардероб* gar·di·*rop* (cloakroom). On arriving at a friend's home, remove your shoes and you'll be offered *тапочки* ta·*pach*·ki (slippers).

I'd like to get cheap tickets.	Я бы хотел/хотела билеты подешевле. m/f ya bih khat·*yel*/khat·ye·la bil·*ye*·tih pa·di·*shev*·lye
I'd like to get the best tickets.	Я бы хотел/хотела билеты получше. m/f ya bih khat·*yel*/khat·ye·la bil·*ye*·tih pa·*luch*·she
What's on at the cinema/theatre tonight?	Что идёт в кино/театре? shto id·*yot* f ki·*no*/ti·*at*·rye
Is there a matinée show?	Есть дневной спектакль? yest' dniv·*noy* spik·*takl*'
Is it in (English)?	Это на (английском)? e·ta na (an·*gli*·skam)
Does it have (English) subtitles?	Этот фильм с субтитрами на (английском)? e·tat film s sub·*ti*·tra·mi na (an·*gli*·skam)
Is this seat taken?	Это место занято? e·ta mye·sta zan·ya·ta
What's he/she saying?	Что он/она говорит? shto on/a·na ga·va·rit
Have you seen ...?	Вы смотрели ...? vih smat·rye·li ...
Q Who's in it?	Кто играет в этом фильме? kto i·*gra*·yit v e·tam film·ye
A It stars ...	Главную роль играет ... glav·nu·yu rol' i·*gra*·yet ...

I (don't) like ...		Я (не) люблю ... ya (nye) lyub·*lyu* ...
action movies	боевики	ba·i·vi·*ki*
animated films	мультфильмы	mult·*fil*'·mih
comedies	комедии	kam·*ye*·di
docu-mentaries	документальные фильмы	da·ku·min·*tal*'·nih·ye *fil*'·mih
drama	драму	*dra*·mu
horror movies	фильмы ужасов	*fil*'·mih u·*zha*·saf
(Russian) cinema	(русское) кино	(*rus*·ka·ye) ki·*no*
sci-fi	научную фантастику	na·*uch*·nu·yu fan·*tas*·ti·ku
short films	коротко-метражные фильмы	ka·rat·ka·mi·*trazh*·nih·ye *fil*'·mih
thrillers	сенсационные фильмы	sin·sat·sih·o·nih·ye *fil*'·mih
war movies	фильмы о войне	*fil*'·mih a veyn·ye

box (in theatre)	ложа f *lo*·zha
concert hall	концертный зал m kant·*sert*·nih zal
drama theatre	драматический театр m dra·ma·*ti*·chi·ski ti·*atr*
dress circle	бельэтаж m byel'·i·*tash*
inconvenient place	неудобное место n nyi·u·*dob*·na·ye *mye*·sta

row	ряд m
	ryat
stalls	партер m
	par·ter
(1st/2nd/3rd) tier	(первый/второй/третий)
	ярус m
	(pyer·vih/fta·roy/trye·ti) ya·rus

Volunteering

I'd like to volunteer my skills.	Я бы хотел/хотела предлогать мои услуги. m/f
	ya bih kha·tyel/khat·ye·la pryed·la·gat' ma·yi u·slu·gi
Are there any volunteer programs available in the area?	Есть добровольческие программы в этом районе?
	yest' da·bra·val'·chye·ski·ye pra·gra·mih v e·tam ra·yon·ye

CULTURE TIP

Astrology

A favourite topic of conversation in Russia is
астрология ast·ra·lo·gi·ya (astrology) and the
зодиак zo·di·ak (zodiac).

Q What's your star sign?	Какой ваш знак? pol
	ka·koy vash znak
	Какой твой знак? inf
	ka·koy tvoy znak
A My star sign is ...	Мой знак ...
	moy znak ...
I'm on the cusp.	Я на стыке знаков.
	ya na stih·kye zna·kaf
We're compatible!	Мы идеально подходим друг другу!
	mih i·di·al'·na pat·kho·dim drug dru·gu

Feelings & Opinions

KEY PHRASES

I'm (not) ...	Я (не) ...	ya (nye) ...
What about you?	А вы?	a vih
How do you like it?	Как вы думаете об этом?	kak vih du·ma·yit·ye ab e·tam
I thought it was OK.	По-моему, было нормально.	pa·mo·i·mu bih·la nar·mal'·na
Did you hear about ...?	Вы слышали про ...?	vih slih·sha·li pra ...

Feelings

I'm (not) ...	Я (не) ... ya (nye) ...	
afraid	боюсь	ba·yus'
cold	замёрз m	zam·yors
	замёрзла f	zam·yorz·la
happy	счастлив m	shas·lif
	счастлива f	shas·li·va
hot	умираю от	u·mi·ra·yu ad
	жары	zha·rih
hungry	голоден m	go·la·din
	голодна f	ga·lad·na
in a hurry	спешу	spi·shu
sad	грущу	gru·shu
thirsty	хочу пить	kha·chu pit'
worried	беспокоюсь	bis·pa·ko·yus'

What about you?	А вы? a vih
a little	немного nim·*no*·ga
I'm a little tired.	Я немного устал/ устала. **m/f** ya nim·*no*·ga u·*stal*/ u·*sta*·la
very	очень *o*·chin'
I'm very surprised.	Я очень удивляюсь. ya *o*·chin' u·div·*lya*·yus'

If you're not feeling well, see **health** (p173).

Opinions

Q Did you like it?	Вам это понравилось? vam e·ta pan·*ra*·vi·las'
Q How do you like it?	Как вы думаете об этом? kak vih *du*·ma·yit·ye ab e·tam
A I thought it was ...	По-моему, было ... pa·*mo*·i·mu *bih*·la ...
A It's ...	Это ... e·ta ...

awful	ужасно	u·*zhas*·na
beautiful	красиво	kra·*si*·va
boring	скучно	*skush*·na
great	здорово	*zdo*·ra·va
interesting	интересно	in·tir·*yes*·na
OK	нормально	nar·*mal'*·na
too expensive	слишком дорого	*slish*·kam *do*·ra·ga
strange	странно	*stra*·na

Politics & Social Issues

🅀 **Who do you vote for?**	За кого вы голосуете?	za ka·vo vih ga·la·su·yit·ye
🅀 **Do you support ...?**	Вы поддерживаете ...?	vih pad·yer·zhih·va·yit·ye ...
🅰 **I support the ....**	Я поддерживаю ...	ya pad·yer·zhih·va·yu ...
🅰 **I'm a member of the ... party.**	Я член ... партии.	ya chlyen ... par·ti

communist	коммунистической	ka·mu·ni·sti·chi·skey
conservative	консервативной	kan·sir·va·tiv·ney
democratic	демократической	di·ma·kra·ti·chi·skey
green	зелёной	zil·yo·ney
liberal	либеральной	li·bi·ral'·ney
social democratic	социал-демократической	sat·sih·al· di·ma·kra·ti·chi·skey
socialist	социалистической	sat·sih·a·li·sti·chi·skey

Did you hear about ...?	Вы слышали про ...?	vih slih·sha·li pra ...
How do people feel about ...?	Как думают про ...?	kak du·ma·yut pra ...
🅀 **Do you agree with it?**	Вы согласны?	vih sa·glas·nih
🅰 **I (don't) agree with ...**	Я (не) согласен/ согласна с ... m/f	ya (nye) sa·gla·sin/ sa·glas·na s ...
How can we protest against ...?	Как мы можем протестовать против ...?	kak mih mo·zhihm pra·ti·sta·vat' pro·tif ...

LANGUAGE TIP	**Idioms**

To find out how Russian speakers really feel about life, you should get familiar with some of their idioms ...

You've got no hope in hell!	Руки коротки. (lit: your hands are too short) *ru·ki ko·rat·ki*
Don't mess with them!	Пальца в рот не клади! (lit: don't put your finger in their mouth) *palt·sa v rot nye kla·di*
This is impossible to pronounce!	Язык сломаешь! (lit: you'll break your tongue) *yi·zihk sla·ma·yish*
Like getting blood from a stone.	Как от козла молока. (lit: like milk from a he-goat) *kak at kaz·la ma·la·ka*
This is the root of the problem.	Вот где собака зарыта. (lit: here's where the dog's buried) *vot gdye sa·ba·ka za·rih·ta*
They've disappeared into thin air.	Как корова языком слизала. (lit: like a cow licked them away) *kak ka·ro·va yi·zih·kom sli·za·la*
It's totally packed.	Как сельдей в бочке. (lit: like herrings in a barrel) *kak sil'·dyey v boch·kye*
Living in the lap of luxury.	Полная чаша. (lit: full cup) *pol·na·ya cha·sha*
Unexpected problems.	Подводные камни. (lit: underwater rocks) *pad·vod·nih·ye kam·ni*

> ## Это красиво.
> *e*·ta kra·*si*·va
> *It's beautiful.*

How can we support ...?	Как мы можем поддерживать ...? kak mih *mo*·zhim pad·*yer*·zhih·vat' ...
the economy	экономика f e·ka·*no*·mi·ka
the environment	окружающая среда f a·kru·*zha*·yu·sha·ya sri·*da*
human rights	права человека n pl pra·*va* chi·lav·*ye*·ka
immigration	иммиграция f i·mi·*grat*·sih·ya
the Soviet era	советский период m sav·*yet*·ski pi·ri·ot
the war in ...	война в ... f vey·*na* f ...

CULTURE TIP

Polite & Informal
Russian has a polite and an informal word for the singular 'you' form. The informal *мы* tih can be used with friends or relatives, while the polite *вы* vih should be used for strangers or officials. As a traveller, it's best to use the *вы* form with new people you meet. Nouns and verbs will change depending on which form is used. In this book we've chosen the form appropriate for the situation, ie normally the polite form unless marked otherwise. If either form might be suitable, we've given both.

See also **personal pronouns** in the **grammar** chapter (p19).

The Environment

Where can I recycle this?	Где можно перерабатывать это? gdye *mozh*·na pye·rye·ra·*ba*·tih·vat' *e*·ta
Is this a protected forest/park?	Это заповедный лес/парк? *e*·ta za·pav·*yed*·nih lyes/park
Is this a protected species?	Это заповедный вид? *e*·ta za·pav·*yed*·nih vit
Is there a ... problem here?	Здесь есть проблема ...? zdyes' yest' prab·*lye*·ma ...
What should be done about ...?	Как быть с ...? kag biht' s ...
nuclear energy	ядерная энергия f *ya*·dir·na·ya in·*yer*·gi·ya
pollution	загрязнение n za·griz·*nye*·ni·ye
recycling programme	рециклирование n rit·sih·kli·ra·*va*·ni·ye

Going Out

KEY PHRASES

What's on tonight?	Что идёт сегодня вечером?	shto id·*yot* si·*vod*·nya *vye*·chi·ram
Where can I find clubs?	Где находятся клубы?	gdye na·*kho*·dit·sa *klu*·bih
Would you like to go for a coffee?	Вы не хотите пойти в кафе?	vih nye kha·*tit*·ye pey·*ti* f ka·*fe*
Where will we meet?	Где встретимся?	gdye fstrye·tim·sa
What time will we meet?	Во сколько встретимся?	va skol'·ka fstrye·tim·sa

Where to Go

What's there to do in the evenings?	Что можно делать по вечерам? shto *mozh*·na *dye*·lat' pa vi·chi·*ram*
What's on ...?	Что идёт ...? shto id·*yot* ...

locally	в этом районе	v *e*·tam ra·*yon*·ye
today	сегодня	si·*vod*·nya
tonight	сегодня вечером	si·*vod*·nya *vye*·chi·ram
this weekend	на этих выходных	na *e*·tikh vih·khad·*nihkh*

Where can I find ...?	Где находятся ...? gdye na·*kho*·dit·sa ...	
clubs	клубы	*klu*·bih
gay venues	гей-клубы	gyey·*klu*·bih
places to eat	рестораны	ri·sta·*ra*·nih
pubs	пивные	piv·*nih*·ye

I feel like going to a ...	Мне хочется пойти ... mnye *kho*·chit·sa pey·*ti* ...	
bathhouse	в баню	v *ban*·yu
bar	в бар	v bar
cafe	в кафе	f ka·*fe*
concert	на концерт	na kant·*sert*
film	в кино	v ki·*no*
football/soccer match	на футбольный матч	na fud·*bol'*·nih mach
party	на тусовку	na tu·*sof*·ku

For more on bars, drinks and partying, see **romance** (p147) and **eating out** (p184). For more forms of entertainment, see **interests** (p129) and **sports** (p155).

Invitations

Are you free now?	Вы свободны сейчас? vih sva·*bod*·nih si·*chas*
Are you free tonight?	Вы свободны сегодня вечером? vih sva·*bod*·nih si·*vod*·nya *vye*·chi·ram
Are you free this weekend?	Вы свободны в субботу? vih sva·*bod*·nih f su·*bo*·tu

Would you like to go (for a) ...?	Вы не хотите пойти ...?	vih nye kha·*tit*·ye pey·*ti* ...

coffee	в кафе	f ka·*fe*
dancing	потанцевать	pa·tant·sih·*vat'*
drink	в бар	v bar
meal	в ресторан	v ri·sta·*ran*
out somewhere	куда-нибудь	ku·*da*·ni·bud'
walk	погулять	pa·gul·*yat'*

SOCIAL   GOING OUT

Do you know a good restaurant?	Вы знаете, где хороший ресторан? vih *zna*·it·ye gdye kha·*ro*·shih ri·sta·*ran*
Do you want to go to a (disco) with me?	Вы не хотите пойти со мной в (дискотеку)? vih nye kha·*tit*·ye pey·*ti* sa mnoy v (di·skat·*ye*·ku)
Come to our place for a party.	Поедем к нам на тусовку. pa·*yed*·yem k nam na tu·*sof*·ku
You should come.	Приезжайте! pri·i·*zheyt*·ye
Drop in sometime!	Заходите как-нибудь! za·kha·*dit*·ye *kak*·ni·bud'

For other invitations, see **romance** (p147).

Responding to Invitations

Sure!	Обязательно! ab·ya·za·til'·na
Yes, I'd love to.	Я с удовольствием. ya s u·da·*volst*·vi·yem
That's very kind of you.	Благодарю вас. bla·ga·dar·*yu* vas

Where shall we go?	Куда? ku·*da*
It's a date.	Договорились. da·ga·va·*ri*·lis'
No, I'm afraid I can't.	Спасибо, но я не могу. spa·*si*·ba no ya nye ma·*gu*
Sorry, I can't sing/dance.	К сожалению, я не умею петь/танцевать. k sa·zhal·*ye*·ni·yu ya nye um·*ye*·yu pyet'/tant·sih·*vat'*
What about (tomorrow)?	Как насчёт (завтра)? kak na·*shot* (*zaf*·tra)

Arranging to Meet

Q	**What time will we meet?**	Во сколько встретимся? va *skol'*·ka fstrye·*tim*·sa
A	**Let's meet at (seven) o'clock.**	Встретимся в (семь) часов. fstrye·*tim*·sa f (syem') chi·*sof*
Q	**Where will we meet?**	Где встретимся? gdye fstrye·*tim*·sa
A	**Let's meet at the (entrance).**	Встретимся перед (входом). fstrye·*tim*·sa *pye*·rit (*fkho*·dam)

🔊 LISTEN FOR

За ваше здоровье!	za *va*·shih zda·*rov*·ye	To your health!
За вечную дружбу!	za *vyech*·nu·yu *druzh*·bu	To eternal friendship!
За любовь!	za lyu·*bov'*	To love!
За успех!	za usp·*yekh*	To success!

Что идёт сегодня вечером?
shto id·*yot* si·*vod*·nya *vye*·chi·ram

What's on tonight?

Q **Where will you be?**	Где вы будете ждать? gdye vih *bu*·dit·ye zhdat'	
A **I'll pick you up.**	Я зайду за вами. ya zey·*du* za *va*·mi	
Q **Are you ready?**	Вы готовы? vih ga·*to*·vih	
A **I'm ready.**	Я готов. m ya ga·*tof* Я готова. f ya ga·*to*·va	
See you later/tomorrow!	До встречи/завтра! da *fstrye*·chi/*zaf*·tra	
Sorry I'm late.	Извините, что я опоздал/ опоздала. m/f iz·vi·*nit*·ye shto ya a·paz·*dal*/ a·paz·*da*·la	

CULTURE TIP

Bathhouses
Going to the *баня* ban·ya (communal bathhouse) is a ritual enjoyed by many Russians, who go to the same bathhouse at the same time each week to meet up with friends. Russian *баня* participants thrash themselves or their friends with a *веник* vye·nik (a bunch of oak or birch twigs) which detoxifies the body while releasing delightful forest aromas. The sexes are segregated, either by coming to the *баня* on alternate days or bathing on different floors of the same building.

When you go to a *баня,* take a *полотенце* pa·lat·yent·se (towel), *шампунь* sham·pun' (shampoo), *туфли* tuf·li (plastic shoes) and some *чай* chey (tea) or *пиво* pi·va (beer). Strip in the change room, buy your twigs and move to the *парилка* pa·ril·ka (steam room). Sit on a wooden bench and dip your twig-bundle into a bucket of hot water to soften it before the thrashing. After five minutes or so of steam, immerse yourself in the *бассейн* bas·yeyn (cold pool). Then drink your tea or beer and have a chat before starting all over again.

Russians wish each other good health after the bathhouse experience with the expression *С лёгким паром!* s lyokh·kim pa·ram (With light steam!).

Drugs

Do you have a light?	Дай мне прикурить! dey mnye pri·ku·rit'
Do you want to have a smoke?	Хочешь покурить? kho·chish' pa·ku·rit'
I take ... occasionally.	Я иногда принимаю ... ya i·nag·da pri·ni·ma·yu ...
I don't take drugs.	Я не принимаю наркотик. ya nye pri·ni·ma·yu nar·ko·tik

If the police are talking to you about drugs, see **police** (p170).

Romance

KEY PHRASES

Would you like to do something?	Хотите, пойдём куда-нибудь?	kha·*tit*·ye peyd·*yom* ku·*da*·ni·but'
I love you.	Я люблю тебя.	ya lyub·*lyu* tib·*ya*
Leave me alone!	Приваливай!	pri·*va*·li·vey

We've given phrases in the polite *вы* vih form in **asking someone out**, **pick-up lines** and **rejections**. For the rest of this chapter, phrases are in the informal *ты* tih (you) form only. If you're not sure what this means, see the box on page 140.

Asking Someone Out

Where would you like to go (tonight)?	Куда вы хотите пойти (сегодня вечером)? ku·*da* vih kha·*tit*·ye pey·*ti* (si·*vod*·nya *vye*·chi·ram)
Q Would you like to do something (tomorrow)?	Хотите, пойдём куда-нибудь (завтра)? kha·*tit*·ye peyd·*yom* ku·*da*·ni·but' (*zaf*·tra)
A Yes, I'd love to.	С удовольствием. s u·da·*volst*·vi·yem
A Sorry, I can't.	К сожалению, я не могу. k sa·zhal·*ye*·ni·yu ya nye ma·*gu*

SOCIAL ROMANCE

ROMANCE

Pick-Up Lines

Isn't this place great/terrible?	Здесь классно/паршиво, правда? zdyes' *klas*·na/par·*shih*·va *prav*·da
Would you like a drink?	Хотите выпить со мной? kha·*tit*·ye *vih*·pit' sa mnoy
What are you having?	Что вы хотите пить? shto vih kha·*tit*·ye pit'
Can I have a light?	Можно прикурить? *mozh*·na pri·ku·*rit'*
Let's dance.	Давайте потанцуем. da·*veyt*·ye pa·tant·*su*·yem
You look great!	Вы классно выглядите! vih *klas*·na *vih*·gli·dit·ye
What are they selling? **(when waiting in a queue)**	Что дают? shto da·*yut*
This isn't how I normally meet people.	Для меня это весьма необычный способ знакомства. dlya min·*ya* e·ta vis'·*ma* ni·a·*bihch*·nih *spo*·sap zna·*komst*·va

Rejections

No, thank you.	Нет, спасибо. nyet spa·*si*·ba
I'd rather not.	Я не хочу. ya nye kha·*chu*
I'm here with my girlfriend.	Я здесь с подругой. ya zdyes' z pa·*dru*·goy
I'm here with my boyfriend.	Я здесь с другом. ya zdyes' z pa·*dru*·gam

SOCIAL ROMANCE

> **CULTURE TIP**
>
> **Etiquette Tips**
> Russian men are very traditional by a modern girl's standards. They offer *Разрешите вам помочь!* raz·re·*shiht*·ye vam pa·*moch'* (Let me help you!) to women for just about everything – opening a door, taking a coat, lighting a cigarette. You can respond with *Вы очень добры!* vih o·chin' dab·*rih* (You're very kind).

Excuse me, I have to go now.	Извините, мне пора идти. iz·vi·*nit*·ye mnye pa·*ra* i·*ti*
Leave me alone!	Приваливай! pri·*va*·li·vey
Piss off!	Отвали! at·ye·*bis'*

Getting Closer

I like you very much.	Ты мне очень нравишься. tih mnye o·chin' *nra*·vish'·sa
You're good-looking.	Ты красивый/красивая. **m/f** tih kra·*si*·vih/kra·*si*·va·ya
You're great.	Ты классный/классная. **m/f** tih *klas*·nih/*klas*·na·ya
I want to get to know you better.	Мне бы хотелось узнать о тебе побольше. mnye bih khat·*ye*·las' uz·*nat'* a tib·*ye* pa·*bol'*·she
Can I kiss you?	Можно тебя поцеловать? *mozh*·na tib·*ya* pat·se·la·*vat'*
Do you want to come inside for a while?	Хочешь зайти на время? *kho*·chish' zey·*ti* na *vryem*·ya
Can I stay over?	Можно мне остаться? *mozh*·na mnye a·*stat'*·sa

150

SOCIAL ROMANCE

> **CULTURE TIP** **Superstitions**
> Don't give an even number of flowers to your Russian love interest, as superstition says this is only suitable for a funeral. Always give an odd number.

Sex

Hold me.	Обними меня. ab·ni·*mi* min·ya
Kiss me.	Поцелуй меня. pat·se·*luy* min·ya
I want you.	Я хочу тебя. ya kha·*chu* tib·ya
Let's go to bed.	Давай в постель. da·*vey* f past·*yel'*
Touch me here.	Трогай меня здесь. *tro*·gey min·ya zdyes'
Q Do you like this?	Это тебе нравится? e·ta tib·ye *nra*·vit·sa
A I (don't) like that.	Это мне (не) нравится. e·ta mnye (nye) *nra*·vit·sa
I think we should stop now.	Мы должны остановиться. mih dalzh·*nih* a·sta·na·*vit'*·sa
I won't do it without protection.	Ничего не сделаю без защиты. ni·chi·*vo* nye *zdye*·la·yu byez zash·*chi*·tih
Do you have a (condom)?	У тебя есть (презерватив)? u tib·*ya* yest' (pri·zir·va·*tif*)
Let's use a (condom).	Одень (презерватив). ad·*yen'* (pri·zir·va·*tif*)
That's great!	Это здорово! e·ta *zdo*·ra·va

| Don't stop! | Не останавливайся! |
| | nye a·sta·*nav*·li·vey·sa |

| Stop! | Стой! |
| | stoy |

| That was amazing. | Было чудесно. |
| | *bih*·la chud·*yes*·na |

| That was romantic. | Было романтично. |
| | *bih*·la ra·man·*tich*·na |

| That was wild. | Было дико. |
| | *bih*·la *di*·ka |

Love

| I'm serious about you. | Я серьёзен/серьёзна. **m/f** |
| | ya sir·*yo*·zin/sir·*yoz*·na |

I need you.	Ты мне нужен. (to a man)
	tih mnye *nu*·zhihn
	Ты мне нужна. (to a woman)
	tih mnye nuzh·*na*

| I love you. | Я люблю тебя. |
| | ya lyub·*lyu* tib·*ya* |

| I see you in my dreams. | Я вижу тебя во сне. |
| | ya vi·*zhu* tib·*ya* va snye |

| I'll die without your love! | Я умру без твоей любви! |
| | ya um·*ru* byes tva·*yey* lyub·*vi* |

SOCIAL

ROMANCE

LANGUAGE TIP

Diminutives

Russians have an extensive range of 'diminutives' – shortened affectionate forms – for most first names, which are used by friends, family and loved ones. *Инна* *i*·na (Inna) for example, may be called *Иннуся* *i*·*nus*·ya (Innusya), *Инночка* *i*·*nach*·ka (Innochka), *Инка* *in*·ka (Inka) or *Иннуля* *i*·*nul*·ya (Innulya), to name a few variations.

SOCIAL ROMANCE

ангел мой	*an*·gil moy	my angel
голубчик m	ga·*lup*·chik	little pigeon
голубушка f	ga·*lu*·bush·ka	little pigeon
зайчик мой	*zey*·chik moy	my rabbit
крошка f	*krosh*·ka	crumb
любовь моя	lyu·*bof*' ma·*ya*	my love
солнышко моё	*sol*·nihsh·ka ma·*yo*	my sunshine

There is no greater happiness than being close to you.	Нет большего счастья, чем близость с тобой. nyet *bol*'·she·va *shast*·ya chem *bli*·zast' s ta·*boy*
Will you go out with me?	Ты будешь встречаться со мной? tih *bu*·dish fstri·*chat*'·sa sa mnoy
Will you meet my parents?	Ты познакомишься с моими родителями? tih paz·na·*ko*·mish'·sa s ma·*i*·mi ra·*di*·til·ya·mi
Will you marry me?	Ты выйдешь за меня? tih *vih*·dish' za min·*ya*

Leaving

I have to leave (tomorrow).	Я (завтра) уезжаю. ya (*zaf*·tra) u·iz·*zha*·yu
I'll keep in touch.	Я буду писать. ya *bu*·du pi·*sat*'
I'll miss you.	Я буду скучать. ya *bu*·du sku·*chat*'
I'll visit you.	Я буду приезжать. ya *bu*·du pri·yiz·*zhat*'

Beliefs & Culture

KEY PHRASES

What's your religion?	Какая ваша религия?	ka·*ka*·ya *va*·sha ri·*li*·gi·ya
I'm ...	Я ...	ya ...
I'm sorry, it's against my beliefs.	Извините, но это не по моим верованиям.	iz·vi·*nit*·ye no *e*·ta nye po ma·*im vye*·ra·va·ni·yam

Religion

Where can I (attend a service)?	Где можно (ходить к церковной службе)? gdye *mozh*·na (kha·*dit*' k tsir·*kov*·ney *sluzh*·bye)
Can I (pray) here?	Можно здесь (молиться)? *mozh*·na zdyes' (ma·*lit*'·sa)
Q What's your religion?	Какая ваша религия? ka·*ka*·ya *va*·sha ri·*li*·gi·ya
Q Are you a believer?	Вы верующий? m vih *vye*·ru·yu·shi Вы верующая? f vih *vye*·ru·yu·sha·ya
A I'm not religious.	Я неверующий? m ya nyev·*ye*·ru·yu·shi Я неверующая. f ya nyev·*ye*·ru·yu·sha·ya
A I (don't) believe in God.	Я (не) верю в Бога. ya (nye) *vyer*·yu v *bo*·ga
A I (don't) believe in fate.	Я (не) верю в судьбу. ya (nye) *vyer*·yu v sud'·*bu*

🅰 I'm (a/an) ...   Я ...
ya ...

atheist	атеист	at·ye·ist
agnostic	агностик	ag·no·stik
Buddhist	будист m	bu·dist
	будистка f	bu·dist·ka
Catholic	католик m	ka·to·lik
	католичка f	ka·to·lich·ka
Jewish	еврей m	yev·ryey
	еврейка f	yev·ryey·ka
Muslim	мусульманин m	mu·sul'·ma·nin
	мусульманка f	mu·sul'·man·ka
Orthodox	православный m	pra·vas·lav·nih
	православная f	pra·vas·lav·na·ya

Cultural Differences

Is this a local custom?	Это местный обычай? e·ta myes·nih a·bih·chey
I didn't mean to do anything wrong.	Я не хотел/хотела сделать что-то не правильно. m/f ya nye khat·yel/khat·ye·la zdye·lat' shto·ta nye pra·vil'·na
I'm not used to this.	Я не привык/привыкла к этому. m/f ya nye pri·vihk/pri·vih·kla k e·ta·mu
I'd rather not join in.	Я предпочитаю не участвовать. ya prit·pa·chi·ta·yu nye u·chast·va·vat'
I'm sorry, it's against my beliefs.	Извините, но это не по моим верованиям. iz·vi·nit·ye no e·ta nye po ma·im vye·ra·va·ni·yam

Sports

KEY PHRASES

Which sport do you play?	Занимаетесь каким видом спорта вы?	za·ni·*ma*·it·yes' ka·*kim vi*·dam *spor*·ta vih
Who are you supporting?	За кого вы болеете?	za ka·*vo* vih bal·*ye*·it·ye
What's the score?	Какой счёт?	ka·*koy* shot

Sporting Interests

Q Which sport do you play?	Занимаетесь каким видом спорта вы? za·ni·*ma*·it·yes' ka·*kim vi*·dam *spor*·ta vih
Q Which sport do you follow?	Интересуетесь каким видом спорта вы? in·ti·ri·*su*·it·yes' ka·*kim vi*·dam *spor*·ta vih
A I play ...	Я играю в ... ya i·*gra*·yu v ...
A I watch ...	Я смотрю ... ya smat·*ryu* ...

basketball	баскетбол	bas·kid·*bol*
football (soccer)	футбол	fud·*bol*
ice hockey	хоккей	khak·*yey*
tennis	теннис	*tye*·nis
volleyball	волейбол	val·yey·*bol*

A I do/go ...		Я занимаюсь ... ya za·ni·*ma*·yus' ...
cycling	велоспортом	vye·la·*spor*·tam
gymnastics	гимнастикой	gim·*na*·sti·key
running	бегом	*bye*·gam
to the gym	фитнесом	*fit*·ni·sam

A I go skating.	Я катаюсь на коньках. ya ka·*ta*·yus' na kan'·*kakh*
A I go skiing.	Я катаюсь на лыжах. ya ka·*ta*·yus' na lih·zhakh
Q Do you like (football/ soccer)?	Вам нравится (футбол)? vam *nra*·vit·sa (fud·*bol*)
A Yes, very much.	Да, очень. da o·*chin'*
A Not really.	Не очень. nye o·*chin'*
A I like watching it.	Я предпочитаю смотреть. ya prit·pa·chi·*ta*·yu smat·*ryet'*

Going to a Game

Would you like to go to a game?	Хотите пойти на матч? kha·*tit*·ye pey·*ti* na match
Who are you supporting?	За кого вы болеете? za ka·*vo* vih bal·*ye*·it·ye
Who's playing?	Кто играет? kto i·*gra*·yet
Who's winning?	Кто ведёт? kto vid·*yot*
What's the score?	Какой счёт? ka·*koy* shot

What a ...!		Какой ...!
		ka·*koy* ...
goal	гол	gol
hit/kick	удар	u·*dar*
pass	пас	pas
shot	удар	u·*dar*

That was a bad game!	Был плохой матч!
	bihl pla·*khoy* mach
That was a boring game!	Был скучный матч!
	bihl *skuch*·nih match
That was a great game!	Был отличный матч!
	bihl at·*lich*·nih match

Playing Sport

Q Do you want to play?	Вы хотите играть?
	vih kha·*tit*·ye i·*grat'*
Q Can I join in?	Можно присоединиться?
	mozh·na pri·sa·ye·di·*nit'*·sa
A I'd love to.	С удовольствием!
	s u·da·*volst*·vi·yem
A I have an injury.	Я ранен/ранена. **m/f**
	ya *ra*·nin/*ra*·ni·na
Your/My point.	Ваше/Моё очко.
	va·shih/ma·*yo* ach·*ko*
(Kick/Pass it) to me!	Мне!
	mnye
You're a good player.	Вы хорошо играете.
	vih kha·ra·*sho* i·*gra*·it·ye
Thanks for the game.	Спасибо за игру.
	spa·*si*·ba za i·*gru*

◀)) LISTEN FOR

матч-пойнт	mach·*poynt*	match point
ничья	ni·*cha*	draw/even
ноль	nol'	nil/love
сухой счёт	su·*khoy* shot	nil all

How much does it cost to go bowling?	Сколько стоит играть в боулинг? skol'·ka sto·it i·*grat'* v bo·u·link
How much does it cost to play pool?	Сколько стоит играть в бильярд? skol'·ka sto·it i·*grat'* v bil·*yart*
Where's the nearest ...?	Где здесь ...? gdye zdyes' ...

golf course	корт для гольфа	kort dlya *gol'*·fa
gym	спортзал	spart·*zal*
swimming pool	бассейн	bas·*yeyn*
tennis court	теннисный корт	*tye*·nis·nih kort

Where do you work out?	Где вы занимаетесь фитнесом? gdye vih za·ni·*ma*·it·yes' *fit*·ni·sam
Do I have to be a member to attend?	Нужно быть членом? *nuzh*·na biht' *chlye*·nam
Is there a women-only session?	Есть сессия только для женщин? yest' *sye*·si·ya *tol'*·ka dlya *zhensh*·chin
Where are the changing rooms?	Где раздевалка? gdye raz·di·*val*·ka

What's the charge per ...? | Сколько стоит билет на ...?
skol'·ka sto·it bil·yet na ...

day	день	dyen'
game	игру	i·*gru*
hour	час	chas
visit	один раз	a·*din* ras

Can I hire a ...? | Можно взять ... напрокат?
mozh·na vzyat' ... na·pra·kat

ball	мяч	myach
bicycle	велосипед	vi·la·sip·*yet*
court	корт	kort
racquet	ракетку	rak·*yet*·ku

Football/Soccer

Who plays for (Torpedo)?	Кто играет за (Торпедо)? kto i·*gra*·yet za (tarp·*ye*·do)
He's a great player.	Он классный футболист. on *klas*·nih fud·ba·*list*
He played brilliantly in the match against (Italy).	Он прекрасно играл против (Италии). on pri·*kras*·na i·*gral* pro·tif (i·*ta*·li)
Which team is at the top of the league?	Какая команда – лидер чемпионата? ka·*ka*·ya ka·*man*·da *li*·dir chim·pi·a·*na*·ta
What a great/terrible team!	Какая прекрасная/ужасная команда! ka·*ka*·ya pri·*kras*·na·ya/u·*zhas*·na·ya ka·*man*·da

SOCIAL SPORTS

🔊 LISTEN FOR

болельщик m	bal·*yel'*·shik	fan
болельщица f	bal·*yel*·shit·sa	fan
бомбардир m	bam·bar·*dir*	striker
гол m	gol	goal
голкипер m	gol·*ki*·pir	goalkeeper
жёлтая карточка f	*zhol*·ta·ya *kar*·tach·ka	yellow card
игрок m	i·*grok*	player
корнер m	*kor*·nir	corner (kick)
красная карточка f	*kras*·na·ya *kar*·tach·ka	red card
менеджер m	*mye*·nid·zhihr	manager
мяч m	myach	ball
нарушение n	na·ru·*she*·ni·ye	foul
офсайд m	of·*seyt*	offside
пенальти m	pi·*nal'*·ti	penalty
рефери m	ri·fi·*ri*	referee
свободный удар m	sva·*bod*·nih u·*dar*	free kick
стрикер m	*stri*·kir	streaker
тренер m	*tre*·nir	coach
удаление с поля n	u·dal·*ye*·ni·ye s *pol*·ya	expulsion
хулиган m	khu·li·*gan*	hooligan

Go (Spartak)!	(Спартак) – чемпион! (spar·*tak*) chim·pi·*on*
Scum!	На мыло! na *mih*·la

Off to see a match? Check out **going to a game** (p156).

Outdoors

Where can I buy supplies?	Где можно купить продукты?	gdye *mozh*·na ku·*pit'* pra·*duk*·tih
Do we need a guide?	Нам нужен проводник?	nam *nu*·zhihn pra·vad·*nik*
Is it safe?	Безопасно?	bi·za·*pas*·na
I'm lost.	Я потерялся. m Я потерялась. f	ya pa·tir·*yal*·sa ya pa·tir·*ya*·las'
What's the weather like?	Какая погода?	ka·*ka*·ya pa·go·da

Hiking

Where can I ...?	Где можно ...? gdye *mozh*·na ...

buy supplies	купить продукты	ku·*pit'* pra·*duk*·tih
find someone who knows this area	найти кого-нибудь, кто знает местность	nay·*ti* ka·*vo*·ni·but' kto *zna*·yet *myes*·nast'
get a map	достать карту	da·*stat'* *kar*·tu
hire hiking gear	взять в прокат обмундирование для туризма	vzyat' f pra·*kat'* ab·mun·di·ra·*va*·ni·ye dlya tu·*riz*·ma

Which is the easiest/ shortest route?	Какой маршрут самый лёгкий/быстрый? ka·*koy* marsh·*rut* sa·mih *lyokh*·ki/*bih*·strih
Which is the most interesting route?	Какой маршрут самый интересный? ka·*koy* marsh·*rut* sa·mih in·tir·*yes*·nih
Is the track (well-) marked?	Маршрут (хорошо) помечен? marsh·*rut* (kha·ra·*sho*) pam·*ye*·chin
Is the track open?	Маршрут открыт marsh·*rut* at·*kriht*
Is the track scenic?	Маршрут сценический? marsh·*rut* tsih·*ni*·chi·ski
Do we need to take bedding?	Нужно взять спальный мешок? *nuzh*·na vzyat' *spal'*·nih mi·*shok*
Do we need to take food?	Нужно взять еду? *nuzh*·na vzyat' ye·*du*
Do we need to take water?	Нужно взять воду? *nuzh*·na vzyat' *vo*·du
Where can I find the ...?	Где ...? gdye ...

campsite	кемпинг	*kyem*·pink
nearest village	ближайшая деревня	bli·*zhay*·sha·ya dir·*yev*·nya
showers	душ	dush
toilets	туалет	tu·al·*yet*

| Is it safe? | Безопасно?
 bi·za·*pas*·na |

Do we need a guide?	Нам нужен проводник? nam *nu*·zhihn pra·vad·*nik*
How high is the climb?	Как высоко мы поднимимся? kak vih·sa·*ko* mih pad·*ni*·mim·sa
How long is the trail?	Какова протяжённость маршрута? ka·ka·*va* prat·ya·*zho*·nast' marsh·*ru*·ta
Is there a hut?	Есть сторожка? yest' sta·*rosh*·ka
When does it get dark?	Когда темнеет? kag·*da* tim·*nye*·yet

SOCIAL OUTDOORS

Какая погода?
ka·*ka*·ya pa·*go*·da

What's the weather like?

Where have you come from?	Откуда вы пришли? ot·ku·da vih prish·li
How long did it take?	Сколько времени это заняло? skol'·ka vrye·mi·ni e·ta zan·ya·la
Does this path go to ...?	Эта тропа ведёт к ...? e·ta tra·pa vid·yot k ...
Can I go through here?	Можно пройти? mozh·na pray·ti
Is the water OK to drink?	Вода питьевая? va·da pi·ti·va·ya
I'm lost.	Я потерялся/потерялась. m/f ya pa·tir·yal·sa/pa·tir·ya·las'

Weather

🔲 **What's the weather like (tomorrow)?** Какая (завтра) погода?
ka·ka·ya (zaf·tra) pa·go·da

🔲 **It's ...**

cloudy	Облачно.	ob·lach·na
cold	Холодно.	kho·lad·na
fine	Прекрасно.	pri·kras·na
freezing	Морозный.	ma·roz·nih
frozen	Замёрзший.	zam·yors·shih
hot	Жарко.	zhar·ka
humid	Влажно.	vlazh·na
raining	Идёт дождь.	id·yot dozhd'
snowing	Идёт снег.	id·yot snyek
sunny	Солнечно.	sol·nich·na
warm	Тепло.	ti·plo
windy	Ветрено.	vye·tri·na

🔊 LISTEN FOR

белый медведь m	bye·lih mid·vyed'	polar bear
берёза f	bir·yo·za	fir
волк m	volk	wolf
ель f	yel'	spruce
лиса f	li·sa	fox
лиственница f	list·vi·nit·sa	larch
орёл m	ar·yol	eagle
северный олень m	sye·vir·nih al·yen'	reindeer
сибирский тигр m	si·bir·ski tigr	Siberian tiger
сосна f	sas·na	pine
степь f	styep'	steppe
тайга f	tey·ga	taiga
тундра f	tun·dra	tundra
тюлень m	tyul·yen'	seal

Where can I buy a rain jacket?	Где можно купить плащ? gdye mozh·na ku·pit' plash
Where can I buy an umbrella?	Где можно купить зонтик? gdye mozh·na ku·pit' zon·tik

Flora & Fauna

What ... is that?	Что это за ...? shto e·ta za ...

animal	животное	zhih·vot·na·ye
flower	цветок	tsvi·tok
plant	растение	rast·ye·ni·ye
tree	дерево	dye·ri·va

🔊 LISTEN FOR

Эй!	ey	Hey!
Ой!	oy	Oh!
Ай-ай-ай!	ey·ey·ey	Shame!
Отлично!	at·*lich*·na	Great!
Нормально!	nar·*mal*·na	Fine!
Конечно!	kan·*yesh*·na	Sure!
Может быть.	*mo*·zhiht biht'	Maybe.
Ничего!	ni·chi·vo	No problem!
Вы шутите!	vih *shu*·tit·ye	No way!
Что нового?	shto *no*·va·va	What's new?
Минутку!	mi·*nut*·ku	Just a minute!
Я шучу!	ya shu·*chu*	Just joking!
Разве это жизнь?	*raz*·vye e·ta zhihzn'	Is this really life?
Не жизнь, а мученье!	nye zhihzn' a mu·*chen*·ye	This isn't life, this is torment!

| **Is it ...?** | **Он ...?** |
| | on ... |

common	обыкновенный	a·bihk·nav·ye·nih
dangerous	опасный	a·*pas*·nih
endangered	вымирающий	vih·mi·*ra*·yu·shi
poisonous	ядовитый	yi·da·*vi*·tih
protected	заповедный	za·pav·*yed*·nih

| **What's it used for?** | **Для чего это использует?** |
| | dlya chi·vo e·ta is·*pol*'·zu·yit |

| **Can you eat the fruit?** | **Фрукты можно есть?** |
| | *fruk*·tih *mozh*·na yest' |

For geographical and agricultural terms, and more names of animals and plants, see the **dictionary**.

Safe Travel

Emergencies

KEY PHRASES

Help!	Помогите!	pa·ma·*gi*·tye
There's been an accident.	Произошёл несчастный случай.	pra·i·za·*shol* nye·*shas*·nih *slu*·chey
It's an emergency!	Это срочно!	*e*·ta *sroch*·na

Help!	Помогите! pa·ma·*gi*·tye
Stop!	Прекратите! pri·kra·*ti*·tye
Go away!	Идите отсюда! i·*dit*·ye at·*syu*·da
Thief!	Вор! vor
Fire!	Пожар! pa·*zhar*
Watch out!	Осторожно! a·sta·*rozh*·na
Call the police!	Вызовите милицию! *vih*·za·vit·ye mi·*lit*·sih·yu
Call a doctor!	Вызовите врача! *vih*·za·vit·ye vra·*cha*
Call an ambulance!	Вызовите скорую помощь! *vih*·za·vit·ye *sko*·ru·yu *po*·mash'
It's an emergency!	Это срочно! *e*·ta *sroch*·na

🔍 LOOK FOR

БОЛЬНИЦА	*bal'*·nit·sa Hospital
МИЛИЦИЯ	mi·*lit*·sih·ya Police
ОТДЕЛЕНИЕ МИЛИЦИИ	a·dil·*ye*·ni·ye mi·*lit*·sih Police Station
СКОРАЯ ПОМОЩЬ	*sko*·ra·ya *po*·mash' Emergency Department

There's been an accident.	Произошёл несчастный случай. pra·i·za·*shol* nye·*shas*·nih *slu*·chey
Could you please help?	Помогите, пожалуйста! pa·ma·*git*·ye pa·*zhal*·sta
Can I use your phone?	Можно воспользоваться телефоном? *mozh*·na vas·*pol'*·za·vat'·sa ti·li·*fo*·nam
I'm lost.	Я потерялся/потерялась. m/f ya pa·tir·*yal*·sa/pa·tir·*ya*·las'
Where are the toilets?	Где здесь туалет? gdye zdyes' tu·al·*yet*
Is it safe ...?	... безопасно? ... bye·za·*pas*·na

at night	Ночью	*no*·chu
for gay people	Для геев	dlya *gye*·yef
for travellers	Для путешест- венников	dlya pu·ti·*shest*· vi·ni·kaf
for women	Для женщин	dlya *zhen*·shin
on your own	Одному m Одной f	ad·na·*mu* ad·*noy*

Police

KEY PHRASES

Where's the police station?	Где милицейский участок?	gdye mi·lit·*sey*·ski u·*cha*·stak
I want to contact my consulate/ embassy.	Я хочу обратиться в своё посольство/ консульство.	ya kha·*chu* a·bra·*tit'*·sa f sva·*yo* pa·*solst*·va/ kan·sulst·*vo*
My bag was stolen.	У меня украли сумку.	u min·*ya* u·*kra*·li *sum*·ku

Where's the police station?	Где милицейский участок? gdye mi·lit·*sey*·ski u·*cha*·stak
Are there police on this train?	В этом поезде есть милиция? v e·tam *po*·iz·dye yest' mi·*lit*·sih·ya
I want to report an offence.	Я хочу заявить в милицию. ya kha·*chu* za·ya·*vit'* v mi·*lit*·sih·yu
I have insurance.	У меня есть страховка. u min·*ya* yest' stra·*khof*·ka
I've been (assaulted).	Меня (побили). min·*ya* (pa·*bi*·li)
She has been (raped).	Её (изнасиловали). yi·*yo* (iz·na·*si*·la·va·li)
He has been (robbed).	Его (ограбили). yi·*vo* (a·*gra*·bi·li)

| **My ... was/were stolen.** | У меня украли ...
u min·ya u·*kra*·li ... |
| **I've lost my ...** | Я потерял/потеряла ... **m/f**
ya pa·tir·*yal*/pa·tir·*ya*·la ... |

backpack	рюкзак	ryug·*zak*
handbag	сумку	*sum*·ku
money	деньги	*dyen*'·gi
passport	паспорт	*pas*·part
wallet	бумажник	bu·*mazh*·nik

It was him.	Это сделал он. e·ta *zdye*·lal on
It was her.	Это сделала она. e·ta *zdye*·la·la a·*na*
What am I accused of?	В чём меня обвиняют? f chom min·ya ab·vin·*ya*·yut
I didn't do it.	Я этого не делал/делала. **m/f** ya e·ta·va nye *dye*·lal/*dye*·la·la
Can I pay an on-the-spot fine?	Можно заплатить штраф на месте? *mozh*·na za·pla·*tit*' shtraf na *mye*·stye
I want to contact my embassy/consulate.	Я хочу обратиться в своё посольство/консульство. ya kha·*chu* a·bra·*tit*'·sa f sva·*yo* pa·*solst*·va/kan·*sulst*·vo
Can I make a phone call?	Можно позвонить? *mozh*·na paz·va·*nit*'
I need a lawyer (who speaks English).	Мне нужен адвокат (говорящий на английском якыке). mnye *nu*·zhihn ad·va·*kat* (ga·var·*ya*·shi na an·*gli*·skam ya·zihk·ye)

🔊 LISTEN FOR

безвизовый въезд	byez·*vi*·za·vih vyest
	not having a visa
воровство в магазине	va·rafst·*vo* v ma·ga·*zin*·ye
	shoplifting
нарушение покоя	na·ru·*she*·ni·ye pa·*ko*·ya
	disturbing the peace
насилие	na·*si*·li·ye
	assault
ограбление	a·grab·*lye*·ni·ye
	theft
просроченную визу	pras·*ro*·chi·nu·yu *vi*·zu
	overstaying a visa
хранение (запрещённых предметов)	khran·*ye*·ni·ye (za·pri·*sho*·nihkh prid·*mye*·taf)
	possession (of illegal substances)
Это штраф за нарушение правил парковки.	*e*·ta shtraf za na·ru·*she*·ni·ye *pra*·vil par·*kof*·ki
	It's a parking fine.
Это штраф за превышение скорости.	*e*·ta shtraf za pri·vih·*she*·ni·ye *sko*·ra·sti
	It's a speeding fine.

I have a prescription for this drug.	У меня есть рецепт на это лекарство. u min·*ya* yest' rit·*sept* na *e*·ta li·*karst*·va
This drug is for personal use.	Это лекарство для личного пользования. *e*·ta li·*karst*·va dlya *lich*·na·va *pol'*·za·va·ni·ya
I didn't realise I was doing anything wrong.	Я не знал/знала, что я делаю что-то неправильно. **m/f** ya nye znal/*zna*·la shto ya *dye*·la·yu *shto*·ta nye·*pra*·vil'·na

Health

KEY PHRASES

Where's the nearest hospital?	Где здесь больница?	gdye zdyes' *bal'*·nit·sa
I'm sick.	Я болею.	ya bal·*ye*·yu
I need a doctor.	Мне нужен врач.	mnye *nu*·zhihn vrach
I'm on medication for ...	Я принимаю лекарство от ...	ya pri·ni·*ma*·yu li·*karst*·va at ...
I'm allergic to ...	У меня аллергия на...	u min·*ya* a·lir·*gi*·ya na ...

Doctor

Where's the nearest ...?   Где здесь ...?
gdye zdyes' ...

dentist	зубной врач	zub·*noy* vrach
doctor	врач	vrach
emergency department	палата скорой помощи	pa·*la*·ta *sko*·rey *po*·ma·shi
hospital	больница	*bal'*·nit·sa
medical centre	поликлиника	pa·li·*kli*·ni·ka
optometrist	оптик	*op*·tik
(night) pharmacist	(ночная) аптека	(nach·*na*·ya) ap·*tye*·ka

Is there an after-hours number?   Есть круглосуточный номер?
yest' kru·gla·*su*·tach·nih *no*·mir

I need a doctor (who speaks English).	Мне нужен врач, (говорящий на английском языке). mnye *nu*·zhihn vrach (ga·var·*ya*·shi na an·*gli*·skam ya·zihk·*ye*)
Could I see a female doctor?	Можно записаться на приём к женщине-врачу? *mozh*·na za·pi·*sat*'·sa na pri·*yom* k *zhen*·shin·ye·vra·*chu*
I've run out of my medication.	У меня кончилось лекарство. u min·*ya* kon·chi·las' li·*karst*·va
This is my usual medicine.	Я обычно принимаю это лекарство. ya a·*bihch*·na pri·ni·*ma*·yu *e*·ta li·*karst*·va
What's the correct dosage?	Какова правильная доза? ka·ka·va pra·*vil*'·na·ya *do*·za

🔊 **LISTEN FOR**

Вы сексуально активны?	vih syeks·u·*al*'·na ak·*tiv*·nih Are you sexually active?
У вас был незащищённый половой контакт?	u vas bihl nye·za·shi·*sho*·nih pa·la·*voy* kan·*takt* Have you had unprotected sex?
Вы принимаете лекарство?	vih pri·ni·*ma*·it·ye li·*karst*·vo Are you on medication?
У вас есть аллергия на что-нибудь?	u vas yest' a·lir·*gi*·ya na *shto*·ni·but' Are you allergic to anything?

I've been vaccinated against hepatitis A/B/C.	Мне делали прививку против гепатита A/B/C. mnye dye·la·li pri·vif·ku pro·tif gi·pa·ti·ta a/be/tse
I've been vaccinated against tetanus.	Мне делали прививку против столбняка. mnye dye·la·li pri·vif·ku pro·tif stalb·nya·ka
I've been vaccinated against typhoid.	Мне делали прививку против брюшного тифа. mnye dye·la·li pri·vif·ku pro·tif bryush·no·va ti·fa
I need new contact lenses.	Мне нужны контактные линзы. mnye nuzh·nih kan·takt·nih·ye lin·zih
I need new glasses.	Мне нужны очки. mnye nuzh·nih ach·ki
My prescription is ...	Мой рецепт ... moy rit·sept ...
Can I have a receipt for my insurance?	Можно квитанцию для моей страховки? mozh·na kvi·tant·sih·yu dlya ma·yey stra·khof·ki

Symptoms & Conditions

I'm (very) sick.	Я (очень) болею. ya (o·chin') bal·ye·yu
My child is sick.	Мой ребёнок болеет. moy rib·yo·nak bal·ye·yet
He's been injured.	Он ушибся. on u·shihp·sa
She's been injured.	Она ушиблась. a·na u·shihb·las'

🔊 LISTEN FOR

Где болит?	gdye ba·*lit* Where does it hurt?
Есть температура?	yest' tim·pi·ra·*tu*·ra Do you have a temperature?
Как давно у вас это состояние?	kag dav·*no* u vas e·ta sa·sta·*ya*·ni·ye How long have you been like this?
У вас это было раньше?	u vas e·ta *bih*·la ran'·she Have you had this before?
Вы пьёте/курите?	vih *pyot*·ye/*ku*·rit·ye Do you drink/smoke?
Вы употребляете наркотики?	vih u·pa·trib·*lya*·it·ye nar·*ko*·ti·ki Do you take drugs?

He/She is having a/an ...	У него/неё ... u nyi·*vo*/nyi·yo ...	
allergic reaction	аллергическая реакция	a·lir·*gi*·chi·ska·ya ri·*akt*·sih·ya
asthma attack	астматическая реакция	ast·ma·*ti*·chi·ska·ya ri·*akt*·sih·ya
epileptic fit	эпилептический припадок	e·pi·lip·*ti*·chi·ski pri·*pa*·dak
heart attack	сердечный приступ	sird·*yech*·nih *pri*·stup

He/She has been vomiting.	Его/Её тошнило. yi·*vo*/yi·yo tash·*ni*·la
He/She has been bitten.	У него/неё укус. u nyi·*vo*/nyi·yo u·*kus*

I feel ...

anxious	У меня не в порядке нервы.	u min·*ya* nye f par·*yat*·kye *nyer*·vih
dizzy	У меня кружится голова.	u min·*ya* kru·zhiht·sa ga·la·*va*
hot and cold	У меня приступ лихорадки.	u min·*ya* pri·stup li·kha·*rat*·ki
nauseous	Меня тошнит.	min·*ya* tash·*nit*
shivery	У меня озноб.	u min·*ya* az·*nop*
weak	У меня слабость.	u min·*ya* sla·bast'

It hurts here.	Здесь болит. zdyes' ba·*lit*
I'm dehydrated.	У меня обезвоживание организма. u min·*ya* a·bis·vo·zhih·va·ni·ye ar·ga·*niz*·ma
I can't sleep.	Мне не спится. mnye nye *spit*·sa
I'm on medication for ...	Я принимаю лекарство от ... ya pri·ni·*ma*·yu li·*karst*·va at ...
I have (a/an) ...	У меня ... u min·*ya* ...
He/She has (a/an) ...	У него/неё ... u nyi·*vo*/nyi·*yo* ...

Allergies

I have a skin allergy.	У меня кожная аллергия. u min·*ya kozh*·na·ya a·lir·*gi*·ya
He/She is allergic to ...	У него/неё аллергия на ... u nyi·*vo*/nyi·*yo* al·*yer*·gi·ya na ...

I'm allergic to ...   У меня аллергия на...
u min·*ya* a·lir·*gi*·ya na ...

anti-inflammatories	противо-воспалительные препараты	*pra·ti·va*·va·spa·*li*·til'·nih·ye pri·pa·*ra*·tih
bees	пчелиный укус	pchi·*li*·nih *u*·kus
codeine	кодеин	kad·ye·*in*
penicillin	пеницилин	pi·nit·*sih*·lin
sulphur-based drugs	серные препараты	*syer*·nih·ye pri·pa·*ra*·tih

For food-related allergies, see **special diets & allergies** (p206).

Women's Health

(I think) I'm pregnant.	(Я думаю, что) Я беременна. (ya *du*·ma·yu shto) ya bir·ye·mi·na
I'm on the Pill.	Я принимаю противозачаточные таблетки. ya pri·ni·*ma*·yu *pra*·ti·va·za·*cha*·tach·nih·ye tab·*lyet*·ki
I haven't had my period for (six) weeks.	У меня (шесть) недель задержка. u min·*ya* (shest') nid·*yel*' zad·*yersh*·ka
I've noticed a lump here.	У меня здесь опухоль. u min·*ya* zdyes' *o*·pu·khal'
Do you have something for (period pain)?	У вас есть что-нибудь от (боли при менструации)? u vas yest' *shto*·ni·but' at (*bo*·li pri mins·tru·*at*·sih)

🔊 LISTEN FOR

Вы употребляете противо-зачаточные средства?	vih u·pa·trib·*lya*·it·ye pra·ti·va·za·*cha*·tach·nih·ye *sryets*·tva Are you using contraception?
У вас есть месячные?	u vas yest' *mye*·sich·nih·ye Are you menstruating?
Когда были последние месячные?	kag·*da* bih·li pa·*sled*·ni·ye *mye*·sich·nih·ye When did you last have your period?
Вы беременны?	vih bir·*ye*·mi·nih Are you pregnant?
Вы беременны.	vih bir·*ye*·mi·nih You're pregnant.

I have a urinary tract infection.	У меня воспаление мочевого канала. u min·*ya* vas·pal·*ye*·ni·ye ma·chi·*vo*·va ka·*na*·la
I have a yeast infection.	У меня воспаление влагалища. u min·*ya* vas·pal·*ye*·ni·ye vla·*ga*·li·sha
I need a pregnancy test.	Я хочу анализ на беременность. ya kha·*chu* a·*na*·lis na bir·*ye*·mi·nast'
I need contraception.	Я хочу противо-зачаточные средства. ya kha·*chu* pra·ti·va·za·*cha*·tach·nih·ye *sryets*·tva
I need the morning-after pill.	Я хочу утреннюю таблетку. ya kha·*chu* ut·rin·yu·yu tab·*lyet*·ku

Alternative Treatments

I don't use (Western medicine).	Я не употребляю (западную медицину). ya nye u·pa·trib·*lya*·yu (*za*·pad·nu·yu mi·dit·*sih*·nu)
I prefer (alternative medicine).	Я предпочитаю (альтернативную медицину). ya prit·pa·chi·*ta*·yu (al'·tir·na·*tiv*·nu·yu mi·di·*tsih*·nu)
Can I see someone who practises ...?	Можно видеть кого-нибудь, который занимается ...? *mozh*·na *vid*·yet' ka·*vo*·ni·but' ka·*to*·rih za·ni·*ma*·it·sa ...

acupuncture	акупунктурой	a·ku·punk·*tu*·rey
naturopathy	натуропатией	na·tu·ra·*pa*·ti·yey
reflexology	рефлексологией	ri·fleks·a·*lo*·gi·yey
reiki	рейки	*ryey*·ki

Parts of the Body

My ... hurts.	У меня болит ... u min·*ya* ba·*lit* ...
I can't move my ...	Я не могу двигать ... ya nye ma·*gu dvi*·gat' ...

> **LANGUAGE TIP**
>
> **Multiple Meanings**
> Russians say *рука* ru·*ka* for both 'arm' and 'hand', *нога* na·*ga* for 'leg' and 'foot', and *палец* *pa*·lits for 'finger' and 'toe'.

SAFE TRAVEL | HEALTH

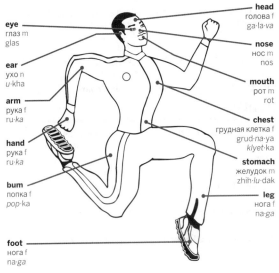

eye
глаз m
glas

ear
ухо n
u·kha

arm
рука f
ru·*ka*

hand
рука f
ru·*ka*

bum
попка f
pop·ka

foot
нога f
na·ga

head
голова f
ga·la·*va*

nose
нос m
nos

mouth
рот m
rot

chest
грудная клетка f
grud·*na*·ya
klyet·ka

stomach
желудок m
zhih·*lu*·dak

leg
нога f
na·*ga*

I have a cramp in my ...	У меня судорога в ... u min·*ya su*·da·ra·ga v ...
My ... is swollen.	У меня распух ... u min·*ya* ras·*pukh* ...

For other parts of the body, see the **dictionary**.

Pharmacist

I need something for (a headache).	Мне нужно что-нибудь от (головной боли). mnye *nuzh*·na *shto*·ni·bud' at (ga·lav·*noy* bo·li)
I have a prescription.	У меня есть рецепт. u min·*ya* yest' rit·*sept*

| Do I need a prescription for (antibiotics)? | Для (антибиотиков) нужен рецепт?
dlya (an·ti·bi·o·ti·kaf) *nu*·zhihn rit·*sept* |
| How many times a day? | Сколько раз в день?
skol'·ka raz v dyen' |

For more pharmaceutical items, see the **dictionary**.

Dentist

I have a broken tooth.	У меня сломался зуб. u min·*ya* sla·*mal*·sa zup
I have a cavity.	У меня дыра в зубе. u min·*ya* dih·*ra* v *zub*·ye
I have a toothache.	У меня болит зуб. u min·*ya* ba·*lit* zup
I've lost a filling.	У меня выпала пломба. u min·*ya* vih·pa·la *plom*·ba
My dentures are broken.	Я сломал/сломала протез. m/f ya sla·*mal*/sla·*ma*·la prat·*yes*
My gums hurt.	У меня болят дёсны. u min·*ya* bal·*yat* *dyos*·nih
I don't want it extracted.	Я не хочу удалять зуб. ya nye kha·*chu* u·dal·*yat'* zup
Please give me an anaesthetic.	Обезбольте, пожалуйста. a·biz·*bolt*·ye pa·*zhal*·sta

LISTEN FOR

Откройте рот.	at·*kroyt*·ye rot	Open wide.
временно	*vrye*·mi·na	temporary
удалить	u·da·*lit'*	extract
укол m	u·*kol*	injection

Food

Eating Out

KEY PHRASES

Can you recommend a restaurant?	Вы можете порекомендовать ресторан?	vih *mo*·zhiht·ye pa·ri·ka·min·da·*vat'* ri·sta·*ran*
A table for two, please.	Столик на двоих, пожалуйста.	*sto*·lik na dva·*ikh* pa·*zhal*·sta
I'd like the menu, please.	Я бы хотел/ хотела меню. **m/f**	ya bih khat·*yel*/ khat·*ye*·la min·*yu*
I'd like a beer, please.	Я бы хотел/ хотела пиво. **m/f**	ya bih khat·*yel*/ khat·*ye*·la *pi*·va
Please bring the bill.	Принесите, пожалуйста счёт.	pri·ni·*sit*·ye pa·*zhal*·sta shot

Basics

breakfast	завтрак **m** *zaf*·trak
lunch	обед **m** ab·*yet*
dinner	ужин **m** *u*·zhihn
snack	закуска **f** za·*kus*·ka
eat v	есть yest'
drink v	пить pit'
I'm starving!	Я умираю с голоду! ya u·mi·*ra*·yu z *go*·la·du

Enjoy your meal!	Приятного аппетита! pri·*yat*·na·va a·pi·*ti*·ta

Finding a Place to Eat

Dining out in Russia offers specialist cafes as well as *столовая*
sta·*lo*·va·ya – a type of cheap and (often) cheerful canteen found in
stations or market areas. Many stations and hotels also have small
буфет buf·*yet* (buffets) or *шведский стол* shvyet·ski stol (smorgas-
bords). Some of these eateries do *с собой* s sa·*boy* (take away).

Can you recommend a ...?	Вы можете порекомендовать ...? vih *mo*·zhiht·ye pa·ri·ka·min·da·*vat'* ...

cafe	кафе	ka·*fe*
canteen	столовую	sta·*lo*·vu·yu
dumpling cafe	пельменную	pilm·ye·nu·yu
kebab cafe	шашлычную	shash·*lihch*·nu·yu
pastry cafe	кондитерскую	kan·*di*·tir·sku·yu
restaurant	ресторан	ri·sta·*ran*
snack bar	закусочную	za·*ku*·sach·nu·yu

Are you still serving food?	Кухня открыта? *kukh*·nya at·*krih*·ta
How long is the wait?	Как долго ждать? kak *dol*·ga zhdat'

🔊 **LISTEN FOR**

Ресторан закрыт.	ri·sta·*ran* za·*kriht*	We're closed.
Мест нет.	myest nyet	We're full.
Одну минуту.	ad·*nu* mi·*nu*·tu	One moment.

FOOD EATING OUT

FOOD **EATING OUT**

CULTURE TIP

Snack Bars

For *уличная пища* u·lich·na·ya *pish*·cha (street food) try a *закусочная* za·*ku*·sach·na·ya (snack bar) like the ones below.

блинная f   *bli*·na·ya
serves pancakes with savoury or sweet fillings

бутербродная f   bu·tir·*brod*·na·ya
prepares small open sandwiches

закусочная f   za·ku·*sach*·na·ya
offers miscellaneous snacks such as *кебаб* ki·*bap* (kebab), *пирожок* pi·ra·*zhok* (spicy mutton pie) or *сосиски* sa·*sis*·ki (fried or boiled sausage)

пельменная f   pilm·*ye*·na·ya
specialises in meat ravioli

пирожковая f   pi·rash·*ko*·va·ya
sells deep-fried meat or vegetable turnovers

чебуречная f   chi·bur·*yech*·na·ya
cooks Armenian or Georgian spicy, deep-fried mutton pies

шашлычная f   shash·*lihch*·na·ya
serves up charcoal-grilled meat kebabs

I'd like to reserve a table for two people.	Я бы хотел/хотела заказать столик на двоих. **m/f** ya bih khat·*yel*/khat·*ye*·la za·ka·*zat'* sto·lik na dva·*ikh*

✂	**For two, please.**	На двоих, пожалуйста.
		na dva·*ikh* pa·*zhal*·sta

I'd like to reserve a table for (eight) o'clock.
Я бы хотел/хотела
заказать столик на
(восемь) часов. **m/f**
ya bih khat·*yel*/khat·*ye*·la
za·ka·*zat' sto*·lik na
(*vo*·sim') chi·*sof*

At the Restaurant

Russian menus may show additional prices for *пол-порция* pal·*port*·sih·ya (half portion) and figures that include *налог* na·*lok* (tax).

I'd like (a/the) ..., please. Я бы хотел/хотела ... **m/f**
ya bih khat·*yel*/khat·*ye*·la ...

children's menu	детское меню	*dyet*·ska·ye min·*yu*
drink list	карту вин	*kar*·tu vin
half portion	пол-порцию	pol·*port*·sih·yu
local speciality	местную специальность	*myes*·nu·yu spit·sih·*al'*·nast'
menu (in English)	меню (на английском)	min·*yu* (na an·*gli*·skam)
(non)smoking	(не)курящий	(nye·)kur·*yash*·chi
table for (three)	столик на (троих)	*sto*·lik na (tra·*ikh*)
that dish	это блюдо	e·ta *blyu*·da

✂	**Menu, please.**	Меню, пожалуйста.	min·*yu* pa·*zhal*·sta

What would you recommend?
Что вы рекомендуете?
shto vih ri·ka·min·*du*·it·ye

What's in that dish?
Что входит в это блюдо?
shto *fkho*·dit v e·ta *blyu*·da

FOOD EATING OUT

 **LISTEN FOR**

Куда вы хотите сесть?	ku·*da* vih kha·*tit*·ye syest'
	Where would you like to sit?
Что вы хотите?	shto vih kha·*tit*·ye
	What can I get for you?
Вам ...?	vam ...
	Would you like ...?
Я рекомендую ...	ya ri·ka·min·*du*·yu ...
	I suggest the ...
Пожалуйста.	pa·*zhal*·sta
	Here you go!

What's that called?	Как это называется?
	kak *e*·ta na·zih·*va*·it·sa

Requests

I'd like it with ...	Можно мне с ...
	mozh·na mnye s ...

cheese	сыром	*sih*·ram
chilli	перцом	*pyert*·sam
garlic	чесноком	chis·na·*kom*
nuts	орехами	ar·ye·kha·mi
oil	маслом	*mas*·lam
pepper	перцом	*pyert*·sam
sauce	соусом	*sou*·sam
tomato sauce	кетчупом	*kyet*·chu·pam
vinegar	уксусом	*uk*·su·sam

Eating Out

Can I see the menu, please?

Могу ли я посмотреть меню, пожалуйста?
ma·*gu*·li ya pa·sma·*tryet'* min·*yu* pa·*zhal*·sta

What would you recommend for ...?

Что бы вы порекомендовали ...?
shto bih vih pa·re·ka·men·da·*va*·li ...

 the main meal
для основного блюда
dlya as·*nov*·na·vo *blyu*·da

 dessert
на десерт
na di·*sert*

 drinks
для напитков
dlya na·*piht*·kov

Can you bring me some ..., please?

Принесите, пожалуйста ...
pri·ni·*sit*·ye pa·*zhal*·sta ...

I'd like the bill, please.

Я бы хотел/хотела счёт. m/f
ya bih khat·*yel*/khat·ye·la shot

I'd like it without ...	Можно мне без ...	*mozh·*na mnye byes ...
cheese	сыра	*sih·*ra
chilli	перца	*pyert·*sa
garlic	чеснока	chis·na·*ka*
nuts	орехов	ar·ye·khaf
oil	масла	*mas·*la
pepper	перца	*pyert·*sa
sauce	соуса	*sou·*sa
tomato sauce	кетчупа	*kyet·*chu·pa
vinegar	уксуса	*uk·*su·sa

I'd like it ...	..., пожалуйста.	... pa·*zhal·*sta
(deep-)fried	(Сильно) Жареное	(*sil'·*na) *zha·*ri·na·ye
grilled	В гриле	v *gril·*ye
rare	Поджаренное	pad·*zha·*ri·na·ye
raw	Сырое	sih·*ro·*ye
steamed	Паровое	pa·ra·*vo·*ye
well-done	Хорошо прожаренное	kha·ra·*sho* pra·*zha·*ri·na·ye

Please bring (a/the) ...	Принесите, пожалуйста ...	pri·ni·*sit·*ye pa·*zhal·*sta ...
cloth	тряпку	*tryap·*ku
glass	стакан	sta·*kan*
serviette	салфетку	salf·*yet·*ku
wineglass	рюмку	*ryum·*ku

For other meal requests, see **vegetarian & special meals** (p206).

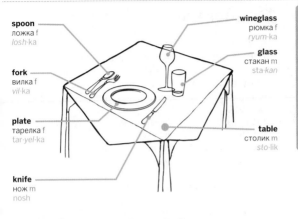

spoon
ложка f
losh·ka

wineglass
рюмка f
ryum·ka

glass
стакан m
sta·kan

fork
вилка f
vil·ka

plate
тарелка f
tar·yel·ka

table
столик m
sto·lik

knife
нож m
nosh

Compliments & Complaints

I love this dish.	Это блюдо очень вкусное. *e·ta blyu·da o·chin' fkus·na·ye*
I love the local cuisine.	Мне очень нравится местная кухня. *mnye o·chin' nra·vit·sa* *myes·na·ya kukhn·ya*
This is superb.	Это великолепное. *e·ta vi·li·kal·yep·na·ye*
That was delicious!	Было очень вкусно! *bih·la o·chin' fkus·na*
My compliments to the chef.	Похвалу повару! *pakh·va·lu po·va·ru*
I'm full.	Я наелся/наелась. **m/f** *ya na·yel·sa/na·ye·las'*

FOOD

EATING OUT

 LOOK FOR

ЗАКУСКИ	za·*kus*·ki	Appetisers
ПЕРВЫЕ БЛЮДА	*pyer*·vih·ye *blyu*·da	First Courses
САЛАТЫ	sa·*la*·tih	Salads
ВТОРЫЕ БЛЮДА	fta·*rih*·ye *blyu*·da	Main Courses
МУЧНЫЕ БЛЮДА	much·*nih*·ye *blyu*·da	Grain Dishes
ОВОЩНЫЕ БЛЮДА	a·vash·*nih*·ye *blyu*·da	Vegetables
РЫБНЫЕ БЛЮДА	*rihb*·nih·ye *blyu*·da	Fish
ДИЧЬ И ПТИЦА	*dyich*· i *ptit*·sa	Game & Poultry
МЯСНЫЕ БЛЮДА	mis·*nih*·ye *blyu*·da	Meat
ЯИЧНЫЕ БЛЮДА	yi·*ich*·nih·ye *blyu*·da	Egg Dishes
СЫР И ТВОРОГ	sihr i tva·*rok*	Cheese & Dairy
ПИРОЖКИ	pi·rash·*ki*	Pies
ПЕЛЬМЕНИ	pilm·*ye*·nih	Dumplings
ФИРМЕННЫЕ БЛЮДА	*fir*·mi·nih·ye *blyu*·da	House Specials
ДОМАШНИЕ БЛЮДА	da·*mash*·ni·ye *blyu*·da	Home-style Dishes
НАЦИОНАЛЬНЫЕ БЛЮДА	nat·sih·a·*nal'*·nih·ye *blyu*·da	National & Ethnic Dishes
ДИЕТИЧЕСКИЕ БЛЮДА	di·ye·*ti*·chi·ski·ye *blyu*·da	Special Diets
СЛАДКИЕ БЛЮДА	*slat*·ki·ye *blyu*·da	Desserts

This is (too) cold.	Это (слишком) холодное. *e*·ta (*slish*·kam) kha·*lod*·na·ye
This is spicy.	Это острое. *e*·ta o·*stra*·ye

Paying the Bill

It's bad form to try splitting the bill for meals when eating out, so fight to pay for everyone – say *Уберите деньги, я угощаю!* u·bi·*rit*·ye *dyen'*·gi ya u·ga·*sha*·yu, which means 'Put your money away, it's my shout'. If you lose, return the compliment later.

| **Please bring the bill.** | Принесите, пожалуйста счёт.
pri·ni·*sit*·ye pa·*zhal*·sta shot |

| ✂ | **Bill, please.** | Счёт, пожалуйста. | shot pa·*zhal*·sta |

| **There's a mistake in the bill.** | Меня обсчитали.
min·*ya* ap·shi·*ta*·li |

Nonalcoholic Drinks

boiled water	кипячёная вода f ki·pi·*cho*·na·ya va·*da*
cup of tea	чашка чаю f *chash*·ka *cha*·yu
fruit juice	фруктовый сок m fruk·*to*·vih sok
herbal tea	чай из трав m chey is traf
lemonade	лимонад m li·ma·*nat*
(sparkling) mineral water	(шипучая) минеральная вода f (shih·*pu*·cha·ya) mi·ni·*ral'*·na·ya va·*da*
soda water	газированная вода f ga·zi·*ro*·va·na·ya va·*da*

CULTURE TIP

Coffee

Getting *кофе kof*·ye (coffee) the way you want it is traditionally difficult in Russia. It's often brewed in pre-mixed batches with milk and/or sugar, so you'd be wise to order *с молоком/сахаром* s ma·la·*kom/sa*·kha·ram (with milk/sugar) or *без молока/сахару* byez ma·la·*ka/ sa*·kha·ru (without milk/sugar). Here are some other options for the coffee aficionado.

coffee	кофе n	*kof*·ye
cup of coffee	чашка кофе f	*chash*·ka kof·ye
decaffeinated	без кафеина	byes kaf·ye·*i*·na
iced	со льдом	sa l'dom
strong	крепкий	*krep*·ki
Turkish	по-турецки	pa·tur·*yets*·ki
weak	слабый	*sla*·bih

soft drink	безалкогольный напиток m bye·zal·ka·*gol'*·nih na·*pi*·tak
tea	чай m chey
with lemon	с лимоном s li·*mo*·nam
with honey	с мёдом s *myo*·dam
with jam	с вареньем s var·*ye*·nim

Alcoholic Drinks

Russians measure their spirits in grams, not shots. The equivalent of a shot is *пятьдесят грамм* pi·dis·*yat* gram (50g), and a double is about *сто грамм* sto gram (100g). If you don't want to order a whole bottle of spirits, you can order by weight – a common amount to share over a meal is *двести грамм* dvye·sti gram (200g).

brandy	коньяк m	kan·*yak*
champagne	шампанское n	sham·*pan*·ska·ye
cocktail	коктейль m	kak·*teyl*
50/100 grams of ...	пятьдесят/сто грамм ...	pi·dis·*yat*/sto gram ...

gin	джина	*dzhih*·na
rum	рома	*ro*·ma
sherry	хереса	*khye*·ri·sa
vodka	водки	*vot*·ki
whisky	виски	*vis*·ki

... beer	... пиво	... *pi*·va

draught	бочковое	*boch*·ka·va·ye
lager	светлое	*svyet*·la·ye
light	лёгкое	*lyokh*·ka·ye
stout	тёмное	*tyom*·na·ye

a ... of beer	... пива	... *pi*·va

glass	стакан	sta·*kan*
jug	кувшин	kuf·*shihn*
large/small bottle	большая/маленькая бутылка	bal'·*sha*·ya/ma·*lin*'·ka·ya bu·*tihl*·ka
mug	кружка	*krush*·ka
pint	пинта	*pin*·ta

a bottle/glass of ... wine	бутылка/рюмка ... вина
	bu·*tihl*·ka/*ryum*·ka ... vi·*na*

dessert	дессертного	dis·*yert*·na·va
dry	сухого	su·*kho*·va
red	красного	*kras*·na·va
rosé	розового	*ro*·za·va·va
semidry	полусухого	pa·lu·su·*kho*·va
semisweet	полусладкого	pa·lus·*lat*·ka·va
sparkling	шипучего	shih·*pu*·chi·va
sweet	сладкого	*slat*·ka·va
white	белого	*bye*·la·va

In the Bar

A lot of public drinking happens in a *кафе* ka·*fe* (cafe), *ресторан* ri·sta·*ran* (restaurant) or *бар* bar (bar). Russians can also be found in the local *трактир* trak·*tir*, which is more like a typical pub, or in a *пивная* piv·*na*·ya (tavern). During the Soviet era the *пивная* was where you'd line up to collect your ration of vodka, and it's still considered the place to go to get under the table fast.

Can you recommend a bar?	Вы можете порекомендовать бар? vih *mo*·zhiht·ye pa·ri·ka·min·da·*vat'* bar
Can you recommend a pub?	Вы можете порекомендовать трактир? vih *mo*·zhiht·ye pa·ri·ka·min·da·*vat'* trak·*tir*
Can you recommend a tavern?	Вы можете порекомендовать пивную? vih *mo*·zhiht·ye pa·ri·ka·min·da·*vat'* piv·*nu*·yu

CULTURE TIP

Vodka

The clichéd Russian drink is, of course, *водка* *vot·ka* – your average Russian drinks more than a bottle of 'little water' per week. Vodka is perfect, according to the locals, when chilled to 10°C and sculled by the *пятьдесят* pit'·dis·*yat* (50 gram shot). Mixing or sipping vodka is considered both cowardly and in poor form.

When toasting with vodka or *самогон* sa·ma·*gon* (home-made vodka), say *Пей до дна!* pyey da dna (Drink to the bottom!) then empty your glass. Beware – you need to do this for every toast. A bottle of vodka is traditionally shared between three, so if there are only two of you, you can ask a potential drinking partner *Третьим будешь?* trye·tim bu·dish' (Will you be the third?).

Vodka is considered the universal remedy, guaranteed to cure everything from the common cold to a hangover. You'll also see Russians participating in a bread-and-vodka ritual. To try it yourself, get a *пятьдесят* (50 gram shot) and a piece of *хлеб чёрный* khlyep *chor*·nih (rye bread). Breathe in and out quickly, bringing your food to the tip of your nose in a kind of blessing. Down your vodka in one shot, and eat your food.

Here are some vodkas available in Russia:

зубровка	zu·*brof*·ka	with cinnamon, lemon & bison grass
лимонная	li·mo·na·ya	with lemon
московская	mas·*kof*·ska·ya	with sodium bicarbonate
охотничья	a·*khot*·ni·cha	with peppers, berries, ginger & cloves
перцовка	pirt·*sof*·ka	with pepper
рябиновка	rya·bi·*naf*·ka	with ash berries
столичная	sta·*lich*·na·ya	with infused sugar
тминная	tmi·na·ya	with caraway
яблочная	ya·blach·na·ya	with apple

LOOK FOR

АПЕРИТИВЫ	a·pi·ra·*ti*·vih	Apéritifs
НАПИТКИ	na·*pit*·ki	Drinks
БЕЗАЛКОГОЛЬНЫЕ НАПИТКИ	bi·zal·ka·*gol'*·nih·ye na·*pit*·ki	Soft Drinks
ПИВО	*pi*·va	Beers
ШАМПАНСКОЕ	sham·*pan*·ska·ye	Sparkling Wines & Champagnes
БЕЛОЕ ВИНО	*bye*·la·ye vi·*no*	White Wines
КРАСНОЕ ВИНО	*kras*·na·ye vi·*no*	Red Wines
ДЕССЕРТНОЕ ВИНО	di·*sert*·na·ye vi·*no*	Dessert Wines
СПИРТНЫЕ НАПИТКИ	spirt·*nih*·ye na·*pit*·ki	Spirits
ВОДКА	*vot*·ka	Vodkas

Is anyone serving?	Кто здесь подаёт? kto zdyes' pa·da·*yot*
I'm next.	Я следующий. m ya *slye*·du·yu·shi Я следующая. f ya *slye*·du·yu·sha·ya
Q What would you like?	Что вы хотите? shto vih kha·*ti*·tye
A I'll have ...	..., пожалуйста. ... pa·*zhal*·sta
Same again, please.	Ещё то же самое! ye·*sho* to zhe *sa*·ma·ye
No ice, thanks.	Безо льда. *bye*·za lda
Let's have a drink!	Давайте выпьем! da·*veyt*·ye *vih*·pim

My round.	Я угощаю. ya u·ga·*sha*·yu
I don't drink alcohol.	Я не пью спиртного. ya nye pyu spirt·*no*·va
Do you have any cold drinks?	У вас есть холодное? u vas yest' kha·*lod*·na·ye
Are these complimentary?	Это бесплатно? e·ta bis·*plat*·na

CULTURE TIP **Local Brews**

кефир m   ki·*fir*
buttermilk – served cold as a breakfast drink and
recommended as a cure for hangovers

компот m   kam·*pot*
a brew of boiled water with fruits and sugar, served
either hot or cold

молочный коктейль m   ma·*loch*·nih kak·*teyl*
'milk cocktails' – milkshakes made with ice cream and
fruit syrup

морс m   mors
a fresh fruit juice made from blackberries, cranberries
or raspberries

простокваша f   pra·stak·*va*·sha
fermented sour milk – a traditional Russian elixir for
good health

сбитень m   zbi·tin'
a drink made from honey, treacle, cinnamon and mint
boiled in water, usually served hot with cakes and
biscuits

Drinking Up

This is hitting the spot.	Это как раз! e·ta kak ras
I feel fantastic!	Я чувствую себя отлично! ya *chust*·vu·yu sib·*ya* at·*lich*·na
I think I've had one too many.	Я напился. **m** ya na·*pil*·sa Я напилась. **f** ya na·*pi*·las'
I'm feeling drunk.	Я пьяный/пьяная. **m/f** ya *pya*·nih/*pya*·na·ya
I'm pissed.	Я мертвецки пьяный/ пьяная. **m/f** ya mirt·*vyet*·ski *pya*·nih/ *pya*·na·ya
I'm going to throw up.	Меня будет мутить. min·*ya* bu·dit mu·*tit'*
Where's the toilet?	Где туалет? gdye tu·al·*yet*
I'm tired, I'd better go home.	Я устал/устала, пора идти домой. **m/f** ya u·*stal*/u·*sta*·la pa·*ra* i·ti da·*moy*
Can you call a taxi for me?	Закажите мне такси. za·ka·*zhiht*·ye mnye tak·si
I don't think you should drive.	Вы не должны водить машину. vih nye dalzh·*nih* va·*dit'* ma·*shih*·nu
I have a hangover.	Я с похмелья. ya s pakh·*myel*·ya

CULTURE TIP

Drinking with the Locals

A Russian celebration is considered incomplete without *советское шампанское* sav·*yet*·ska·ye sham·*pan*·ska·ye or 'Soviet-brand' champagne or another kind of *пойло* poy·la (booze). Another classic is *квас* kvas (kvass), Russia's most popular summer drink. It's a sweet-and-sour blend of sugar and rye flour believed to quench thirst, improve digestion and even benefit the human spirit.

Other typical drinks you might like to sample:

мёд m   myot
mead – a dense, sweet honey beer served hot

медовуха f   mi·da·*vu*·kha
мёд served cold

ряженка f   rya·*zhihn*·ka
coffee-coloured baked, fermented milk

When you simply can't take another vodka hangover, you need to know how to fend off the alcohol you'll be so generously served. It's not acceptable to only drink some of what you're given, but you can say *чуть-чуть* chut'·*chut'* (just a little) when your glass is being refilled – that way you're only forced to down half as much. And if your protests are still to no avail, try the moral high ground of *Я лечусь от алкоголя* ya li·*chus'* at al·ka·*gol*·ya (I'm a recovering alcoholic). The praise you'll earn from this confession will add a lovely touch of irony to your drinking tales when you get home ...

Self-Catering

KEY PHRASES

What's the local speciality?	Что типично местное?	shto ti·*pich*·na *myes*·na·ye
Where can I find the ... section?	Где продают ...?	gdye pra·da·*yut* ...
I'd like some ...	Дайте немного ...	*deyt*·ye nim·*no*·ga ...

Buying Food

What's the local speciality?	Что типично местное? shto ti·*pich*·na *myes*·na·ye
Do you sell locally produced food?	Вы продаёте пищевые продукты в местном масштабе? vih pra·da·*yo*·tye pi·*she*·vih·ye pra·*duk*·tih v *myest*·nam mash·*ta*·bye
Do you sell organic produce?	Вы продаёте натуральные пищевые продукты? vih pra·da·*yo*·tye na·tu·*ral'*·nih·ye pi·*she*·vih·ye pra·*duk*·tih
What's that?	Что это? shto e·ta
Can I taste it?	Дайте мне попробовать. *deyt*·ye mnye pa·*pro*·ba·vat'
Can I have a bag, please?	Дайте, пожалуйста, пакет. *deyt*·ye pa·*zhal*·sta pak·*yet*

How much is (a kilo of cheese)?	Сколько стоит (кило сыра)?	
	skol'·ka sto·it (ki·lo sih·ra)	
I'd like (a) ...	Дайте ...	
	deyt·ye ...	

10 (of them)	десяток	*dis·ya·tak*
(200) grams	(двести) грамм	*(dvye·sti) gram*
half a kilo	полкило	*pol·ki·lo*
(two) kilos	(два) кило	*(dva) ki·lo*
bottle	бутылку	*bu·tihl·ku*
jar/tin	банку	*ban·ku*
packet	пакет	*pak·yet*
piece	кусок	*ku·sok*
(three) pieces	(три) куска	*(tri) kus·ka*
slice	ломтик	*lom·tik*
(six) slices	(шесть) ломтика	*(shest') lom·ti·ka*
(just) a little	(только) немного	*(tol'·ka) nim·no·ga*
more	ещё	*yi·sho*
some ...	немного ...	*nim·no·ga ...*
that one	то	*to*
this one	это	*e·ta*

Less.	Меньше.
	myen'·shih
A bit more.	Ещё немного.
	yi·sho nim·no·ga
Enough.	Достаточно.
	da·sta·tach·na
Do you have anything cheaper?	У вас есть что-нибудь подешевле?
	u vas yest' shto·ni·but' pa·di·shev·lye

FOOD

SELF-CATERING

Do you have other kinds?	У вас есть другие?
	u vas yest' dru·gi·ye
Where can I find the ... section?	Где продают ...?
	gdye pra·da·yut ...

bread	хлеб	khlyep
dairy	молоко	ma·la·ko
dried goods	сушёные продукты	su·sho·nih·ye pra·duk·tih
fish	рыбу	rih·bu
frozen goods	замороженные продукты	za·ma·ro·zhih·nih·ye pra·duk·tih
fruit and vegetable	овощи и фрукты	o·va·shi i fruk·tih
meat	мясо	mya·sa

Cooking

Could I please borrow a ...?	Можно взять ...?
	mozh·na vzyat' ...

frying pan	сковороду	ska·va·ra·du
knife	нож	nosh
samovar	самовар	sa·ma·var
saucepan	кастрюлю	kast·ryul·yu

CULTURE TIP

Food Fashions
Relatively recent food fashions in Russia are *суши* su·shih (sushi) and *в стиле фьюжн* f sti·lye fyu·zhan (fusion) restaurants. Other good food options are *Среднеазиатский ресторан* srid·ni·a·zi·at·ski ri·sta·ran (Central Asian restaurants) or *Индийский ресторан* in·di·ski ri·sta·ran (Indian restaurants).

cured/salted	солёный sal·*yo*·nih
dried	сушёный su·*sho*·nih
fresh	свежий *svye*·zhih
frozen	замороженный za·ma·*ro*·zhih·nih
marinated	маринованый ma·ri·*no*·va·nih
smoked	копчёный kap·*cho*·nih
stuffed	фаршированный far·shih·*ro*·va·nih

For more cooking implements, see the **dictionary**.

Что типично местное?
shto ti·*pich*·na *myes*·na·ye
What's the local speciality?

Vegetarian & Special Meals

KEY PHRASES

I'm a vegetarian.	Я вегетарианец. m	ya vi·gi·ta·ri·a·nits
	Я вегетарианка. f	ya vi·gi·ta·ri·an·ka
Could you prepare a meal without ...?	Вы могли бы приготовить блюдо без ...?	vih ma·gli bih pri·ga·to·vit' blu·da byez ...
I'm allergic to ...	У меня аллергия на ...	u min·ya a·lir·gi·ya na ...

Special Diets & Allergies

Is there a vegetarian restaurant nearby?	Здесь есть вегетарианский ресторан? zdyes' yest' vi·gi·ta·ri·an·ski ri·sta·ran
Is there a halal restaurant nearby?	Здесь есть халал ресторан? zdyes' yest' kha·lal ri·sta·ran
Is there a kosher restaurant nearby?	Здесь есть кошерный ресторан? zdyes' yest' ka·sher·nih ri·sta·ran
I'm on a special/strict diet.	Я на особенной/строгой диете. ya na a·so·bi·ney/stro·gey di·yet·ye
I'm a vegan.	Я веган/веганка. m/f ya vye·gan/vye·gan·ka

CULTURE TIP

Russian Breakfast
Russian food is simple, generous, and appetising.
A typical Russian breakfast, for instance, consists
of каша ka·sha (buckwheat porridge), хлеб khlyep (bread)
and кефир ki·fir (sour milk).

I'm a vegetarian.	Я вегетарианец. m
	ya vi·gi·ta·ri·a·nits
	Я вегетарианка. f
	ya vi·gi·ta·ri·an·ka

| I'm allergic to ... | У меня аллергия на ... |
| | u min·ya a·lir·gi·ya na ... |

crustaceans	ракообразных	ra·ka·a·braz·nihkh
dairy produce	молочные	ma·loch·nih·ye
	продукты	pra·duk·tih
eggs	яйца	yeyt·sa
gelatine	желатин	zhih·la·tin
gluten	клейковину	klyey·ka·vi·nu
honey	мёд	myot
molluscs	моллюсков	mal·yu·skaf
MSG	МНГ	em·en·ge
nuts	орехи	ar·ye·khi
peanuts	арахисы	a·ra·khi·sih
seafood	морепродукты	mor·ye·pra·duk·tih

Ordering Food

| Could you prepare a meal without ...? | Вы могли бы приготовить блюдо без ...? |
| | vih ma·gli bih pri·ga·to·vit' blu·da byez ... |

I don't eat ... Я не ем ...
ya nye yem ...

butter	масла	*mas*·la
eggs	яиц	*ya*·its
fish	рыбы	*rih*·bih
fish/meat stock	рыбного/ мясного бульона	*rihb*·na·va/ myas·*no*·va bu·*lo*·na
oil	масла	*mas*·la
pork	свинины	svi·*ni*·nih
poultry	птицы	*ptit*·sih
red meat	мяса	*mya*·sa

Is this ...? Это ...?
e·ta ...

decaffeinated	без кофеина	byes kaf·ye·*i*·na
free of animal produce	без животных продуктов	byes zhih·*vot*·nihkh pra·*duk*·taf
free-range	от курицы, живущей на свободном выгуле	at *ku*·rit·sih zhih·*vush*·chey na sva·*bod*·nam *vih*·gu·li
genetically modified	генетически модифицировано	gi·ni·*ti*·chi·ski mo·di·fit·*sih*·ra·va·na
gluten-free	без клейковины	byes kli·ka·*vi*·nih
low-fat	маложирно	ma·la·*zhihr*·na
low in sugar	с низким содержанием сахара	s *nis*·kim sa·dir·*zha*·ni·yem *sa*·kha·ra
organic	органически	ar·ga·*ni*·chi·ski
salt-free	без соли	byes *so*·li

Menu
~ DECODER ~
кулинарный словарь

This miniguide to Russian cuisine is designed to help you get the most out of your gastronomic experience by providing you with food terms that you may see on menus. Nouns have their gender indicated by ⑩, ① or ⑩, while adjectives are given in the masculine form only. Both nouns and adjectives are provided in the nominative case. For an explanation of case, and how to form feminine and neuter adjectives, see the **grammar** chapter, pages 16 and 14 respectively.

This chapter has been ordered according to the Cyrillic alphabet (see **pronunciation**, p13).

~ А ~

абрикос ⑩ *a·bri·kos* apricot

авсень ⑩ *af·syen'* beef or pork brain & tongue cooked with vegetables & spices

авюторга ① *av·yu·tor·ga* pickled mullet

азербайджанский плов ⑩ *a·zir·bey·dzhan·ski plof* Azerbaijan pilau with almonds, sesame seeds & ginger

азу из говядины ⑩ *a·zu iz gav·ya·di·nih* beef stew with vegetables & spices

антрекот ⑩ *an·tri·kot* entrecôte (boned sirloin steak)

апельсин ⑩ *a·pil'·sin* orange

апельсиновый сок ⑩ *a·pil'·si·na·vih sok* orange juice

арахис ⑩ *a·ra·khis* peanut

арбуз ⑩ *ar·bus* melon • rockmelon • watermelon

~ Б ~

бабка ① *bap·ka* baked meat & potato • cake

— ромовая ① *ro·ma·va·ya* rum cake

— яблочная ① *ya·blach·na·ya* apple cake

баклажан ⑩ *ba·kla·zhan* aubergine • eggplant

— в сметане f *smi·tan·ye* fried eggplant & onions with sour cream

— фаршированный *far·shih·ro·va·nih* eggplant stuffed with vegetables

балык сорпа ① *ba·lihk sor·pa* stew of mutton, sheep tail fat, rice & sour milk

банан ⑩ *ba·nan* banana

баранина ① *ba·ra·ni·na* lamb • mutton

булочка ⓕ *bu*·lach·ka bread rolls

бекон ⓜ *bi*·kon bacon

бефстроганов ⓜ bif·stra·ga·*nof* beef stroganoff – braised beef with sour cream & mushrooms

биточки ⓕ pl bi·*toch*·ki meatballs, often served in tomato sauce

бифштекс ⓜ bif·*shteks* steak – usually glorified hamburger filling

блинчики ⓜ pl blin·*chi*·ki pancakes – either rolled around meat or cheese & or filled with jam or another sweet filling

— с мясом s *mya*·sam pancakes & meat

блины ⓜ pl bli·*nih* buckwheat pancakes

— картофельные с икрой kar·to·fil'·*nih*·ye s i·*kroy* potato pancakes with red caviar

— со сметаной sa smi·*ta*·ney baked pancakes with sour cream

бобовые ⓜ pl ba·bo·*vih*·ye legumes

борщ ⓜ borsh beetroot soup with vegetables & meat

— зелёный zil·*yo*·nih green beetroot soup with sorrel & sour cream

— московский mas·*kof*·ski Moscow beetroot soup with beef & frankfurters

— постный *post*·nih meatless beetroot soup

— украинский u·kra·*in*·ski Ukrainian beetroot soup with vegetables

ботвинья ⓕ bat·*vi*·nya fish soup with green vegetables & **квас**

брокколи ⓕ *bro*·ka·li broccoli

брусника ⓕ brus·*ni*·ka cranberries

брынза ⓕ *brihn*·za salty white cheese

бульон ⓜ bu·*lon* chicken broth

~ В ~

в гриле v *gril*·ye grilled

в сметане f smi·*tan*·ye in sour cream

в томате f ta·*mat*·ye in tomato

варево ⓝ *va*·ri·va liquid dishes

вареники ⓜ pl var·ye·ni·ki dumplings with berries inside, then topped with sugar

— с картофелем s kar·*to*·fil·yem fried potato **вареники**

варёное мясо поруски ⓝ var·yo·na·ye mya·sa pa·rus·ki Russian-style boiled beef

варёный var·*yo*·nih boiled • poached

варенье ⓝ var·*yen*·ye jam • fruit cooked in sugar

ватрушки pl vat·*rush*·ki pastries with cottage cheese & sour cream

вегетарианский vi·gi·ta·ri·*an*·ski vegetarian

вермишель ⓕ vir·mi·*shel'* noodles

ветчина ⓕ vit·chi·*na* ham

взвар ⓜ vzvar vegetable or herb sauce

винегрет ⓜ vi·nig·*ryet* 'winter salad' – potato, carrot, beetroot, onion & pickles

виноград ⓜ vi·na·*grat* grapes

вишня ⓕ *vish*·nya cherry

вырезка по-таёжному ⓕ *vih*·ris·ka pa·ta·*yozh*·na·mu cubed steak with herbs

~ Г ~

говядина ⓕ gav·ya·di·na beef

гоголь-моголь ⓜ go·gal' *mo*·gal' whipped egg yolks with alcohol & sugar

голубь ⓜ go·lub' pigeon

голубцы ⓜ pl ga·lub·*tsih* cabbage rolls stuffed with meat & rice

— вегетарианские vi·gi·ta·ri·an·ski·ye cabbage rolls with mushrooms & carrots

горох ⓜ ga·*rokh* peas

гребешки ⓜ pl gri·bish·ki scallops

гренки ⓜ pl grin·ki toast fried in butter

грецкий орех ⓜ *gryets·ki ar·yekh* walnut

грибы ⓜ pl *gri·bih* mushrooms

— в сметане f *smi·tan·ye* mushrooms baked in sour cream

груша ⓕ *gru·sha* pear

гурьевская каша ⓕ *gur·yef·ska·ya ka·sha* porridge with caramelised nuts & fruits

гусь ⓜ *gus'* goose

~ Д ~

дары моря ⓜ pl *da·rih mor·ya* seafood

дзеренина ⓕ *dzir·ye·ni·na* wild goat cutlets, served with fried potatoes, mushrooms & pickled fruits

деруны ⓜ pl *di·ru·nih* potato pancakes with cream & preserves

драники ⓕ pl *dra·ni·ki* potato pancakes

драчона ⓕ *dra·cho·na* baked egg & milk mix served with parsley

дыня ⓕ *dihn·ya* melon

~ Ж ~

жаренина ⓕ *zha·ri·ni·na* potatoes baked in milk & buckwheat

жареница ⓕ *zha·ri·nit·sa* fish pie

жареный *zha·ri·nih* fried • roasted

— поросёнок ⓜ pa·ras·yo·nak roasted suckling pig

жаркое ⓝ *zhar·ko·ye* meat or poultry stewed in a clay pot

— из медвежатины is *mid·vi·zha·ti·na* bear-meat stew

— по-домашнему pa·da·mash·ni·mu 'home-style' meat stew with vegetables

харчо ⓝ *zhar·cho* lamb soup with cherries, walnuts, rice & vegetables

житие ⓕ *zhiht·nya* rye porridge

жюльен куриный в кокотницах *zhyul·yen ku·ri·nih f ka·kot·ni·tsakh* chicken, mushroom & cheese bake

~ З ~

зайчатина ⓕ *zey·cha·ti·na* rabbit meat

запеканка ⓕ *za·pi·kan·ka* pie of cottage cheese, semolina, sour cream & raisins

запечёный *za·pi·cho·nih* baked

заяц ⓜ *za·yits* hare

зелень ⓕ *zye·lin'* greens • herbs

землянika ⓕ *zim·li·ni·ka* wild strawberries

зразы картофельные ⓕ pl *zra·zih kar·to·fil'·nih·ye* boiled potatoes mixed with mince & fried in small cakes

~ И ~

изюм ⓕ *iz·yum* raisins

икра ⓕ *i·kra* caviar

— баклажанная ba·kla·zha·na·ya eggplant caviar – baked eggplant blended with tomato & onion (like baba ghanooj)

— красная kras·na·ya red caviar (salmon)

— чёрная chor·na·ya black caviar (sturgeon)

индейка ⓕ *in·dyey·ka* turkey

инжир ⓜ *in·zhihr* figs

~ К ~

кабачок ⓜ *ka·ba·chok* courgette • zucchini

казахский плов *ka·zakh·ski plof* pilau with lamb, carrots & apricots

какао ⓝ *ka·ka·o* milky cocoa

кальмары ⓜ pl *kal'·ma·rih* squid

капуста ⓕ *ka·pu·sta* cabbage • sauerkraut

— с помидорами s pa·mi·do·ra·mi cabbage with thickened tomato sauce

карп ⓜ *karp* carp

карри ⓝ *ka·ri* curry

Л

картофель ⓜ kar·to·fil' potato
— в мундире v mun·dir·ye baked jacket potatoes
— фаршированный грибами far·shih·ro·va·nih gri·ba·mi potatoes stuffed with mushroom & onion, drizzled with sour cream then baked
картофлянки ⓜ pl kar·tof·lyan·ki baked potato dumplings
картошка ⓕ kar·tosh·ka potato
картошник ⓜ kar·tosh·nik potatoes boiled, mixed with cheeses, cream & baking powder then baked
катык ⓖ ka·tihk fermented clotted milk
каша ⓕ ka·sha buckwheat porridge
— сименуха si·mi·nu·kha porridge with mushrooms, eggs & onions
каштан ⓜ kash·tan chestnut
квас ⓜ kvas kvass – a beer-like drink made from sugar & rye flour
квашеная капуста ⓕ kva·shih·na·ya ka·pu·sta pickled cabbage • sauerkraut
кешью ⓜ kye·shu cashew
кисель ⓜ kis·yel' fruit jelly
кишмиш ⓜ kish·mish sultana
клубника ⓕ klub·ni·ka strawberry
клёцки ⓕ pl klyots·ki dumplings
коза ⓕ ka·za goat
козинаки ⓕ pl ka·zi·na·ki walnut honey toffee
колбаса ⓕ kal·ba·sa salami • sausage
— копчёная kap·cho·na·ya smoked sausage
компот ⓜ kam·pot fruit in syrup
копчёный kap·cho·nih smoked
корица ⓕ ka·rit·sa cinnamon
котлета ⓕ kat·lye·ta ground meat croquette
— пожарская pa·zhar·ska·ya croquette with minced chicken or turkey
— по-киевски pa·ki·if·ski chicken Kiev –rolled boneless chicken stuffed with butter, crumbed & deep-fried

крабы ⓜ pl kra·bih crab
красная рыба ⓕ kras·na·ya rih·ba red fish
красная смородина ⓕ kras·na·ya sma·ro·di·na redcurrant
креветка ⓕ kriv·yet·ka prawn
креветки ⓕ pl kriv·yet·ki shrimp
кровавый kra·va·vih rare (food)
кролик ⓜ kro·lik rabbit
кукуруза ⓕ ku·ku·ru·za corn
кулебяка ⓕ ku·lib·ya·ka pastry filled with cabbage, eggs & herbs • salmon cooked in wine with eggs, rice & vegetables
кулич ⓜ kul·yich Easter cake with raisins & nutmeg
курица ⓕ ku·rit·sa chicken
курник ⓜ kur·nik pancakes filled with rice & egg, chicken or mushrooms, then baked
кэрри ⓕ ke·ri curry

~ Л ~

лайм ⓜ leym lime
лапша ⓕ lap·sha chicken noodle soup
латкес ⓕ lat·kis fried pancakes with pumpkin or squash
лесной орех ⓜ lis·noy ar·yekh hazelnut
лещ ⓜ lyesh bream
лимон ⓜ li·mon lemon
лобио ⓕ lo·bi·o spiced bean stew with capsicum & tomato
лососина ⓕ la·sa·si·na salmon
лосось ⓜ lo·sos' salmon
лук ⓜ luk onions
лук-порей ⓜ luk·pa·rey leek
люля-кебаб ⓜ lyul·ya·ki·bap ground lamb sausages

~ М ~

майонез ⓜ ma·yan·yez mayonnaise
малина ⓕ ma·li·na raspberry
манная каша ⓕ ma·na·ya ka·sha porridge with semolina

манты ⓜ pl *man·*tih steamed, palm-sized version of meat dumplings
маринованый ma·ri·no·va·nih marinated
маринованные грибы ⓜ pl ma·ri·*no·*va·nih·ye gri·*bih* pickled mushrooms
маринованный ma·ri·*no·*va·nih pickled
маслины ① pl mas·*li·*nih olives
масло ⓝ *mas·*la butter • oil
мёд ⓜ myot honey
медвежатина ① mid·vi·*zha·*ti·na bear
мёдивник ⓜ *myo·*div·nik honey cake with raisins
медовуха ① mi·da·*vu·*kha honey **квас**
мидия ① *mi·*di·ya mussel
миндаль min·*dal'* almond
молоко ⓝ ma·la·*ko* milk
морковь ① mar·*kof'* carrot
мороженое ⓝ ma·ro·*zhih·*na·ye ice cream
мясной фарш ⓜ mis·*noy* farsh mince
мясное ассорти ⓝ mis·*no·*ye a·sar·*ti* selection of cold meats
мясо ⓝ *mya·*sa meat
— по-сибирски pa·si·*bir·*ski Siberian-style beef topped with cheese
мята ① *mya·*ta mint

~ О ~

овощи ⓜ pl o·*va·*shi vegetables
овощная окрошка ① a·vash·*na·*ya a·*krosh·*ka cold vegetable soup with potatoes, carrots, turnips & radish
овощной пирог ⓜ a·vash·*noy* pi·*rok* vegetable pie with cabbage, mushrooms, cream cheese & eggs
овощной плов ⓜ a·vash·*noy* plof vegetable pilau
овсянка ① af·*syan·*ka oats
овёс ⓜ av·*yos* oats
огурец ⓜ a·gur·*yets* cucumber

огурцы ⓜ pl a·gurt·*sih* pickles
окрошка ① a·*krosh·*ka soup of cucumber, sour cream, potato, egg, meat & kvass
окунь ⓜ o·kun' perch
оладьи из тыквы ⓜ pl a·*la·*di is *tihk·*vih pumpkin fritters
оладьи ① pl a·*la·*di fritters topped with syrup or sour cream, often fried with fruit
оленина ① a·li·*ni·*na venison
оливка ① a·*lif·*ka olive
оливковое масло ⓝ a·*lif·*ka·va·ye *mas·*la olive oil
оливье ⓝ a·li·*vye* 'Olivier salad' – meat & vegetables with sour cream
омуль ⓜ o·mul' salmon-like fish
орех ⓜ ar·*yekh* nut
осетрина ① a·si·*tri·*na sturgeon
— отварная at·var·*na·*ya poached sturgeon
— с грибами z gri·*ba·*mi sturgeon with mushrooms
— с майонезом s ma·yan·ye·zam sturgeon with mayonnaise
отбивная ① at·biv·*na·*ya beef or pork steak
отварной at·var·*noy* boiled • poached

~ П ~

палтус ⓜ *pal·*tus halibut
папоротник ⓜ pa·pa·*rat·*nik fern tips
паровый *pa·*ra·vih steamed
пасха ① pas·kha Easter cake made from cottage cheese, nuts & candied fruits
патока ① pa·ta·ka treacle
паштет ⓜ pasht·*yet* meat paste similar to liver sausage
персик ⓜ *pyer·*sik peach
перец ⓜ *pye·*rits black pepper • capsicum
пельмени ⓜ pl pilm·*ye·*ni meat dumplings

петрушка ① pi·*trush*·ka parsley
печёный pi·*cho*·nih baked
печень ① *pye*·chin' liver
пирог ⑩ pi·*rok* pie
— из тыквы ⑩ pi·*rok* is *tihk*·vih pumpkin pie – baked whole pumpkin filled with rice, apples, raisins & cherries
пирожное ⑪ pi·*rozh*·na·ye biscuits • pastries • small cakes
печёная тыква ① pi·*cho*·na·ya *tihk*·va baked pumpkin with eggs & almonds
печенье ⑪ pi·*chen*·ye biscuit • cookie • cracker
пирожки ⑩ pl pi·*rash*·ki spicy, deep-fried mutton pies
— картофельные kar·to·*fil*'·nih·ye potato pies
— с капустой s ka·*pus*·toy meat & cabbage pies
плов ⑩ plof pilau – rice with mutton
— из кролика is *kro*·li·ka rabbit pilau
поджарка ① pad·*zhar*·ka roast meat, usually beef or pork
помидор ⑩ pa·mi·*dor* tomato
пончики ⑩ pl *pon*·chi·ki sugared doughnuts
почки ① pl *poch*·ki kidneys
— в мадере v mad·*yer*·ye kidneys in Madeira wine & sour cream sauce
простокваша ① pra·stak·*va*·sha sour milk
пряник ⑩ *prya*·nik gingerbread
птица ① *ptit*·sa poultry
пшённая каша с черносливом ① psho·na·ya *ka*·sha s chir·na·*sli*·vam millet porridge with prunes

~ P ~

рагу ⑩ ra·*gu* stew
рассольник ⑩ ra·*sol*'·nik soup with chopped pickles & kidney

расстегай ⑩ ra·sti·*gey* small pies
редиска ① ri·*dis*·ka radish
рис ⑩ ris rice
рисовая запеканка ① *ri*·sa·va·ya za·pi·*kan*·ka porridge with rice & cheese
рыба ① *rih*·ba fish
— солёная sal·*yo*·na·ya salted fish
рыбное ассорти ⑪ *rihb*·na·ye a·sar·*ti* selection of cold fish delicacies

~ C ~

салат ⑩ sa·*lat* salad – usually tomato, onion & cucumber
— из капусты is ka·*pus*·tih cabbage, apple & carrot salad
— из картофеля kar·to·*fil*·ya potato salad with onions & mayonnaise
— из помидоров is pa·mi·*do*·raf tomato salad
— из огурцов iz a·gurt·*sof* cucumber salad
— из редиса is ri·*di*·sa radish & onion salad
— из яиц iz ya·*its* egg salad with mayonnaise, garlic, pimiento & scallion
— оливье a·liv·*ye* see **оливье**
— столичный sta·*lich*·nih vegetable, beef, potato & egg salad
самбук ⑩ sam·*buk* plum & sugar mousse
самса ① *sam*·sa baked walnut parcels
сардина ① sar·*di*·na sardine
сардины с лимоном ① pl sar·*di*·nih s li·*mo*·nam sardines with lemon
сахар ⑩ *sa*·khar sugar
сациви ⑩ sat·*sih*·vi chicken in walnut sauce
свёкла ① *svyol*·ka beetroot
свинина ① svi·*ni*·na pork
севрюга ① siv·*ryu*·ga sturgeon

селёдка ① sil·*yot*·ka pickled herrings
— **под шубой** pat *shu*·bey salad with herring, potato, beet, carrot & mayonnaise
сельдерей ⓜ sil'·*dir*·yey celery
сельдь ① syelt' herring
сёмга ① *syom*·ga salmon
— **копчёная** kap·*cho*·na·ya smoked salmon
сименуха ① si·mi·*nu*·kha porridge with mushrooms
скумбрия ① *skum*·bri·ya mackerel
слива ① *sli*·va plum
сливки ⓜ pl *slif*·ki cream
сметана ① smi·*ta*·na sour cream
сметаник ⓜ smi·*ta*·nik pie with almonds, berries & jam
соевый соус ⓜ so·i·vih so·us soy sauce
солёные огурцы ⓜ sal·*yo*·nih·ye a·gurt·*sih* pickled cucumber
солёный sal·*yo*·nih cured • salted
— **арбуз** ⓜ ar·*bus* pickled watermelon
солёные грибы ⓜ pl sal·*yo*·nih·ye gri·*bih* marinated mushrooms
солянка ① sal·*yan*·ka 'salted' soup – meat or fish soup with salted cucumbers & other vegetables
— **мясная** myas·*na*·ya 'salted' soup with meat
— **рыбная** rihb·*na*·ya 'salted' soup with fish
сосиски ① pl sa·*sis*·ki fried/boiled sausages
соус ⓜ sous sauce
судак ⓜ su·*dak* pikeperch
суп ⓜ sup soup
— **вермишелевый** vir·mi·*shel*·i·vih noodle soup
— **грибной** grib·*noy* mushroom soup with vegetables
— **с мясом** s *mya*·sam soup with meat
— **с рыбой** s *rih*·bey soup with fish
— **с фрикадельками** s fri·kad·*yel*'·ka·mi soup with meatballs

сыр ⓜ sihr cheese
сырники ① pl *sihr*·ni·ki cottage cheese fritters

~ Т ~

табака ① ta·ba·*ka* seasoned chicken (fried or grilled)
творог ⓜ tva·*rok* cottage cheese
телятина ① til·*ya*·ti·na veal
тефтели ① pl *tyef*·ti·li meatballs
толма ① *tol*·ma dolma – meat & rice stuffed in vine leaves
торт ⓜ tort large cake
требуха ① tri·bu·*kha* tripe
треска ① tris·*ka* trout
тунец ⓜ tun·*yets* tuna
турецкий горох ⓜ tu·*rets*·ki ga·*rokh* chickpea
туря ① *tur*·ya sauerkraut mixed with bread & onion & covered with **квас**
тушёный tu·*sho*·nih stewed
тыква ① *tihk*·va pumpkin

~ У ~

устрица ① *ust*·rit·sa oyster
утка ① *ut*·ka duck
уха ① u·*kha* fish soup with potato & carrot
ушное ① ush·*no*·ye stew

~ Ф ~

фаршированный far·shih·*ro*·va·nih stuffed
фасоль ① fa·*sol*' bean
финики ⓜ pl fi·ni·ki dates
фисташка ① fis·*tash*·ka pistachio
форель ① far·*yel*' trout
форшмак ⓜ farsh·*mak* baked liquefied beef & lamb with herrings soaked in milk
фри fri fried
фруктовый торт ⓜ fruk·*to*·vih tort fruit cake with raisins, almonds, apricots, candied fruits & sherry
фрукты ⓜ pl *fruk*·tih fruit

T

MENU DECODER

~ X ~

хачапури ⓜ kha·cha·*pu*·ri rich, cheesy bread
хаш ⓜ khash tripe soup
херес ⓜ *khye*·ris sherry
хинкали ⓘ pl khin·*ka*·li lamb dumplings
хлеб ⓜ khlyep bread
— белый *bye*·lih white bread
— чёрный *chor*·nih black rye bread
— с фруктами s *fruk*·ta·mi rye bread with fruit
— ячменно-пшеничный yach·*mye*·na·pshe·*nich*·nih wheat & barley bread
хрен ⓜ khryen horseradish

~ Ц ~

цветная капуста ⓘ tsvit·*na*·ya ka·*pu*·sta cauliflower
— с картофелем ⓘ s kar·*to*·fil·yem baked cauliflower & potato dish
цыплёнок табака ⓜ tsihp·*lyo*·nak ta·ba·*ka* Caucasian-style grilled chicken
цитрусовый джем ⓜ *tsih*·tra·sa·vey dzhem marmalade

~ Ч ~

чахохбили ⓘ pl cha·*khokh*·bi·li steamed dumplings
черешня ⓘ chir·*yesh*·nya cherry
чёрная редька ⓘ *chor*·na·ya ryet'·ka black radish
чёрная смородина ⓘ *chor*·na·ya sma·ro·di·na blackcurrant
черника ⓘ chir·*ni*·ka blackberries
чернослив ⓜ chir·nas·*lif* prunes
чебуреки ⓜ pl chi·bur·*ye*·ki fried beef & pork dumplings
чров плав ⓜ chrof plof rice pilau with dried fruit & nuts

чучкелла ⓘ chuch·*kye*·la looped, sugar-coated grape and walnut candies

~ Ш ~

шаверма ⓘ shav·*yer*·ma shawarma – rotisserie meat served in pita bread
шаурма ⓘ *sha*·ur·ma see **шаверма**
шашлык ⓜ shash·*lihk* skewered meat
шишки ⓘ pl *shihsh*·ki cedar nuts
шницель ⓜ *shnit*·sel' Wiener schnitzel
шоколад ⓜ sha·ka·*lat* chocolate
шпинат ⓜ shpi·*nat* spinach
— по-армянски pa·arm·*yan*·ski Armenian spinach – baked fried spinach with milk, cheese & eggs
шпроты ⓘ pl *shpro*·tih sprats (like herring)

~ Щ ~

щавель ⓜ shav·*yel'* sorrel
щи ⓜ pl shi fresh or pickled cabbage soup, usually with meat & potato
— постные *post*·nih·ye cabbage soup without meat
— с грибами z gri·*ba*·mi cabbage soup with mushrooms
щука ⓘ *shu*·ka pike

~ Я ~

яблоко ⓜ *ya*·bla·ka apple
яблочный пирог ⓜ *ya*·blach·nih pi·*rok* apple pie
ягоды ⓘ pl *ya*·ga·dih berries
язык с гарниром ⓜ yi·*zihk* z gar·*ni*·ram tongue with garnish
яйцо ⓘ yiyt·*so* egg
— всмятку *fsmyat*·ku soft-boiled egg
— крутое kru·*to*·ye hard-boiled egg
яичница ⓘ ya·*ich*·nit·sa fried egg

Dictionary

ENGLISH *to* RUSSIAN

английский–русский

Russian nouns in this dictionary have their gender indicated by
ⓜ, ⓕ or ⓝ. If it's a plural noun you'll also see pl. When a word that
could be either a noun or a verb has no gender indicated, it's a verb.
For added clarity, certain words are marked as adjectives a, verbs v
or adverbs adv. Adjectives are given in the masculine form only.
Nouns and adjectives are given in the nominative case only.

Verbs are mostly given in two forms: perfective and imperfective.
The two forms are separated by a slash with the imperfective
form given first (eg 'walk' *гулять/погулять* gul·*yat'*/pa·gul·*yat'*).
If only one verb form is given, it's used for both perfective and
imperfective.

For more information, refer to the **grammar** chapter.

A

aboard на борту na bar·*tu*

abortion аборт ⓜ a·*bort*

about около o·ka·la

above над nat

abroad за границей za gra·*nit*·sey

accident авария ⓕ a·*va*·ri·ya

accommodation помещение ⓝ
pa·mi·*she*·ni·ye

account (bank) счёт ⓜ shot

across через *che*·ris

actor актёр/актриса ⓜ/ⓕ akt·*yor*/
ak·*tri*·sa

adaptor адаптер ⓜ a·*dap*·tir

address адрес ⓜ a·dris

administration администрация ⓕ
ad·mi·nist·*rat*·sih·ya

admission (price) вход ⓜ fkhot

admit впускать/впустить fpu·*skat'*/
fpu·*stit'*

adult взрослый/взрослая ⓜ/ⓕ
vzros·lih/vzros·la·ya

advertisement реклама ⓕ
ri·*kla*·ma

advice совет ⓜ sav·*yet*

(be) afraid бояться ba·*yat'*·sa

after после *pos*·lye

(this) afternoon (сегодня) днём
(si·*vod*·nya) dnyom

aftershave одеколон ⓜ
a·di·ka·*lon*

again ещё раз yi·*sho* ras

age возраст ⓜ *voz*·rast

... ago ... тому назад ... ta·*mu* na·*zat*

A

agree соглашаться/согласиться
sa·gla·*shat*'·sa/sa·gla·*sit*'·sa

agriculture сельское хозяйство ⓝ
syel'·ska·ye khaz·*yeyst*·va

ahead вперёд fpir·*yot*

AIDS СПИД ⓜ spit

air воздух ⓜ *voz*·dukh

air conditioning
кондиционирование ⓝ
kan·dit·sih·a·*ni*·ra·va·ni·ye

airline авиакомпания ⓕ
a·vi·a·kam·*pa*·ni·ya

airmail авиапочта ⓕ a·vi·a·*poch*·ta

airplane самолёт ⓜ sa·mal·*yot*

airport аэропорт ⓜ a·e·ra·*port*

airport tax налог на вылет ⓜ na·*lok*
na *vih*·lit

aisle (plane etc) проход ⓜ pra·*khot*

alarm clock будильник ⓜ bu·*dil*'·nik

alcohol алкоголь ⓜ al·ka·*gol*'

all все fsye

allergy аллергия ⓕ al·*yer*·gi·ya

almond миндаль ⓜ min·*dal*'

almost почти pach·*ti*

alone один/одна ⓜ/ⓕ a·*din*/ad·*na*

already уже u·*zhe*

also тоже *to*·zhih

altar алтарь ⓜ al·*tar*'

altitude высота ⓕ vih·sa·*ta*

always всегда fsig·*da*

ambassador посол ⓜ pa·*sol*

amber янтарь ⓜ yin·*tar*'

ambulance скорая помощь ⓕ
sko·ra·ya *po*·mash

anaemia анемия ⓕ an·*ye*·mi·ya

ancient древний *dryev*·ni

and и i

angry сердитый sir·*di*·tih

animal животное ⓝ zhih·*vot*·na·ye

ankle лодыжка ⓕ la·*dihsh*·ka

another ещё один/одна ⓜ/ⓕ yi·*sho*
a·*din*/ad·*na*

answer ответ ⓜ at·*vyet*

ant муравей ⓜ mu·rav·*yey*

antibiotics антибиотики ⓕ pl
an·ti·bi·*o*·ti·ki

antihistamines антигистаминные
средства ⓝ pl an·ti·gi·sta·*mi*·nih·ye
sryets·tva

antinuclear противоядерный
pra·ti·va·*ya*·dir·nih

antique антиквариат ⓜ
an·tik·*var*·yat

antiseptic антисептик ⓜ
an·tis·*yep*·tik

any любой lyu·*boy*

apartment квартира ⓕ kvar·*ti*·ra

apple яблоко ⓝ *yab*·la·ka

appointment встреча ⓕ *fstre*·cha

apricot абрикос ⓜ a·bri·*kos*

archaeological археологический
ar·khi·a·la·*gi*·chi·ski

architect архитектор ⓜ
ar·khit·*yek*·tar

architecture архитектура ⓕ
ar·khi·tik·*tu*·ra

argue спорить *spo*·rit'

arm рука ⓕ ru·*ka*

arrest арестовывать/арестовать
a·ri·sto·vih·*vat*'/a·ri·sta·*vat*'

arrivals прибытие ⓝ pri·*bih*·ti·ye

arrive приезжать/приехать
pri·i·*zhat*'/pri·ye·*khat*'

art искусство ⓝ is·*kust*·va

art gallery галлерея ⓕ ga·lir·*ye*·ya

artist художник/художница ⓜ/ⓕ
khu·*dozh*·nik/khu·*dozh*·nit·sa

ashtray пепельница ⓕ pye·*pil*'·nit·sa

ask (a question) спрашивать/
спросить *spra*·shih·vat'/spra·*sit*'

ask (for something) просить/
попросить pra·*sit*'/pa·pra·*sit*'

aspirin аспирин ⓜ a·spi·*rin*

asthma астма ⓕ *ast*·ma

astrology астрология ⓕ
ast·ra·*lo*·gi·ya

at в v

atheism атеизм ⓜ a·ti·*izm*

atheist атеист ⓜ a·ti·*ist*

atmosphere атмосфера ⓕ
at·mas·*fye*·ra

aubergine баклажан ⓜ ba·kla·*zhan*

B

aunt тётя ① *tyot·*ya
Australia Австралия ① af·*stra·*li·ya
ATM банкомат ⓜ ban·ka·*mat*
autumn осень ① *o·*sin'
avenue проспект ⓜ prasp·*yekt*
awful ужасный u·*zhas·*nih

B

B&W (film) чёрно-белый
chor·nab·ye·*lih*
baby ребёнок ⓜ rib·yo·*nak*
baby food детское питание ⓝ
dyet·ska·ye pi·*ta·*ni·ye
baby powder тальк ⓜ talk
babysitter приходящая няня ①
pri·khad·ya·sha·ya *nyan·*ya
back (body) спина ① spi·*na*
back (position) задняя часть ①
zad·nya·ya chast'
backpack рюкзак ⓜ ryug·*zak*
bacon бекон ⓜ bi·*kon*
badge значок ⓜ zna·*chok*
bad плохой pla·*khoy*
bag мешок ⓜ mi·*shok*
baggage багаж ⓜ ba·*gash*
baggage allowance норма багажа ①
nor·ma ba·ga·*zha*
baggage claim выдача багажа ①
vih·da·cha ba·ga·*zha*
bakery булочная ① bu·lach·na·ya
balance (account) баланс ⓜ
ba·*lans*
balcony балкон ⓜ bal·*kon*
ball (sport) мяч ⓜ myach
ballet балет ⓜ bal·*yet*
banana банан ⓜ ba·*nan*
band (music) группа ① *gru·*pa
bandage бинт ⓜ bint
Band-Aid пластырь ⓜ *pla·*stihr
bank банк ⓜ bank
bank account банковский счёт ⓜ
ban·kaf·ski shot
banknote банкнот ⓜ bank·*not*
barber парикмахер ⓜ pa·rik·ma·*khir*
basket корзина ① kar·*zi·*na
bath ванна ① *va·*na

bathhouse баня ① *ban·*ya
bathing suit купальный костюм ⓜ
ku·*pal'·*nih kast·*yum*
bathroom ванная ① *va·*na·ya
battery (general) батарея ①
ba·tar·ye·ya
be быть biht'
beach пляж ⓜ plyash
bean фасоль ① fa·*sol'*
beautiful красивый kra·*si·*vih
because потому что pa·ta·*mu* shta
bed кровать ① kra·*vat'*
bedding постельное бельё ⓝ
past·yel'·na·ye bil·yo
bedroom спальня ① *spaln·*ya
bee пчела ① pchi·*la*
beef говядина ① gav·ya·di·na
beer пиво ⓝ *pi·*va
beetroot свёкла ① *svyo·*kla
before до do
beggar нищий/нищая ⓜ/① *ni·*shi/
*ni·*sha·ya
behind за za
Belarus Белоруссия ① bi·la·*ru·*si·ya
Belgium Бельгия ① byel'·*gi·*ya
below под pot
berth (train) полка ① *pol·*ka
berth (ship) койка ① *koy·*ka
beside рядом с rya·dam s
best самый лучший sa·mih *luch·*shih
bet пари ① pl pa·*ri*
between между *myezh·*du
bicycle велосипед ⓜ vi·la·sip·*yet*
big большой bal'·*shoy*
bike велосипед ⓜ vi·la·sip·*yet*
bike chain цепь для велосипеда ①
tsep' dlya vi·la·sip·ye·da
bike lock замок для велосипеда ⓜ
za·*mok* dlya vi·la·sip·ye·da
bike path велодорожка ①
vi·la·da·*rosh·*ka
bike shop велосипедный магазин ⓜ
vi·la·sip·*yed·*nih ma·ga·*zin*
bill (restaurant etc) счёт ⓜ shot
binoculars бинокль ⓜ bi·*nokl'*
bird птица ① *ptit·*sa

B

birthday день рождения Ⓜ dyen'·razh·dye·ni

biscuit печенье Ⓝ pi·chen·ye

bite (dog/insect) укус Ⓜ u·kus

bitter горький gor'·ki

black чёрный a chor·nih

black market чёрный рынок Ⓜ chor·nih rih·nak

bladder мочевой пузырь Ⓜ ma·chi·voy pu·zihr'

blanket одеяло Ⓝ a·di·ya·la

blind слепой a sli·poy

blister волдырь Ⓜ val·dihr'

blood кровь ① krof'

blood group группа крови ① gru·pa kro·vi

blood pressure кровяное давление Ⓝ kra·vi·no·ye dav·lye·ni·ye

blood test анализ крови Ⓜ a·na·lis kro·vi

(dark) blue синий si·ni

(light) blue голубой ga·lu·boy

board (plane/ship) садиться/сесть sa·dit'·sa/syest'

boarding house пансионат Ⓜ pan·si·a·nat

boarding pass посадочный талон Ⓜ pa·sa·dach·nih ta·lon

boat лодка ① lot·ka

body тело Ⓝ tye·la

bone кость ① kost'

book книга ① kni·ga

book заказывать/заказать za·ka·zih·vat'/za·ka·zat'

booked out распроданы ras·pro·da·nih

bookshop книжный магазин Ⓜ knizh·nih ma·ga·zin

boots (footwear) сапоги Ⓜ sa·pa·gi

border граница ① gra·nit·sa

bored скучно skush·na

boring скучный skuch·nih

borrow брать/взять на время brat'/vzyat' na vryem·ya

botanic garden ботанический сад Ⓜ ba·ta·ni·chi·ski sat

both оба/обе Ⓜ/① o·ba/ob·ye

bottle бутылка ① bu·tihl·ka

bottle opener (beer) открывалка ① at·krih·val·ka

bottle opener (wine) штопор Ⓜ shto·par

bottle shop винный магазин Ⓜ vi·nih ma·ga·zin

bottom (body) зад Ⓜ zat

bottom (position) дно Ⓝ dno

boulevard бульвар Ⓜ bul'·var

bowl миска ① mis·ka

box коробка ① ka·rop·ka

boxer shorts удлинённые шорты Ⓜ pl u·dil·nyo·nih·ye shor·tih

boxing бокс Ⓜ boks

boy мальчик Ⓜ mal'·chik

boyfriend друг Ⓜ druk

bra лифчик Ⓜ lif·chik

brakes тормоза Ⓜ pl tar·ma·za

brandy коньяк Ⓜ kan·yak

brave a смелый smye·lih

bread хлеб Ⓜ khlyep

bread rolls булочка ① bu·lach·ka

break ломать/сломать la·mat'/sla·mat'

breakfast завтрак Ⓜ zaf·trak

breast (body) грудь ① grud'

breathe дышать dih·shat'

bribe взятка ① vzyat·ka

bribe давать/дать взятку da·vat'/dat' vzyat·ku

bridge мост Ⓜ most

briefcase портфель Ⓜ part·fyel'

bring приносить/принести pri·na·sit'/pri·ni·sti

broken (down) сломанный slo·ma·nih

bronchitis бронхит Ⓜ bran·khit

brother брат Ⓜ brat

brown коричневый ka·rich·ni·vih

bruise синяк Ⓜ sin·yak

brush щётка ① shot·ka

bucket ведро Ⓝ vi·dro

Buddhist буддист/буддистка Ⓜ/① bu·dist/bu·dist·ka

budget бюджет ⓜ byud-*zhet*

buffet буфет ⓜ buf-*yet*

bug жук ⓜ zhuk

build строить/построить *stro*-it'/ past-*ro*-it'

builder строитель ⓜ *stra*-i-til'

building здание ⓝ *zda*-ni-ye

bumbag поясной кошелёк ⓜ pa-yas-*noy* ka-shal-*yok*

burn ожог ⓜ a-*zhok*

bus автобус ⓜ af-*to*-bus

bus station автовокзал ⓜ af-ta-vag-*zal*

bus stop остановка ⓕ a-sta-*nof*-ka

business бизнес ⓜ *biz*-nis

business class бизнес-класс ⓜ *biz*-nis-klas

business person бизнесмен ⓜ biz-nis-*myen*

business trip командировка ⓕ ka-man-di-*rof*-ka

busker уличный музыкант ⓜ *u*-lich-nih mu-zih-*kant*

busy занят/занята ⓜ/ⓕ *za*-nit/ za-ni-*ta*

but но no

butcher мясник ⓜ mis-*nik*

butter масло ⓝ *mas*-la

butterfly бабочка ⓕ *ba*-bach-ka

button пуговица ⓕ *pu*-ga-vit-sa

buy покупать/купить pa-ku-*pat'*/ ku-*pit'*

C

cabbage капуста ⓕ ka-*pu*-sta

cable car фуникулёр ⓜ fu-ni-kul-*yor*

cake (large) торт ⓜ tort

cake (small) пирожное ⓝ pi-*rozh*-na-ye

cake shop кондитерская ⓕ kan-di-*tir*-ska-ya

calculator калькулятор ⓜ kal'-kul-*ya*-tar

calendar календарь ⓜ ka-lin-*dar'*

call звонить/позвонить zva-*nit'*/ paz-va-*nit'*

call (phone) звонок ⓜ zva-*nok*

camera фотоаппарат ⓜ fo-to-a-pa-*rat*

camera shop фотографический магазин ⓜ fo-to-gra-*fi*-chi-ski ma-ga-*zin*

camp располагаться/ расположиться ras-pa-la-*gat'*-sa/ ras-pa-la-*zhiht'*-sa

campfire костёр ⓜ kast-*yor*

campsite кемпинг ⓜ *kyem*-pink

can (be able) мочь/смочь moch'/ smoch'

can (have permission) можно *mozh*-na

can (tin) банка ⓕ *ban*-ka

can opener открывашка ⓕ at-krih-*vash*-ka

Canada Канада ⓕ ka-*na*-da

cancel отменять/отменить at-min-*yat'*/at-mi-*nit'*

cancer рак ⓜ rak

candle свеча ⓕ svi-*cha*

candy конфеты ⓕ pl kanf-*ye*-tih

capsicum перец ⓜ *pye*-rits

car машина ⓕ ma-*shih*-na

car hire прокат автомобилей pra-*kat* af-ta-ma-*bil*-yey

car park автостоянка ⓕ af-ta-sta-*yan*-ka

car registration регистрация машины ⓕ ri-gist-*rat*-sih-ya ma-*shih*-nih

caravan автоприцеп ⓜ af-ta-prit-*sep*

cardiac arrest сердечный приступ ⓜ sird-*yech*-nih *pri*-stup

cards (playing) карты ⓕ pl *kar*-tih

care for ухаживать за u-*kha*-zhih-vat' za

carpenter плотник ⓜ *plot*-nik

carriage вагон ⓜ va-*gon*

carriage attendant проводник ⓜ pra-vad-*nik*

carrot морковь ⓕ mar-*kof'*

carry нести/понести ni-*sti*/pa-ni-*sti*

cash наличные ⓝ pl na-*lich*-nih-ye

C

cash (a cheque) обменивать/
обменять ab·*mye*·ni·vat'/ab·*min*·yat'
cashew кешью ⓕ *kye*·shu
cashier кассир ⓜ ka·*sir*
cassette кассета ⓕ kas·*ye*·ta
castle замок ⓜ *za*·mak
casual work временная работа ⓕ
vrye·mi·na·ya ra·*bo*·ta
cat кошка ⓕ *kosh*·ka
cathedral собор ⓜ sa·*bor*
Catholic католик/католичка ⓜ/ⓕ
ka·*to*·lik/ka·ta·*lich*·ka
cauliflower цветная капуста ⓕ
tsvit·*na*·ya ka·*pu*·sta
cave пещера ⓕ pi·*she*·ra
CD компакт-диск ⓜ kam·pakt·*disk*
celebration праздник ⓜ *praz*·nik
cell phone мобильный телефон ⓜ
ma·*bil*'·nih ti·li·*fon*
cemetery кладбище ⓝ *klad*·bi·she
cent цент ⓜ tsent
centimetre сантиметр ⓜ
san·tim·*yetr*
centre центр ⓜ tsentr
ceramics керамика ⓝ ki·*ra*·mi·ka
cereal хлопья ⓕ *khlop*·ya
certificate свидетельство ⓝ
svid·*ye*·tilst·va
chain цепь ⓕ tsep'
chair стул ⓜ stul
chairlift (ski) подвесной
подъёмник ⓜ pad·vis·*noy*
pad·*yom*·nik
champagne шампанское ⓝ
sham·*pan*·ska·ye
championships чемпионат ⓜ
chim·pi·a·*nat*
chance шанс ⓜ shans
change перемена ⓕ pi·rim·*ye*·na
change (coins) мелочь ⓕ *mye*·lach'
change (money) обменивать/
обменять ab·*mye*·ni·vat'/ab·*min*·yat'
changing room примерочная ⓕ
prim·*ye*·rach·na·ya
chat up убалтывать/уболтать
u·*bal*·tih·vat'/u·bal·*tat*'

cheap дешёвый di·*sho*·vih
cheat мошенник ⓜ ma·*she*·nik
check (banking) чек ⓜ chek
check (bill) счёт ⓜ shot
check-in (desk) регистрация ⓕ
ri·gist·*rat*·sih·ya
checkpoint контрольный пункт ⓜ
kan·*trol*'·nih punkt
cheese сыр ⓜ sihr
chef шеф-повар ⓜ shef·*po*·var
chemist (pharmacist) фармацевт ⓜ
far·mat·*seft*
chemist (pharmacy) аптека ⓕ
apt·*ye*·ka
cheque (banking) чек ⓜ chek
cherry вишня ⓕ *vish*·nya
chess (set) шахматы ⓜ pl
shakh·ma·tih
chessboard шахматная доска ⓕ
shakh·mat·na·ya da·*ska*
chest (body) грудная клетка ⓕ
grud·*na*·ya klyet·ka
chestnut каштан ⓜ kash·*tan*
chewing gum жевательная
резинка ⓕ zhih·va·*til*'·na·ya ri·*zin*·ka
chicken курица ⓕ *ku*·rit·sa
chicken pox ветрянка ⓕ vit·*ryan*·ka
child ребёнок ⓜ rib·*yo*·nak
child seat детский стульчик ⓜ
dyet·ski stul'·chik
childminding присмотр за детьми ⓜ
pris·*motr* za dit'·mi
children дети ⓝ pl *dye*·ti
China Китай ⓜ ki·*tey*
chocolate шоколад ⓜ sha·ka·*lat*
choose выбирать/выбрать
vih·bi·*rat*'/*vih*·brat'
Christmas Рождество ⓝ razh·dist·*vo*
church церковь ⓕ *tser*·kaf'
cider сидр ⓜ sidr
cigar сигара ⓕ si·*ga*·ra
cigarette сигарета ⓕ si·gar·*ye*·ta
cigarette lighter зажигалка ⓕ
za·zhih·*gal*·ka
cinema кино ⓝ ki·*no*
circus цирк ⓜ tsihrk

citizen гражданин/гражданка ⓜ/ⓕ grazh·da·*nin*/grazh·*dan*·ka

citizenship гражданство ⓝ grazh·*danst*·va

city город ⓜ *go*·rat

city centre центр города ⓜ tsentr *go*·ra·da

civil rights гражданские права ⓝ pl grazh·*dan*·ski·ye pra·*va*

class (category) класс ⓜ klas

classical классический kla·*si*·chi·ski

clean a чистый chi·stih

clean чистить/почистить chi·*stit*'/pa·*chi*·stit'

cleaning уборка ⓕ u·*bor*·ka

client клиент ⓜ kli·*yent*

climb подниматься/подняться pad·ni·*mat*'·sa/pad·*nyat*'·sa

cloakroom гардероб ⓜ gar·di·*rop*

clock часы ⓜ pl chi·*sih*

close закрывать/закрыть za·krih·*vat*'/za·*kriht*'

close (nearby) близкий *blis*·kih

closed закрытый za·*krih*·tih

clothesline верёвка для белья ⓕ vir·*yof*·ka dlya bil·*ya*

clothing одежда ⓕ ad·*yezh*·da

clothing store магазин готового платья ⓜ ma·ga·*zin* ga·*to*·va·va *plat*·ya

cloud облако ⓝ *ob*·la·ka

cloudy облачный *ob*·lach·nih

clutch (car) сцепление ⓝ stsep·*lye*·ni·ye

coach (bus) автобус ⓜ af·*to*·bus

coach (sport) тренер ⓜ *tre*·nir

coast берег ⓜ *bye*·rik

coat пальто ⓝ pal'·*to*

cockroach таракан ⓜ ta·ra·*kan*

cocktail коктейль ⓜ kak·*teyl*

cocoa какао ⓝ ka·*ka*·o

coffee кофе ⓜ *kof*·ye

coins монеты ⓕ pl man·*ye*·tih

cold простуда ⓕ pra·*stu*·da

cold холодный kha·*lod*·nih

colleague коллега ⓜ&ⓕ kal·*lye*·ga

collect call звонок по коллекту ⓜ zva·*nok* pa kal·*yek*·tu

college техникум ⓜ *tyekh*·ni·kum

colour цвет ⓜ tsvyet

comb расчёска ⓕ ras·*chos*·ka

come приходить/прийти pri·kha·*dit*'/pri·*ti*

comfortable удобный u·*dob*·nih

commission комиссионные ⓜ pl ka·mi·si·o·*nih*·ye

compartment (train) купе ⓝ ku·*pe*

communism коммунизм ⓜ ka·mu·*nizm*

communist коммунист/коммунистка ⓜ/ⓕ ka·mu·*nist*/ka·mu·*nist*·ka

companion попутчик/попутчица ⓜ/ⓕ pa·*put*·chik/pa·*put*·chit·sa

company (firm) компания ⓕ kam·*pa*·ni·ya

compass компас ⓜ *kom*·pas

complain жаловаться/пожаловаться zha·la·vat'·sa/pa·zha·la·vat'·sa

complaint жалоба ⓕ *zha*·la·ba

complimentary (free) бесплатный bis·*plat*·nih

computer компьютер ⓜ kam·*pyu*·tir

computer game компьютерная игра ⓕ kam·*pyu*·tir·na·ya i·*gra*

concert концерт ⓜ kant·*sert*

concussion сотрясение мозга ⓝ sat·ris·*ye*·ni·ye *moz*·ga

conditioner (hair) бальзам ⓜ bal'·*zam*

condolence соболезнование ⓝ sa·ba·*lyez*·na·va·ni·ye

condom презерватив ⓜ pri·zir·va·*tif*

conference (big) съезд ⓜ syest

conference (small) конференция ⓕ kan·fir·*yent*·sih·ya

confirm (booking) подтверждать/подтвердить pat·virzh·*dat*'/pat·vir·*dit*'

conjunctivitis конъюнктивит ⓜ kan·yunk·ti·*vit*

D

connection связи ① *svya·zi*

conservative консервативный *kan·sir·va·tiv·nih*

constipation запор ⓜ *za·por*

consulate консульство ⓝ *kon·sulst·vo*

contact lens solution раствор для контактных линз ⓜ *rast·vor dlya kan·takt·nihkh lins*

contact lenses контактные линзы ① pl *kan·takt·nih·ye lin·zih*

contraceptives противозачаточные средства ⓝ pl *pra·ti·va·za·cha·tach·nih·ye sryetst·va*

contract контракт ⓜ *kan·trakt*

convent женский монастырь ⓜ *zhen·skih ma·na·stihr*

cook повар ⓜ *po·var*

cook готовить/приготовить *ga·to·vit'/pri·ga·to·vit'*

cookie печенье ⓝ *pi·chen·ye*

cooking кулинария ① *ku·li·na·ri·ya*

cool (temperature) прохладный *pra·khlad·nih*

corkscrew штопор ⓜ *shto·par*

corn кукуруза ① *ku·ku·ru·za*

corner угол ⓜ *u·gal*

cost v стоить *sto·it'*

cotton хлопок ⓜ *khlo·pak*

cotton balls ватные шарики ⓜ pl *vat·nih·ye sha·ri·ki*

cotton buds ватные палочки ① pl *vat·nih·ye pa·lach·ki*

cough кашель ⓜ *ka·shel'*

cough medicine жидкость от кашля ① *zhiht·kast' at kash·lya*

count считать/посчитать *shi·tat'/pa·shi·tat'*

country страна ① *stra·na*

countryside сельская местность ① *syel'·ska·ya myes·nast'*

coupon талон ⓜ *ta·lon*

courgette кабачок ⓜ *ka·ba·chok*

court (legal) суд ⓜ *sut*

court (tennis) корт ⓜ *kort*

cover charge плата за куверт ① *pla·ta za kuv·yert*

cow корова ① *ka·ro·va*

crafts ремёсла ⓝ pl *rim·yos·la*

crash авария ① *a·va·ri·ya*

crazy сумасшедший *su·ma·shet·shi*

cream (food) сливки ① pl *slif·ki*

cream (ointment) крем ⓜ *kryem*

crèche ясли ⓝ pl *yas·li*

credit кредит ⓜ *kri·dit*

credit card кредитная карточка ① *kri·dit·na·ya kar·tach·ka*

cross (religious) крест ⓜ *kryest*

crowded заполнено людьми *za·pol·ni·na lyud'·mi*

cruise круиз ⓜ *kru·is*

cucumber огурец ⓜ *a·gur·yets*

cup чашка ① *chash·ka*

cupboard шкаф ⓜ *shkaf*

currency exchange обмен валюты ⓜ *ab·myen val·yu·tih*

current (electricity) ток ⓜ *tok*

custom обычай ⓜ *a·bih·chey*

customs таможня ① *ta·mozh·nya*

customs declaration таможенная декларация ① *ta·mo·zhih·na·ya di·kla·rat·sih·ya*

cut резать/нарезать *rye·zat'/na·rye·zat'*

cutlery столовый прибор ⓜ *sta·lo·vih pri·bor*

CV автобиография ① *af·ta·bi·a·gra·fi·ya*

cycle ездить на велосипеде *yez·dit' na vi·la·si·pye·dye*

cycling езда на велосипеде *yiz·da na vi·la·sip·yed·ye*

cyclist велосипедист ⓜ *vi·la·si·pi·dist*

cystitis цистит ⓜ *tsih·stit*

D

dad папа ⓜ *pa·pa*

daily ежедневный *yi·zhih·dnyev·nih*

dance v танцевать *tant·sih·vat'*

D

dancing танцы ⓜ pl *tant*·sih

dangerous опасный a·*pas*·nih

dark тёмный *tyom*·nih

date (appointment) встреча ⓕ *fstrye*·cha

date (day) число ⓝ *chis*·lo

date (person) v встречаться с *fstri*·*chat*'·sa s

date of birth дата рождения ⓕ *da*·ta razh·*dye*·ni·ya

daughter дочка ⓕ *doch*·ka

dawn рассвет ⓜ *ras*·vyet

day день ⓜ dyen'

day after tomorrow послезавтра pas·li·*zaf*·tra

day before yesterday позавчера pa·zaf·chi·*ra*

dead мёртвый *myort*·vih

deaf глухой glu·*khoy*

deal (cards) сдавать/сдать *zda*·vat'/zdat'

decide решать/решить ri·*shat*'/ ri·*shiht*'

deep глубокий glu·*bo*·ki

degrees (temperature) градус ⓜ *gra*·dus

delay задержка ⓕ zad·*yersh*·ka

delicatessen гастроном ⓜ gas·tra·*nom*

deliver доставлять/доставить da·stav·*lyat*'/da·*sta*·vit'

democracy демократия ⓕ di·ma·*kra*·ti·ya

demonstration манифестация ⓕ ma·ni·fi·*stat*·sih·ya

Denmark Дания ⓕ *da*·ni·ya

dental dam латексная салфетка ⓕ *la*·tiks·na·ya sal·*fyet*·ka

dentist зубной врач ⓜ zub·*noy* vrach

deodorant дезодорант ⓜ di·zo·da·*rant*

depart отправляться/отправиться at·prav·*lyat*'·sa/at·*pra*·vit'·sa

department store универмаг ⓜ u·ni·vir·*mak*

departure отъезд ⓜ at·*yest*

departure gate выход на посадку ⓜ *vih*·khat na pa·*sat*·ku

deposit задаток ⓜ za·*da*·tak

descendent потомок ⓜ pa·*to*·mak

desert пустыня ⓕ pu·*stihn*·ya

dessert десерт ⓜ dis·*yert*

destination место назначения ⓝ *mye*·sta naz·na·*che*·ni·ya

details подробности ⓕ pl pa·*drob*·na·sti

diabetes диабет ⓜ di·ab·*yet*

diaper подгузник ⓜ pad·*guz*·nik

diaphragm диафрагма ⓕ di·a·*frag*·ma

diarrhoea понос ⓜ pa·*nos*

diary дневник ⓜ dnyev·*nik*

dictionary словарь ⓜ sla·*var*'

die умереть u·*mir*·yet'

diet диета ⓕ di·*ye*·ta

different другой dru·*goy*

difficult трудный *trud*·nih

dining car вагон-ресторан ⓜ va·*gon*·ri·sta·*ran*

dinner ужин ⓜ *u*·zhin

direct прямой pri·*moy*

direct-dial (by) прямым набором номера pri·*mihm* na·*bo*·ram *no*·mi·ra

direction направление ⓝ na·prav·*lye*·ni·ye

director директор ⓜ dir·*yek*·tar

dirty грязный *gryaz*·nih

disaster катастрофа ⓕ ka·tas·*tro*·fa

disabled инвалид ⓜ in·va·*lit*

disco дискотека ⓕ dis·kat·*ye*·ka

discount скидка ⓕ *skit*·ka

disease болезнь ⓕ bal·*yezn*'

dish блюдо ⓝ *blyu*·da

diving подводное плавание ⓝ pad·*vod*·na·ye pla·va·ni·ye

divorced разведённый raz·vid·*yo*·nih

dizzy кружится голова kru·*zhiht*·sa ga·la·va

do делать/сделать *dye*·lat'/*zdye*·lat'

doctor врач ⓜ vrach

documentary документальный фильм ⓜ da·ku·min·*tal*'·nih film

dog собака ⓕ sa·*ba*·ka
doll кукла ⓕ *kuk*·la
dominoes домино ⓝ da·mi·*no*
door дверь ⓕ dvyer'
double а двойной dvey·*noy*
double bed двуспальная кровать ⓕ dvu·*spal*'·na·ya kra·*vat*'
double room номер на двоих ⓜ *no*·mir na dva·*ikh*
down вниз vnis
downhill под уклон pad u·*klon*
dream сон ⓜ son
dress платье ⓝ *plat*·ye
drink (alcoholic) спиртной напиток ⓜ spirt·*noy* na·*pi*·tak
drink (general) напиток ⓜ na·*pi*·tak
drink пить/выпить pit'/*vih*·pit'
drive v водить машину va·*dit*' ma·*shih*·nu
drivers licence водительские права ⓝ pl va·*di*·til'·ski·ye *pra*·va
drugs (illegal) наркотики ⓕ pl nar·*ko*·ti·ki
drums барабаны ⓜ pl ba·ra·*ba*·nih
drunk пьяный *pya*·nih
dry а сухой su·*khoy*
dry (clothes) сушить/высушить su·*shiht*'/*vih*·su·shiht'
duck утка ⓕ *ut*·ka
dummy (pacifier) соска ⓕ *sos*·ka

E

each каждый *kazh*·dih
ear ухо ⓝ *u*·kha
early ранний *ra*·ni
earn зарабатывать/заработать za·ra·*ba*·tih·vat'/za·ra·bo·*tat*'
earplugs затычки для ушей ⓕ pl za·*tihch*·ki dlya u·*shey*
earrings серёжки ⓕ pl sir·*yosh*·ki
east восток ⓜ va·*stok*
Easter Пасха ⓕ *pas*·kha
easy лёгкий *lyokh*·ki
eat есть/съесть yest'/syest'
economy class пассажирский класс ⓜ pa·sa·*zhihr*·ski klas

eczema экзема ⓕ eg·*zye*·ma
education образование ⓝ a·bra·za·*va*·ni·ye
egg яйцо ⓝ yeyt·*so*
eggplant баклажан ⓜ bak·la·*zhan*
election выборы ⓜ pl *vih*·ba·rih
electrical store электронный универмаг ⓜ e·lik·*tro*·nih u·ni·vir·*mak*
electricity электричество ⓝ e·lik·*tri*·chist·va
elevator лифт ⓜ lift
embarrassed смущённый smu·*sho*·nih
embassy посольство ⓝ pa·*solst*·va
emergency авария ⓕ a·*va*·ri·ya
emotional эмоциональный e·mot·sih·a·*nal*'·nih
employee служащий/служащая ⓜ/ⓕ *slu*·zha·shi/*slu*·zha·sha·ya
employer работодатель ⓜ ra·bo·ta·*dat*'·yel'
empty пустой pu·*stoy*
encephalitis энцефалит ⓜ ent·sih·fa·*lit*
end конец ⓜ kan·*yets*
engaged (person) обручённый ab·ru·*cho*·nih
engaged (phone) занято *zan*·ya·ta
engagement (wedding) обручение ⓝ ab·ru·*che*·ni·ye
engine мотор ⓜ ma·*tor*
engineer инженер ⓜ in·zhih·*nyer*
engineering инженерное дело ⓝ in·zhih·*nyer*·na·ye *dye*·la
England Англия ⓕ *an*·gli·ya
English английский an·*gli*·ski
enjoy (oneself) наслаждаться/насладиться nas·lazh·*dat*'·sa/nas·la·*dit*'·sa
enough достаточно da·*sta*·tach·na
enter входить/войти fkha·*dit*'/*vey*·ti
entertainment guide путеводитель ⓜ pu·ti·va·*di*·til'
entry вход ⓜ fkhot
envelope конверт ⓜ kanv·*yert*

environment окружающая среда ①
a·kru·zha·yu·sha·ya sri·da

epilepsy эпилепсия ① e·pil·yep·si·ya

equality равноправие ⑪
rav·na·pra·vi·ye

equipment оборудование ⑪
a·ba·ru·da·va·ni·ye

escalator эскалатор ⑩ e·ska·la·tar

estate agency риэлтер ⑩ ri·el·tir

Estonia Эстония ① e·sto·ni·ya

ethnic этнический et·ni·chi·ski

euro евро ⑪ yev·ro

Europe Европа ① yev·ro·pa

euthanasia эйтаназия ①
ey·ta·na·zi·ya

evening вечер ⑩ vye·chir

every каждый kazh·dih

everyone все fsye

everything всё fsyo

exactly точно toch·na

excellent отличный at·lich·nih

excess (baggage) перевес ⑩
pi·riv·yes

exchange менять/обменять
min·yat'/ab·min·yat'

exchange rate обменный курс ⑩
ab·mye·nih kurs

exhaust (car) выхлопная труба ①
vih·khlap·na·ya tru·ba

exhibition выставка ① vih·staf·ka

exit выход ⑩ vih·khat

expensive дорогой da·ra·goy

experience опыт ⑩ o·piht

express (mail) экспресс ⑩
eks·pres

extension (visa) продление ⑪
prad·lye·ni·ye

eye drops глазные капли ① pl
glaz·nih·ye ka·pli

eyes глаза ① pl gla·za

F

fabric ткань ① tkan'

face лицо ⑪ lit·so

face cloth личное полотенце ⑪
lich·no·ye pa·lat·yent·se

factory фабрика ① fa·bri·ka

factory worker рабочий/
рабочая ⑩/① ra·bo·chi/
ra·bo·cha·ya

fall (autumn) осень ① o·sin'

fall (down) падать/упасть
pa·dat'/u·past'

family семья ① sim·ya

famous знаменитый zna·mi·ni·tih

fan (machine) вентилятор ⑩
vin·til·ya·tar

fan (sport) болельщик/
болельщица ⑩/① bal·yel'·shik/
bal·yel'·shit·sa

far далеко da·li·ko

fare плата ① pla·ta

farm ферма ① fyer·ma

farmer фермер ⑩ fyer·mir

fashion мода ① mo·da

fast быстрый bihst·rih

fat толстый tol·stih

father отец ⑩ at·yets

father-in-law (wife's father)
свёкор ⑩ svyo·kar

father-in-law (husband's father)
тесть ⑩ tyest'

fault (someone's) вина ① vi·na

faulty ошибочный a·shih·bach·nih

feel (touch) трогать/потрогать
tro·gat'/pa·tro·gat'

feelings чувства ⑪ pl chust·va

female женский zhen·ski

ferry паром ⑩ pa·rom

festival фестиваль ⑩ fi·sti·val'

fever лихорадка ① li·kha·rat·ka

few мало ma·la

fiancé жених ⑩ zhih·nikh

fiancée невеста ① niv·ye·sta

fight драка ① dra·ka

fill наполнять/наполнить
na·paln·yat'/na·pol·nit'

film (camera) плёнка ① plyon·ka

film (cinema) фильм ⑩ film

film speed скорость протяжки плёнки ① *sko·rast' prat·yash·ki plyon·*ki

filtered с фильтром s *fil'·*tram

find находить/найти na·kha·*dit'/*ney·*ti*

fine (penalty) штраф ⓜ shtraf

fine a хороший kha·*ro·*shih

finger палец ⓜ *pa·*lits

finish конец ⓜ kan·*yets*

finish кончать/кончить kan·*chat'/*kon·chit'

Finland Финляндия ① fin·*lyan·*di·ya

fire (emergency) пожар ⓜ pa·*zhar*

fire (heat) огонь ⓜ a·*gon'*

firewood дрова ⓝ *dra·*va

first a первый *pyer·*vih

first-aid kit санитарная сумка ① sa·ni·*tar·*na·ya *sum·*ka

first class в первом классе f *pyer·*vam *klas·*ye

fish рыба ① *rih·*ba

fishing рыболовство ⓝ rih·ba·*lofst·*va

fish shop рыбный магазин ⓜ *rihb·*nih ma·ga·*zin*

flag флаг ⓜ flak

flashlight фонарик ⓜ fa·*na·*rik

flat (apartment) квартира ① kvar·*ti·*ra

flat плоский *plo·*ski

flea блоха ① bla·*kha*

fleamarket блошиный рынок ⓜ bla·*shih·*nih *rih·*nak

flight полёт ⓜ pal'·*yot*

flood наводнение ⓝ na·vad·*nye·*ni·ye

floor (room) пол ⓜ pol

floor (storey) этаж ⓜ e·*tash*

flour мука ① mu·*ka*

flower цветок ⓜ tsvi·*tok*

flu грипп ⓜ grip

fly муха ① *mu·*kha

foggy туманно tu·*ma·*na

follow следовать/последовать *slye·*da·vat'/pas·*lye·*da·vat'

food еда ① yi·*da*

food supplies продовольствие ⓝ pra·da·*volst·*vi·ye

foot нога ① na·*ga*

football (soccer) футбол ⓜ fud·*bol*

footpath тротуар ⓜ tra·tu·*ar*

foreign иностранный i·nast·*ra·*nih

forest лес ⓜ lyes

forever навсегда naf·syeg·*da*

forget забывать/забыть za·bih·*vat'/*za·*biht'*

fork вилка ① *vil·*ka

fortnightly две недели dvye nid·*ye·*li

fortune teller гадалка ① ga·*dal·*ka

foul нарушение ⓝ na·ru·*she·*ni·ye

fragile хрупкий *khrup·*ki

France Франция ① *frant·*sih·ya

free (available) свободный sva·*bod·*nih

free (gratis) бесплатный bis·*plat·*nih

fresh свежий svye·zhih

fridge холодильник ⓜ kha·la·*dil'·*nik

friend друг/подруга ⓜ/① druk/pa·*dru·*ga

from от ot

frost мороз ⓜ ma·*ros*

fruit фрукты ⓜ pl *fruk·*tih

fry жарить/пожарить *zha·*rit'/pa·*zha·*rit'

frying pan сковорода ① ska·va·ra·*da*

full полный *pol·*nih

full-time на полной ставке na *pol·*ney *staf·*kye

fun adv весело *vye·*si·la

funeral похороны ⓜ pl *po·*kha·ra·nih

funny смешной smish·*noy*

furniture мебель ① *mye·*bil'

future будущее ⓝ *bu·*du·shi·ye

G

game (match) матч ⓜ mach

game (type of sport) спорт ⓜ sport

garage гараж ⓜ ga·*rash*

garbage мусор ⓜ *mu·*sar

garbage can помойный ящик ⓜ pa·*moy*·nih ya·*shik*

garden сад ⓜ sat

gardener садовод ⓜ sa·da·*vot*

gardening садоводство ⓝ sa·da·*votst*·va

garlic чеснок ⓜ chis·*nok*

gas (cooking) газ ⓜ gas

gas (petrol) бензин ⓜ bin·*zin*

gastroenteritis гастроэнтерит ⓜ ga·stra·en·ti·*rit*

gate (airport) выход на посадку ⓜ *vih*·khat na pa·*sat*·ku

gauze марля ⓕ *marl*·ya

Georgia Грузия ⓕ *gru*·zi·ya

Germany Германия ⓕ gir·*ma*·ni·ya

get получать/получить pa·lu·*chat'*/pa·lu·*chit'*

get off (train, etc) сходить/сойти skha·*dit'*/*sey*·ti

gift подарок ⓜ pa·*da*·rak

girl (teenage) девушка ⓕ *dye*·vush·ka

girl (pre-teen) девочка ⓕ *dye*·vach·ka

girlfriend подруга ⓕ pa·*dru*·ga

give давать/дать da·*vat'*/dat'

glandular fever железистая лихорадка ⓕzhil·*ye*·zi·sta·ya li·kha·*rat*·ka

glass стакан ⓜ sta·*kan*

glasses (spectacles) очки ⓝ pl ach·*ki*

gloves перчатки ⓕ pl pir·*chat*·ki

glue клей ⓜ klyey

go идти/пойти i·*ti*/pey·*ti*

go (by vehicle) ехать/поехать *ye*·khat'/pa·*ye*·khat'

go out выходить/выйти vih·kha·*dit'*/*vih*·ti

go out with встречаться с fstri·*chat*'·sa s

goat козёл ⓜ kaz·*yol*

god (general) бог ⓜ bok

goggles очки ⓝ pl ach·*ki*

gold золото ⓝ *zo*·la·ta

golf ball гольф-мяч ⓜ *golf*·myach

golf course корт для гольфа ⓜ kort dlya *gol'*·fa

good хороший kha·ro·*shih*

government правительство ⓝ pra·*vi*·til'·stva

gram грамм ⓜ gram

granddaughter внучка ⓕ *vnuch*·ka

grandfather дедушка ⓜ *dye*·dush·ka

grandmother бабушка ⓕ *ba*·bush·ka

grandson внук ⓜ vnuk

grass трава ⓕ tra·*va*

grateful благодарный bla·ga·*dar*·nih

grave могила ⓕ ma·*gi*·la

great (fantastic) отличный at·*lich*·nih

green зелёный zil·*yo*·nih

greengrocer зеленщик ⓜ zi·lin·*shik*

grey серый sye·*rih*

grocery гастроном ⓜ gast·ra·*nom*

grow расти/вырасти ra·*sti*/*vih*·ra·sti

guaranteed с гарантией z ga·*ran*·ti·yey

guess догадываться/догадаться da·ga·dih·*vat*'·sa/da·ga·*dat*'·sa

guesthouse гостиница ⓕ ga·*sti*·nit·sa

guide (audio) аудио-путеводитель ⓜ au·di·o·pu·ti·va·*di*·til'

guide (person) гид ⓜ git

guidebook путеводитель ⓜ pu·ti·va·*di*·til'

guide dog собака-поводырь ⓕ sa·*ba*·ka·pa·va·*dihr*

guided tour организованная экскурсия ⓕ ar·ga·ni·*zo*·va·na·ya ik·*skur*·si·ya

guilty виновный vi·*nov*·nih

guitar гитара ⓕ gi·*ta*·ra

gun ружьё ⓝ ruzh·*yo*

gym спортзал ⓜ spart·*zal*

gymnastics гимнастика ⓕ gim·*na*·sti·ka

gynaecologist гинеколог ⓜ gi·ni·*ko*·lak

G

H

H

hair волосы ⓜ pl *vo·la·sih*

hairbrush щётка для волос ⓕ *shot·ka dlya vo·las*

haircut стрижка ⓕ *strish·ka*

hairdresser парикмахер ⓜ *pa·rik·ma·khir*

half половина ⓕ *pa·la·vi·na*

hallucination галлюцинация ⓕ *gal·yut·sih·nat·sih·ya*

ham ветчина ⓕ *vit·chi·na*

hammer молоток ⓜ *ma·la·tok*

hammock гамак ⓜ *ga·mak*

hand рука ⓕ *ru·ka*

handbag сумочка ⓕ *su·mach·ka*

handkerchief носовой платок ⓜ *na·sa·voy pla·tok*

handlebars руль ⓜ *rul'*

handmade ручной работы *ruch·noy ra·bo·tih*

handsome красивый *kra·si·vih*

happy счастливый *shis·li·vih*

harbour гавань ⓕ *ga·van'*

hard (not soft) твёрдый *tvyor·dih*

hard-boiled вкрутую fkru·tu·yu*

hardware store хозяйственный магазин ⓜ *khaz·yeyst·vi·nih ma·ga·zin*

hat шапка ⓕ *shap·ka*

have у ... есть u ... yest'

have a cold простужаться/ простудиться pra·stu·zhat'·sa/ pra·stu·dit'·sa

have fun веселиться/ развеселиться vi·si·lit'·sa/ pa·vi·si·lit'·sa

hay fever сенная лихорадка ⓕ *si·na·ya li·kha·rat·ka*

hazelnut лесной орех ⓜ *lis·noy ar·yekh*

he он on

head голова ⓕ *ga·la·va*

headache головная боль ⓕ *ga·lav·na·ya bol'*

headlights фары ⓕ pl *fa·rih*

health здоровье ⓝ *zda·rov·ye*

hear слышать/услышать *slih·shat'/ us·lih·shat'*

hearing aid слуховой аппарат ⓜ *slu·kha·voy a·pa·rat*

heart сердце ⓝ *syerd·tsih*

heart attack сердечный приступ ⓜ *sird·yech·nih pri·stup*

heart condition болезнь сердца ⓕ *bal·yezn' syerd·tsa*

heat жара ⓕ *zha·ra*

heated обогреваемый *a·ba·gri·ma·i·vih*

heater обогреватель ⓜ *a·ba·gri·va·til'*

heavy тяжёлый tya·zho·lih*

helmet шлем ⓜ *shlyem*

help помощь ⓕ *po·mash'*

help помогать/помочь pa·ma·gat'/ pa·moch'

hepatitis гепатит ⓜ *gi·pa·tit*

her (possession) её yi·yo

herb трава ⓕ *tra·va*

herbal травяной trav·ya·noy

herbalist специалист по травам ⓜ *spit·sih·a·list pa tra·vam*

here здесь zdyes'

high (distance) высокий vih·so·ki

highchair высокий стульчик ⓜ *vih·so·ki stul'·chik*

high school средняя школа ⓕ *sryed·ni·ya shko·la*

highway шоссе ⓝ *sha·se*

hike v ходить пешком kha·dit' pish·kom

hiking поход ⓜ *pa·khot*

hill холм ⓜ *kholm*

Hindu индус/индуска ⓜ/ⓕ *in·dus/ in·dus·ka*

hire v брать/взять напрокат brat'/ vzyat' na·pra·kat

his его yi·vo

historical исторический i·sta·ri·chi·ski

history история ⓕ *i·sto·ri·ya*

HIV ВИЧ ⓜ vich
hockey хоккей ⓜ khak·yey
holiday праздник ⓜ praz·nik
holidays отпуск ⓜ ot·pusk
home дом ⓜ dom
homeless бездомный biz·dom·nih
homemaker домохозяйка ⓕ
do·ma·khaz·yey·ka
homosexual гомосексуалист ⓜ
go·mo·sik·su·a·list
honey мёд ⓜ myot
honeymoon медовый месяц ⓜ
mi·do·vih mye·sits
horoscope гороскоп ⓜ ga·ra·skop
horse лошадь ⓕ lo·shat'
horse riding верховая езда ⓕ
vir·kha·va·ya yiz·da
hospital больница ⓕ bol'·nit·sa
hospitality гостеприимство ⓝ
ga·sti·pri·imst·va
hot жаркий zhar·ki
hot water горячая вода ⓕ
gar·ya·chi·ya va·da
hotel гостиница ⓕ ga·sti·nit·sa
hour час ⓜ chas
house дом ⓜ dom
housework домашние дела ⓝ pl
da·mash·ni·ye dye·la
how как kak
how much сколько skol'·ka
hug обнимать/обнять ab·ni·mat'/
ab·nyat'
human resources управление
персоналом ⓝ u·prav·lye·ni·ye
pir·sa·na·lam
human rights права человека ⓝ pl
pra·va chi·lav·ye·ka
humid влажный vlazh·nih
hungry (be) голоден/голодна
go·la·din/ga·glad·na
hurt v болеть bal·yet'
husband муж ⓜ mush
hypothermia гипотермия ⓕ
gi·pat·yer·mi·ya

I

I я ya
ice лёд ⓜ lyot
ice axe ледоруб ⓜ lye·da·rup
ice cream мороженое ⓝ
ma·ro·zhih·na·ye
ice-cream parlour кафе-
мороженое ⓝ ka·fe·ma·ro·zhih·na·ye
ice hockey хоккей на льду ⓜ
khak·yey na ldu
ice skating катание на коньках ⓝ
ka·ta·ni·ye na kan'·kakh
identification установление
личности ⓝ u·sta·nav·lye·ni·ye
lich·na·sti
ID card идентификационная карта ⓕ
id·yen·ti·fi·kat·sih·o·na·ya kar·ta
idiot дурак ⓜ du·rak
if если yes·li
ill болен bo·lin
immigration иммиграция ⓕ
i·mi·grat·sih·ya
important важный vazh·nih
impossible невозможно
ni·vaz·mozh·na
in в v
(be) in a hurry спешить spi·shiht'
in front of перед pye·rit
included включая fklyu·cha·ya
income tax подоходный налог ⓜ
pa·da·khod·nih na·lok
indicator (car) указатель ⓜ
u·ka·za·til'
indoor закрытый za·krih·tih
industry промышленность ⓕ
pra·mihsh·li·nast'
infection инфекция ⓕ inf·yekt·sih·ya
inflammation воспаление ⓝ
vas·pal·ye·ni·ye
influenza грипп ⓜ grip
information информация ⓕ
in·far·mat·sih·ya
ingredient ингредиент ⓜ
in·gri·di·yent
inhaler ингалятор ⓜ in·gal·ya·tar

J

inject делать/сделать укол ⓜ
dye·lat'/zdye·lat' u·kol

injection инъекция ⓕ in·yekt·sih·ya

injury травма ⓕ trav·ma

innocent невиновный
nye·vi·nov·nih

inside внутри vnu·tri

instructor инструктор ⓜ ins·truk·tar

insurance страхование ⓝ
stra·kha·va·ni·ye

interesting интересный
in·tir·yes·nih

international международный
mizh·du·na·rod·nih

interpreter переводчик ⓜ
pi·ri·vot·chik

interview интервью ⓝ in·tir·vyu

invite приглашать/пригласить
pri·gla·shat'/pri·gla·sit'

Ireland Ирландия ⓕ ir·lan·di·ya

iron (clothes) утюг ⓜ ut·yuk

island остров ⓜ ost·raf

Israel Израиль ⓜ iz·ra·il'

it оно a·no

IT компьютеры ⓜ pl kam·pyu·ti·ri

Italy Италия ⓕ i·ta·li·ya

itch зуд ⓜ zut

itinerary маршрут ⓜ marsh·rut

IUD ВМС ⓜ ve·em·se

J

jacket (for men) куртка ⓕ kurt·ka

jacket (for women) жакет ⓜ
zhak·yet

jail тюрьма ⓕ tyur'·ma

Japan Япония ⓕ ya·po·ni·ya

jar банка ⓕ ban·ka

jaw челюсть ⓕ chel·yust'

jeep джип ⓜ dzhihp

jewellery ювелирные изделия ⓝ pl
yu·vi·lir·ni·ye iz·dye·li·ya

Jewish еврей/еврейка ⓜ/ⓕ
yiv·rey/yiv·rey·ka

job работа ⓕ ra·bo·ta

jogging бег трусцой byek trust·soy

joke анекдот ⓜ a·nik·dot

journalist журналист/
журналистка ⓜ/ⓕ zhur·na·list/
zhur·na·list·ka

journey путешествие ⓝ
pu·ti·shest·vi·ye

judge судья ⓜ sud·ya

juice сок ⓜ sok

jumper (sweater) джемпер ⓜ
dzhem·pir

K

key ключ ⓜ klyuch

keyboard клавиатура ⓕ
kla·vi·a·tu·ra

kidney почка ⓕ poch·ka

kilogram килограмм ⓜ ki·la·gram

kilometre километр ⓜ ki·lam·yetr

kind (nice) добрый dob·rih

kindergarten детский сад ⓜ
dyet·ski sat

king король ⓜ ka·rol'

kiss поцелуй ⓜ pat·sih·luy

kiss целовать/поцеловать
tsih·la·vat'/pat·sih·la·vat'

kitchen кухня ⓕ kukh·nya

knee колено ⓝ kal·ye·na

knife нож ⓜ nosh

know знать znat'

kopeck копейка ⓕ kap·yey·ka

kosher кошерный ko·shihr·nih

L

labourer рабочий/рабочая ⓜ/ⓕ
ra·bo·chi/ra·bo·cha·ya

lace кружево ⓝ kru·zhih·va

lake озеро ⓝ o·zi·ra

lamb баранина ⓕ ba·ra·ni·na

land земля ⓕ zim·lya

landlady хозяйка ⓕ khaz·yey·ka

landlord хозяин ⓜ khaz·ya·in

language язык ⓜ yi·zihk

laptop портативный компьютер ⓜ
par·ta·tiv·nih kam·pyu·tir

large большой bal'·shoy

last (final) последний pas·lyed·ni

L

last (previous) прошлый *prosh*-lih
late поздний *poz*-ni
later позже *po*-zhih
Latvia Латвия ① *lat*-vi-ya
laugh смеяться/рассмеяться
smi-*yat*-sa/ras-mi-*yat*-sa
laundry (clothes) бельё ⑩ bil-*yo*
laundry (place) прачечная ①
pra-chich-na-ya
law (rule) закон ⑪ za-*kon*
law (profession) юриспруденция ①
yu-ris-prud-*yent*-sih-ya
lawyer адвокат ⑪ ad-va-*kat*
laxative слабительное ⑩
sla-*bi*-til'-na-ye
lazy ленивый li-*ni*-vih
leader руководитель ⑪
ru-ka-va-*dit*-yel'
learn учить/выучить u-*chit*'/
vih-u-chit'
leather кожа ① *ko*-zha
left (direction) левый *lye*-vih
left luggage оставленный багаж ⑪
a-*stav*-li-nih ba-*gash*
left luggage (office) камера
хранения ① *ka*-mi-ra khran-ye-ni-ya
left-wing левый *lye*-vih
leg нога ① na-*ga*
legal законный za-*ko*-nih
legislation законодательство ⑩
za-ko-na-da-tilst-va
legumes бобовые ⑪ pl ba-*bo*-vih-ye
lemon лимон ⑪ li-*mon*
lemonade лимонад ⑪ li-ma-*nat*
lens линза ① *lin*-za
lesbian лесбианка ① lis-bi-*an*-ka
less меньше *myen*'-she
letter (mail) письмо ⑩ pis'-*mo*
lettuce салат ⑪ sa-*lat*
liar лгун/лгунья ⑪/① lgun/lgun'-ya
library библиотека ① bib-li-at-ye-ka
lice вши ① pl fshih
licence лицензия ① lit-*sen*-zi-ya
license plate number номерной
знак ⑪ na-mir-*noy* znak
lie (not stand) лежать li-*zhat*'

lie (untruth) лгать/солгать lgat'/
sal-*gat*'
life жизнь ① zhihzn'
life jacket спасательный жилет ⑪
spa-*sa*-til'-nih zhihl-yet
lift (elevator) лифт ⑪ lift
light свет ⑪ svyet
light (colour) светлый *svyet*-lih
light (weight) лёгкий *lyokh*-kih
light bulb лампочка ① *lam*-pach-ka
light meter экспозиметр ⑪
ek-spo-zim-*yetr*
lighter (cigarette) зажигалка ①
za-zhih-*gal*-ka
like v любить *lyu*-bit'
lime (fruit) лайм ⑪ leym
linen (bedding) бельё ⑩ bil-*yo*
lips губы ⑪ pl *gu*-bih
lipstick губная помада ① gub-*na*-ya
pa-*ma*-da
liquor store винный магазин ⑪
vi-nih ma-ga-*zin*
listen слушать *slu*-shat'
Lithuania Литва ① lit-*va*
little (not much) немного nim-*no*-ga
little (size) маленький *ma*-lin'-ki
live (somewhere) жить zhiht'
liver печень ① *pye*-chin'
local местный *myes*-nih
lock замок ⑪ za-*mok*
locked запертый zap-*yer*-tih
lollies конфеты ① pl kanf-ye-tih
long длинный *dli*-nih
look смотреть/посмотреть
smat-*ryet*'/pas-mat-*ryet*'
look for присматривать/
присмотреть pris-*mat*-ri-vat'/
pris-mar-*yet*'
loose change мелочь ① *mye*-lach'
lose терять/потерять tir-*yat*'/
pa-tir-*yat*'
lost пропавший pra-*paf*-shih
lost property office бюро
находок ⑪ byu-ro na-*kho*-dak
(a) lot много *mno*-ga
loud громкий *grom*-ki

love любовь ① lyu·*bof'*
love любить lyu·*bit'*
lover любовник/любовница ⑩/①
lyu·*bov*·nik/lyu·*bov*·nit·sa
low низкий *nis*·ki
lubricant смазка ① *smas*·ka
luck счастье ⑩ *shast*·ye
lucky счастливый shis·*li*·vih
luggage багаж ⑩ ba·*gash*
luggage lockers камера-автомат ①
ka·mi·ra·af·ta·mat
luggage tag багажная бирка ①
ba·*gazh*·na·ya *bir*·ka
lump шишка ① *shihsh*·ka
lunch обед ⑩ ab·*yet*
lung лёгкое ⑩ *lyokh*·ka·ye
luxury роскошь ① *ros*·kash'

M

machine машина ① ma·*shih*·na
magazine журнал ⑩ zhur·*nal*
mail (letters/system) почта ①
poch·ta
mailbox почтовый ящик ⑩
pach·*to*·vih *ya*·shik
main главный *glav*·nih
main road главная дорога ①
glav·na·ya da·*ro*·ga
make делать/сделать *dye*·lat'/
zdye·lat'
make-up косметика ① kas·*mye*·ti·ka
mammogram маммограмма ①
ma·ma·*gra*·ma
man (male) мужчина ⑩ mush·*chi*·na
manager (general) заведующий ⑩
zav·*ye*·du·yu·shi
manager (hotel, restaurant)
администратор ⑩ ad·mi·nist·*ra*·tar
many много *mno*·ga
map карта ① *kar*·ta
margarine маргарин ⑩ mar·ga·*rin*
marital status семейное
положение ⑩ sim·*yey*·na·ye
pa·la·*zhe*·ni·ye
market рынок ⑩ *rih*·nak

marmalade цитрусовый джем ⑩
tsih·tra·sa·vey dzhem
marriage брак ⑩ brak
married женатый/замужняя ⑩/①
zhih·*na*·tih/za·*muzh*·ni·ya
marry (for a man) жениться
zhih·*nit'*·sa
marry (for a woman) выходить/
выйти замуж vih·kha·*dit'*/*vih*·ti
za·mush
martial arts боевые искусства ⑩ pl
ba·i·*vih*·ye is·*kust*·va
massage массаж ⑩ ma·*sash*
masseur массажист ⑩ ma·sa·*zhist*
masseuse массажистка ①
ma·sa·*zhist*·ka
match (sports) матч ⑩ match
matches (fire) спички ⑩ pl *spich*·ki
mattress матрац ⑩ ma·*trats*
maybe может быть *mo*·zhiht biht
mayonnaise майонез ⑩ ma·yan·*yes*
mayor мэр ⑩ mer
me меня min·*ya*
meal еда ① yi·*da*
measles корь ① kor'
meat мясо ⑩ *mya*·sa
mechanic механик ⑩ mi·*kha*·nik
medicine (drugs) лекарство ⑩
li·*karst*·va
medicine (study, profession)
медицина ① mi·dit·*sih*·na
meditation медитация ①
mi·di·*tat*·sih·ya
meet встречать/встретить
fstri·*chat'*/*fstrye*·tit'
meeting собрание ⑩ sa·*bra*·ni·ye
melon арбуз ⑩ ar·*bus*
member член ⑩ chlyen
menstruation менструация ①
minst·ru·at·sih·ya
menu меню ⑩ min·*yu*
message записка ① za·*pis*·ka
metal метал ⑩ mi·*tal*
metre метр ⑩ myetr
metro station станция метро ①
stant·sih·ya mi·*tro*

N

microwave (oven) микроволновка ⓕ
mi·kra·val·*nof*·ka
midday полдень ⓜ *pol*·din'
midnight полночь ⓕ *pol*·noch'
migraine мигрень ⓕ mi·*greyn*'
military военные ⓜ pl va·ye·*nih*·ye
military service военная служба ⓕ
va·*ye*·na·ya *sluzh*·ba
milk молоко ⓝ ma·la·*ko*
milk shake молочный коктейль ⓜ
ma·*loch*·nih kak·*teyl*'
millimetre миллиметр ⓜ mi·*lim*·yetr
mince мясной фарш ⓜ mis·*noy* farsh
mineral water минеральная вода ⓕ
mi·ni·*ral*'·na·ya va·*da*
minute (time) минута ⓕ mi·*nu*·ta
mirror зеркало ⓝ *zyer*·ka·la
miscarriage выкидыш ⓜ
vih·ki·dihsh
miss (person) тосковать по
ta·ska·*vat*' pa
miss (train etc) опаздывать/
опоздать к a·*paz*·dih·vat'/a·paz·*dat*' k
mistake ошибка ⓕ a·*shihp*·ka
mobile phone мобильный
телефон ⓜ ma·*bil*'·nih ti·li·*fon*
modern современный
sa·vrim·*ye*·nih
moisturiser увлажняющий крем ⓜ
uv·lazh·*nya*·yu·shi kryem
monastery монастырь ⓜ
ma·na·*stihr*
money деньги ⓕ pl *dyen*'·gi
monk монах ⓜ ma·*nakh*
month месяц ⓜ *mye*·sits
monument памятник ⓜ *pam*·yit·nik
moon луна ⓕ lu·*na*
more больше *bol*'·she
morning утро ⓝ *u*·tra
morning sickness утренняя
тошнота ⓕ *u*·tri·ni·ya tash·na·*ta*
mosque мечеть ⓕ mi·*chet*'
mosquito комар ⓜ ka·*mar*
mosquito net противомоскитная
сетка ⓕ pra·ti·va·ma·*skit*·na·ya *syet*·ka
motel мотель ⓜ ma·*tel*'

mother мать ⓕ mat'
mother-in-law (husband's mother)
свекровь ⓕ svi·*krof*'
mother-in-law (wife's mother)
тёща ⓕ *tyo*·sha
motorbike мотоцикл ⓜ ma·tat·*sihkl*
motorboat моторная лодка ⓕ
ma·*tor*·na·ya *lot*·ka
motorway шоссе ⓝ sha·*se*
mountain гора ⓕ ga·*ra*
mountain bike горный велосипед ⓜ
gor·nih vi·la·sip·*yet*
mountain range горная гряда ⓕ
gor·na·ya grya·*da*
mountaineering альпинизм ⓜ
al'·pi·*nizm*
mouse мышь ⓕ mihsh'
mouth рот ⓜ rot
movie фильм ⓜ film
Mr господин ⓜ ga·spa·*din*
Mrs/Ms госпожа ⓕ ga·spa·*zha*
mud слякоть ⓕ *slya*·kat'
mum мама ⓕ *ma*·ma
mumps свинка ⓕ *svin*·ka
murder убийство ⓝ u·*bist*·va
murder убивать/убить u·bi·*vat*'/
u·*bit*'
muscle мускул ⓜ *mus*·kul
museum музей ⓜ muz·*yey*
mushroom гриб ⓜ grip
music музыка ⓕ *mu*·zih·ka
musician музыкант ⓜ mu·zih·*kant*
music shop музыкальный
магазин ⓜ mu·zih·*kal*'·nih ma·ga·*zin*
Muslim мусульманин/
мусульманка ⓜ/ⓕ mu·sul'·*ma*·nin/
mu·sul'·*man*·ka
mussel мидия ⓕ *mi*·di·ya
mustard горчица ⓕ gar·*chit*·sa
mute немой ni·*moy*
my мой moy

N

nail clippers ножницы для
ногтей ⓕ pl *nozh*·nit·sih dlya
nakt·*yey*

O

name (given) имя ⓝ *im*·ya
name (of object) название ⓝ na·*zva*·ni·ye
name (family) фамилия ⓕ fa·*mi*·li·ya
napkin салфетка ⓕ salf·*yet*·ka
nappy подгузник ⓜ pad·*guz*·nik
national park заповедник ⓜ za·pav·*yed*·nik
nationality национальность ⓕ nat·sih·a·*nal*'·nast'
nature природа ⓕ pri·*ro*·da
nausea тошнота ⓕ tash·na·*ta*
near(by) близко (от) *blis*·ka (at)
nearest ближайший bli·*zhey*·shi
necessary нужный *nuzh*·nih
neck шея ⓕ *she*·ya
necklace ожерелье ⓝ a·zhihr·*yel*·ye
need нуждаться в nuzh·*dat*'·sa v
needle (sewing) игла ⓕ i·*gla*
needle (syringe) шприц ⓜ shprits
negative негативный ni·ga·*tiv*·nih
neither ... nor ... ни ... ни ... ni ... ni ...
net сеть ⓜ syet'
Netherlands Нидерланды ⓝ pl ni·dir·*lan*·dih
never никогда ni·kag·*da*
new новый *no*·vih
New Year Новый год ⓜ *no*·vih got
New Zealand Новая Зеландия ⓕ *no*·va·ya zi·*lan*·di·ya
news новости ⓕ pl *no*·va·sti
newsagency газетный киоск ⓜ gaz·*yet*·nih ki·*osk*
newspaper газета ⓕ gaz·*ye*·ta
next (following) следующий *slye*·du·yu·shi
next to рядом с *rya*·dam s
nice милый *mi*·lih
nickname прозвище ⓝ *proz*·vi·she
night ночь ⓕ noch'
nightclub ночной клуб ⓜ nach·*noy* klup
no нет nyet
noisy шумный *shum*·nih
none никаких ni·ka·*kikh*

nonsmoking некурящий ni·kur·*ya*·shi
noon полдень ⓜ *pol*·din'
north север ⓜ *sye*·vir
Norway Норвегия ⓕ narv·*ye*·gi·ya
nose нос ⓜ nos
not не nye
notebook блокнот ⓜ blak·*not*
nothing ничего ni·chi·*vo*
now сейчас si·*chas*
nuclear energy ядерная энергия ⓕ *ya*·dir·na·ya e·*nir*·gi·ya
nuclear power station ядерная электростанция ⓕ *ya*·dir·na·ya e·lik·tra·*stant*·sih·ya
nuclear waste ядерные отходы ⓜ pl *ya*·dir·nih·ye at·*kho*·dih
number номер ⓜ *no*·mir
numberplate номерной знак ⓜ na·mir·*noy* znak
nun монахиня ⓕ ma·*na*·khi·ya
nurse медсестра ⓕ mit·sist·*ra*

О

oats овёс ⓜ av·*yos*
ocean океан ⓜ a·ki·*an*
off (spoiled) испорченный is·*por*·chi·nih
office контора ⓕ kan·*to*·ra
office worker служащий/ служащая ⓜ/ⓕ *slu*·zha·shi/ *slu*·zha·shi·ya
often часто *cha*·sta
oil (cooking/fuel) масло ⓝ *mas*·la
old старый *sta*·rih
olive оливка ⓕ a·*lif*·ka
olive oil оливковое масло ⓝ a·*lif*·ka·va·ye *mas*·la
on на na
on time вовремя *vov*·ryem·ya
once один раз a·*din* ras
one один/одна ⓜ/ⓕ a·*din*/ad·*na*
one-way в один конец v a·*din* kan·*yets*
onion лук ⓜ luk

only только *tol'*·ka
open открытый at·*krih*·tih
open открывать/открыть at·krih·*vat'*/at·*kriht'*
opening hours часы работы ⓜ pl chi·*sih* ra·bo·tih
opera опера ⓕ *o*·pi·ra
opera house оперный театр ⓜ *o*·pir·nih ti·*atr*
operation (general) операция ⓕ a·pi·*rat*·sih·ya
operator оператор ⓜ a·pi·*ra*·tar
opinion мнение ⓝ *mnye*·ni·ye
opposite против *pro*·tif
optometrist оптик ⓜ *op*·tik
or или *i*·li
orange (fruit) апельсин ⓜ a·*pil'*·*sin*
orange (colour) оранжевый a·*ran*·zhih·vih
orange juice апельсиновый сок ⓜ a·*pil'*·*si*·na·vih sok
orchestra оркестр ⓜ ar·*kestr*
order заказ ⓜ za·*kas*
order заказывать/заказать za·*ka*·zih·vat'/za·ka·*zat'*
ordinary обыкновенный a·bihk·nav·*ye*·nih
orgasm оргазм ⓜ ar·*gazm*
original оригинальный a·ri·gi·*nal'*·nih
Orthodox православный pra·vas·*lav*·nih
other другой dru·*goy*
our наш nash
outside снаружи sna·*ru*·zhih
ovarian cyst яичниковая киста ⓕ yi·*ich*·ni·ko·va·ya kis·*ta*
ovary яичник ⓜ yi·*ich*·nik
oven духовка ⓕ du·*khof*·ka
overcoat пальто ⓝ *pal'*·to
overdose передозировка ⓕ pi·ri·do·zi·*rof*·ka
overnight всю ночь fsyu noch'
overseas за границей za gra·*nit*·sey
owner владелец ⓜ vlad·*yel*·its
oxygen кислород ⓜ kis·la·*rot*
oyster устрица ⓕ *ust*·rit·sa

pacemaker ритмизатор сердца ⓜ rit·mi·*za*·tar syert·sa
pacifier (dummy) соска ⓕ *sos*·ka
package посылка ⓕ pa·*sihl*·ka
packet пачка ⓕ *pach*·ka
padlock навесной замок ⓜ na·vis·*noy* za·*mok*
page страница ⓕ stra·*nit*·sa
pain боль ⓕ bol'
painful болит ba·*lit*
painkiller болеутоляющие ⓝ pl bo·li·u·tal·*ya*·yu·shi·ye
painter художник ⓜ khu·*dozh*·nik
painting (a work) картина ⓕ kar·*ti*·na
painting (the art) живопись ⓕ *zhih*·va·pis'
pair пара ⓕ *pa*·ra
palace дворец ⓜ dvar·*yets*
pan сковорода ⓕ ska·va·ra·*da*
pants (trousers) брюки ⓜ pl *bryu*·ki
panty liners гигиеническая прокладка ⓕ gi·gi·i·*ni*·chi·ska·ya pra·*klat*·ka
pap smear мазок ⓜ ma·*zok*
paper бумага ⓕ bu·*ma*·ga
paperwork документы ⓜ pl da·kum·*yen*·tih
paraplegic парализованный pa·ra·li·zo·va·nih
parcel посылка ⓕ pa·*sihl*·ka
parents родители ⓜ pl ra·*di*·ti·li
park парк ⓜ park
park (a car) ставить/поставить (машину) *sta*·vit'/pa·*sta*·vit' (ma·*shih*·nu)
parliament дума ⓕ *du*·ma
part (component) деталь ⓕ di·*tal'*
part-time на неполной ставке па ni·*pol*·ney staf·kye
party (fiesta) вечеринка ⓕ vi·chi·*rin*·ka
party (politics) партия ⓕ *par*·ti·ya

pass проходить/пройти
pra·kha·*dit'*/*prey·ti*

passenger пассажир ⓜ pa·sa·*zhihr*

passport паспорт ⓜ *pas·*part

past (time) прошлое ⓝ *prosh·*la·ye

pastry пирожное ⓝ pi·*rozh*·na·ye

path тропинка ⓕ tra·*pin·*ka

pay платить/заплатить pla·*tit'*/
za·pla·*tit'*

pay phone телефон-автомат ⓜ
ti·li·*fon*·af·ta·mat

payment оплата ⓕ a·*pla·*ta

peace мир ⓜ mir

peach персик ⓜ *pyer·*sik

peanut арахис ⓜ a·ra·*khis*

pear груша ⓕ *gru·*sha

peasant крестьянин/
крестьянка ⓜ/ⓕ krist·*ya·*nin/
krist·*yan·*ka

pedal педаль ⓕ pi·*dal'*

pedestrian пешеход ⓜ pi·shih·*khot*

pen ручка ⓕ *ruch·*ka

pencil карандаш ⓜ ka·ran·*dash*

penis пенис ⓜ *pye·*nis

pensioner пенсионер/
пенсионерка ⓜ/ⓕ pin·si·an·*yer*/
pin·si·an·*yer·*ka

people люди ⓜ pl *lyu·*di

pepper (bell/black) перец ⓜ *pye·*rits

per в v

per cent процент ⓜ prat·*sent*

perfect прекрасный pri·*kras·*nih

performance спектакль ⓜ spik·*takl'*

perfume духи ⓜ pl du·*khi*

period pain болезненные
месячные ⓜ pl bal·*yez·*ni·nih·ye
*mye·*sich·nih·ye

permafrost вечная мерзлота ⓕ
*vyech·*na·ya mirz·la·*ta*

permission (permit) разрешение ⓝ
raz·ri·*she·*ni·ye

person человек ⓜ chi·lav·*yek*

petrol бензин ⓜ bin·*zin*

petrol station заправочная
станция ⓕ za·*pra*·vach·na·ye
*stant·*sih·ya

pharmacy аптека ⓕ apt·*ye·*ka

phone book телефонная книга ⓕ
ti·li·*fo*·na·ya *kni·*ga

phone box телефонная будка ⓕ
ti·li·*fo*·na·ya *but·*ka

phonecard телефонная карточка ⓕ
ti·li·*fo*·na·ya *kar·*tach·ka

photo снимок ⓜ *sni·*mak

photographer фотограф ⓜ fa·*to·*graf

photography фотография ⓕ
fa·ta·*gra·*fi·ya

phrasebook разговорник ⓜ
raz·ga·*vor·*nik

pickaxe кирка ⓕ *kir·*ka

pigeon голубь ⓜ *go·*lub'

pie пирог ⓜ pi·*rok*

piece кусок ⓜ ku·*sok*

pig свинья ⓕ svin·*ya*

pill таблетка ⓕ tab·*lyet·*ka

(the) Pill противозачаточная
таблетка ⓕ pra·ti·va·za·*cha·*tach·na·ya
tab·*lyet·*ka

pillow подушка ⓕ pa·*dush·*ka

pillowcase наволочка ⓕ
*na·*va·lach·ka

pink розовый *ro·*za·vih

place место ⓝ *mye·*sta

place of birth место рождения ⓝ
*mye·*sta razh·*dye·*ni·ya

plane самолёт ⓜ sa·mal·*yot*

planet планета ⓕ plan·*ye·*ta

plant растение ⓝ rast·*ye·*ni·ye

plastic пластмассовый
plast·*ma·*sa·vih

plate тарелка ⓕ tar·*yel·*ka

plateau плато ⓝ pla·*to*

platform платформа ⓕ plat·*for·*ma

play (dominoes) играть в (домино)
i·*grat'* v (da·mi·*no*)

play (guitar) играть на (гитаре)
i·*grat'* na (gi·*tar·*ye)

play (theatre) пьеса ⓕ *pye·*sa

plug (bath) пробка ⓕ *prop·*ka

plug (electricity) вилка ⓕ *vil·*ka

plum слива ⓕ *sli·*va

poached варёный var·*yo·*nih

P

pocket карман ⓜ kar·*man*

pocket knife карманный ножик ⓜ kar·*ma*·nih no·*zhik*

poetry поэзия ⓕ pa·e·*zi*·ya

point указывать/указать u·*ka*·zih·vat'/u·ka·*zat*'

poisonous ядовитый ya·da·*vi*·tih

Poland Польша ⓕ *pol*'·sha

police милиция ⓕ mi·*li*·sih·ya

police officer милиционер ⓜ mi·lit·sih·an·*yer*

police station полицейский участок ⓜ pa·lit·*sey*·ski u·*cha*·stak

policy политика ⓕ pa·*li*·ti·ka

politician политик ⓜ pa·*li*·tik

politics политика ⓕ pa·*li*·ti·ka

pollen пыльца ⓕ pihlt·*sa*

pollution загрязнение ⓝ za·griz·*nye*·ni·ye

pool (game) пулька ⓕ *pul*'·ka

pool (swimming) бассейн ⓜ bas·*yeyn*

poor бедный *byed*·nih

popular популярный pa·pul·*yar*·nih

pork свинина ⓕ svi·*ni*·na

port (sea) порт ⓜ port

positive позитивный pa·zi·*tiv*·nih

possible возможный vaz·*mozh*·nih

postage почтовые расходы ⓜ pl pach·*to*·vih·ye ras·*kho*·dih

postcard открытка ⓕ at·*kriht*·ka

postcode почтовый индекс ⓜ pach·*to*·vih *in*·diks

post office почта ⓕ *poch*·ta

pot (ceramic/cooking) горшок ⓜ gar·*shok*

potato картошка ⓕ kar·*tosh*·ka

pottery керамика ⓕ ki·*ra*·mi·ka

pound (money/weight) фунт ⓜ funt

poverty бедность ⓕ *byed*·nast'

powder пудра ⓕ *pud*·ra

power энергия ⓕ en·*yer*·gi·ya

prawn креветка ⓕ kriv·*yet*·ka

prayer молитва ⓕ ma·*lit*·va

prefer предпочитать/предпочесть prit·pa·chi·*tat*'/prit·pa·*chest*'

pregnancy test kit тест на беременность ⓜ tyest na bir·*ye*·mi·nast'

pregnant беременная bir·*ye*·mi·na·ya

prepare приготавливать/приготовить pri·ga·*tav*·li·vat'/pri·ga·*to*·vit'

prescription рецепт ⓜ rit·*sept*

present (gift) подарок ⓜ pa·*da*·rak

present (time) настоящее ⓝ na·sta·*ya*·shi·ye

president президент ⓜ pri·zid·*yent*

pressure давление ⓝ dav·*lye*·ni·ye

pretty хорошенький kha·ro·*shihn*'·ki

price цена ⓕ tse·*na*

priest священник ⓜ svya·*she*·nik

prime minister премьер-министр ⓜ prim·*yer*·mi·*nistr*

printer (computer) принтер ⓜ *prin*·tir

prison тюрьма ⓕ tyur'·*ma*

private частный *chas*·nih

produce производить/произвести pra·iz·va·*dit*'/pra·iz·vi·*sti*

profit прибыль ⓕ *pri*·bihl'

program программа ⓕ pra·*gra*·ma

promise обещать/пообещать a·bi·*shat*'/pa·a·bi·*shat*'

protect защищать/защитить za·shi·*shat*'/za·shi·*tit*'

protest протест ⓜ prat·*yest*

provisions провизия ⓕ pra·*vi*·zi·ya

prune чернослив ⓜ chir·nas·*lif*

pub пивная ⓕ piv·*na*·ya

public gardens публичный сад ⓜ pub·*lich*·nih sat

public relations внешние связи ⓕ pl *vnyesh*·ni·ye *svya*·zi

public telephone публичный телефон ⓜ pub·*lich*·nih ti·li·*fon*

public toilet общественный туалет ⓜ ap·*shest*·vi·nih tu·al·*yet*

pull тянуть/потянуть ti·*nut*'/pi·ti·*nut*'

pump насос ⓜ na·*sos*

pumpkin тыква ⓕ *tihk*·va

Q

puncture прокол ⓜ pra·kol
pure чистый chis·tih
purple пурпурный pur·pur·nih
purse кошелёк ⓜ ka·shal·yok
push толкать/толкнуть tal·kat'/talk·nut'
put ставить/поставить sta·vit'/pa·sta·vit'

Q

qualifications квалификации ⓕ pl kva·li·fi·kat·si
quality качество ⓝ ka·chist·va
quarantine карантин ⓜ ka·ran·tin
quarter четверть ⓕ chet·virt'
queen королева ⓕ ka·ral·ye·va
question вопрос ⓜ va·pros
queue очередь ⓕ o·chi·rit'
quick быстрый bihst·rih
quiet тихий ti·khi
quit бросать/бросить bra·sat'/bro·sit'

R

rabbit кролик ⓜ kro·lik
rabies бешенство ⓝ bye·shinst·va
race (sport) бег ⓜ byek
racetrack ипподром ⓜ i·pa·drom
racing bike гоночный велосипед ⓜ go·nach·nih vi·la·sip·yet
racism расизм ⓜ ra·sizm
racquet ракета ⓕ rak·ye·ta
radiation радиация ⓕ ra·di·at·sih·ya
radiator радиатор ⓜ ra·di·a·tar
radio радио ⓝ ra·di·o
railway station вокзал ⓜ vag·zal
rain дождь ⓜ dozht'
raincoat плащ ⓜ plash
rally манифестация ⓕ ma·ni·fist·at·sih·ya
rape изнасилование ⓝ iz·na·si·la·va·ni·ye
rape насиловать/изнасиловать na·si·la·vat'/iz·na·si·la·vat'
rare (food) кровавый kra·va·vih

rare (uncommon) редкий ryet·ki
rash сыпь ⓕ sihp'
raspberry малина ⓕ ma·li·na
rat крыса ⓕ krih·sa
raw сырой sih·roy
razor бритва ⓕ brit·va
razor blade лезвие ⓝ lyez·vi·ye
read читать/прочитать chi·tat'/pra·chi·tat'
reading чтение ⓝ chtye·ni·ye
ready готов ⓜ ga·tof
real estate agent риэлтер ⓜ ri·el·tir
rear (location) а задний zad·ni
reason причина ⓕ pri·chi·na
receipt квитанция ⓕ kvi·tant·sih·ya
recently недавно ni·dav·na
recommend рекомендовать/порекомендовать ri·ka·min·da·vat'/pa·ri·ka·min·da·vat'
record записывать/записать za·pi·sih·vat'/za·pi·sat'
recycle перерабатывать/переработать pi·ri·ra·ba·tih·vat'/pi·ri·ra·bo·tat'
red красный kras·nih
referee рефери ⓜ ri·fi·ri
reference рекомендация ⓕ ri·ka·min·dat·sih·ya
refrigerator холодильник ⓜ kha·la·dil'·nik
refugee беженец/беженка ⓜ/ⓕ bye·zhih·nits/bye·zhihn·ka
refund возвращение денег ⓝ vaz·vra·she·ni·ye dye·nik
refuse отказывать/отказать at·ka·zih·vat'/at·ka·zat'
regional региональный ri·gi·a·nal'·nih
registered mail ⓕ заказной za·kaz·noy
regret v сожалеть sa·zhal·yet'
rehydration salts нюхательная соль ⓕ nyu·kha·til'·na·ya sol'
relationship связь ⓕ svyas'
relax расслабляться/расслабиться ras·lab·lyat'·sa/ras·la·bit'·sa
relic реликвия ⓕ ri·lik·vi·ya

religion религия ① ri·*li*·gi·ya
religious религиозный ri·li·gi·*oz*·nih
remote дальний *dal*·nih
rent квартирная плата ①
kvar·*tir*·na·ya *pla*·ta
rent v арендовать a·rin·da·*vat'*
repair чинить/починить chi·*nit'*/
pa·chi·*nit'*
republic республика ① ris·*pub*·li·ka
reservation (booking) заказ ⓜ
za·*kas*
rest отдыхать/отдохнуть
a·dih·*khat'*/a·dakh·*nut'*
restaurant ресторан ⓜ ris·ta·*ran*
résumé автобиография ①
af·ta·bi·a·*gra*·fi·ya
retired на пенсии na *pyen*·si
return (come back) возвращаться/
вернуться vaz·vra·*shat'*·sa/vir·*nut'*·sa
return (ticket) обратный a·*brat*·nih
review рецензия ① rit·*sen*·zi·ya
rhythm ритм ⓜ ritm
rib ребро ⑪ ri·*bro*
rice рис ⓜ ris
rich (wealthy) богатый ba·*ga*·tih
ride поездка ① pa·*yest*·ka
ride (horse) ездить/ехать верхом
yez·dit'/*ye*·khat' vir·*khom*
right (correct) правильный
pra·vil'·nih
right (direction) правый *pra*·vih
right-wing правый *pra*·vih
ring (jewellery) кольцо ⓜ *kalt*·so
ring (phone) звонить/позвонить
zva·*nit'*/paz·va·*nit'*
rip-off грабёж ⓜ grab·*yosh*
river река ① ri·*ka*
road дорога ① da·*ro*·ga
road map карта дорог ① *kar*·ta
da·*rok*
rob красть/обокрасть krast'/
a·ba·*krast'*
robbery грабёж ⓜ grab·*yosh*
rock скала ① ska·*la*
rock climbing скалолазание ⑪
ska·la·*la*·za·ni·ye

rockmelon арбуз ⓜ ar·*bus*
romantic романтичный
ra·man·*tich*·nih
room (hotel) номер ⓜ *no*·mir
room (house) комната ① *kom*·na·ta
room number номер комнаты ⓜ
no·mir *kom*·na·tih
rope верёвка ① vir·*yof*·ka
rouble рубль ⓜ rubl'
round круглый *krug*·lih
route путь ⓜ put'
rubbish мусор ⓜ *mu*·sar
rubella краснуха ① kras·*nu*·kha
rug ковёр ⓜ kav·*yor*
ruins развалины ① pl raz·va·li·nih
rule правило ⑪ *pra*·vi·la
rum ром ⓜ rom
run бежать/побежать bi·*zhat'*/
pa·bi·*zhat'*
running бег ⓜ byek
Russia Россия ① ra·*si*·ya
Russian (language) русский ⓜ
rus·ki
Russian (man/woman) а русский/
русская ⓜ/① *rus*·ki/*rus*·ka·ya

S

sad грустный *grus*·nih
safe сейф ⓜ syeyf
safe a безопасный biz·a·*pas*·nih
saint святой ⓜ svi·*toy*
salad салат ⓜ sa·*lat*
salary зарплата ① zar·*pla*·ta
sale (low prices) распродажа ①
ras·pra·*da*·zha
sales tax налог на продажу ⓜ
na·*lok* na pra·*da*·zhu
salmon лососина ① la·sa·*si*·na
salt соль ⓜ sol'
same тот же самый tod zhe sa·*mih*
sand песок ⓜ pi·*sok*
sandal сандалия ① san·*da*·li·ya
sanitary napkin гигиеническая
салфетка ① gi·gi·i·*ni*·chi·ska·ya
salf·*yet*·ka
sauce соус ⓜ *so*·us

S

saucepan кастрюля ① kast·*ryul*·ya
sauna сауна ① *sa*·u·na
sausage (cooked) сосиска ①
sa·*sis*·ka
sausage (salami) колбаса ①
kal·ba·*sa*
say говорить/сказать ga·va·*rit*'/
ska·*zat*'
scalp скальп ⓜ skalp
scarf шарф ⓜ sharf
school школа ① *shko*·la
science наука ① na·*u*·ka
scientist учёный/учёная ⓜ/①
u·*cho*·nih/u·*cho*·na·ya
scissors ножницы ① pl *nozh*·nit·sih
score (sport) забивать/забить
za·bih·*vat*'/za·*biht*'
Scotland Шотландия ①
shat·*lan*·di·ya
sculpture скульптура ① skulp·*tu*·ra
sea море ⓝ *mor*·ye
seal (animal) тюлень ⓜ tyul·*yen*'
seasickness морская болезнь ①
mar·*ska*·ya bal·*yezn*'
seaside берег моря ⓜ *bye*·rik *mor*·ya
season время года ⓝ *vryem*·ya
go·da
seat место ⓝ *myes*·ta
seatbelt ремень ⓜ rim·*yen*'
second (time) секунда ① si·*kun*·da
second a второй fta·*roy*
second class во втором классе va
fta·*rom klas*·ye
second-hand подержанный
pad·*yer*·zha·nih
secretary секретарша ①
si·kri·*tar*·sha
see видеть/увидеть *vi*·dit'/u·*vi*·dit'
self-employed на себя na sib·*ya*
selfish эгоистичный e·go·is·*tich*·nih
self-service самообслуживание ⓝ
sa·ma·aps·*lu*·zhih·va·ni·ye
sell продавать/продать pra·da·*vat*'/
pra·*dat*'
send посылать/послать pa·sih·*lat*'/
pas·*lat*'

sensible разумный ra·*zum*·nih
sensual чувственный *chust*·vi·nih
separate отдельный ad·*yel*'·nih
serious серьёзный sir·*yoz*·nih
service услуга ① us·*lu*·ga
service charge плата за
обслуживание ① *pla*·ta za
aps·*lu*·zhih·va·ni·ye
service station заправочная
станция ① za·*pra*·vach·na·ya
stant·sih·ya
serviette салфетка ① salf·*yet*·ka
several несколько nye·*skal*'·ka
sew шить/сшить shiht'/s·shiht'
sex секс ⓜ syeks
sexism сексизм ⓜ syek·*sizm*
sexy сексуальный syek·su·*al*'·nih
shade (shadow) тень ① tyen'
shampoo шампунь ⓜ sham·*pun*'
shape форма ① *for*·ma
share (item) делить/поделить
di·*lit*'/pa·di·*lit*'
share (room) жить в одной
(комнате) zhiht' v ad·*noy* (*kom*·nat·ye)
shave бриться/побриться *brit*'·sa/
pa·*brit*'·sa
shaving cream крем для бритья
kryem dlya brit·*ya*
she она a·*na*
sheep овца ① aft·*sa*
sheet (bed) простыня ①
pra·stihn·*ya*
ship корабль ⓜ ka·*rabl*'
shirt рубашка ① ru·*bash*·ka
shoes туфли ① pl *tuf*·li
shoe shop обувной магазин ⓜ
a·buv·*noy* ma·ga·*zin*
shoot стрелять/расстрелять
stril·*yat*'/ras·tril·*yat*'
shop магазин ⓜ ma·ga·*zin*
shop ходить по магазинам kha·*dit*'
pa ma·ga·*zi*·nam
shopping centre торговый центр ⓜ
tar·*go*·vih tsentr
short (height) короткий ka·*rot*·ki
shortage дефицит ⓜ di·fit·*siht*

S

shorts шорты ⓜ pl *shor*·tih

shoulder плечо ⓝ pli·*cho*

shout кричать/крикнуть kri·*chat'*/ krik·*nut'*

show спектакль ⓜ spik·*takl*

show показывать/показать pa·*ka*·zih·vat'/pa·ka·*zat'*

shower душ ⓜ dush

shrine святыня ⓕ svya·*tihn*·ya

shut a закрытый za·*krih*·tih

shy застенчивый za·*styen*·chi·vih

Siberia Сибирь ⓕ si·*bir'*

Siberian сибирский si·*bir*·ski

sick болен/больна ⓜ/ⓕ *bo*·lin/ bal'·*na*

side сторона ⓕ sta·ra·*na*

sign знак ⓜ znak

sign (documents) подписывать/ подписать pat·*pi*·sih·vat'/pat·pi·*sat'*

signature подпись ⓕ *pot*·pis'

silk щёлк ⓜ sholk

silver серебро ⓝ si·ri·*bro*

SIM card сим-карта ⓕ *sim*·kar·ta

similar похожий pa·*kho*·zhih

simple простой pra·*stoy*

since ... с ... s ...

sing петь/спеть pyet'/spyet'

singer певец/певица ⓜ/ⓕ piv·*yets*/ pi·*vit*·sa

single (man) холост ⓜ *kho*·last

single (woman) не замужем ⓕ nye za·mu·zhihm

single room одноместный номер ⓜ ad·na·*mes*·nih *no*·mir

singlet майка ⓕ *mey*·ka

sister сестра ⓕ sis·*tra*

sit сидеть sid·*yet'*

size (general) размер ⓜ raz·*myer*

skate кататься на коньках ka·*tat'*·sa na kan'·*kakh*

ski v кататься на лыжах ka·*tat'*·sa na lih·zhakh

skiing катание на лыжах ⓝ ka·ta·ni·ye na lih·zhakh

skim milk снятое молоко ⓝ snya·*to*·ye ma·la·*ko*

skin кожа ⓕ *ko*·zha

skirt юбка ⓕ *yup*·ka

skull череп ⓜ *che*·rip

sky небо ⓝ *nye*·ba

sleep v спать spat'

sleeping bag спальный мешок ⓜ *spal*·nih mi·*shok*

sleeping berth спальное место ⓝ *spal*·na·ye *mye*·sta

sleeping car спальный вагон ⓜ *spal*·nih va·*gon*

sleeping pills снотворные таблетки ⓜ pl snat·*vor*·nih·ye tab·*lyet*·ki

sleepy сонный *so*·nih

slice ломтик ⓜ *lom*·tik

slide (film) слайд ⓜ sleyt

slow медленный *myed*·li·nih

slowly медленно *myed*·li·na

small маленький *ma*·lin'·ki

smell запах ⓜ za·pakh

smile улыбаться/улыбнуться u·lih·*bat'*·sa/u·lihb·*nut'*·sa

smoke курить/покурить ku·*rit'*/ pa·ku·*rit'*

snack закуска ⓕ za·*kus*·ka

snack bar закусочная ⓕ za·*ku*·sach·na·ya

snake змея ⓕ zmi·*ya*

snow снег ⓜ snyek

soap мыло ⓝ *mih*·la

soap opera мыльная опера ⓕ *mihl*·na·ya o·pi·ra

soccer футбол ⓜ fud·*bol*

socialism социализм ⓜ sat·sih·a·*lizm*

socks носки ⓜ pl na·*ski*

soda содовая ⓕ *so*·da·va·ya

soft drink безалкогольный напиток ⓜ biz·al·ka·*gol'*·nih na·*pi*·tak

soft-boiled всмятку vsmyat·ku

soldier солдат ⓜ sal·*dat*

some несколько *nye*·skal'·ka

someone кто-то *kto*·ta

something что-то *shto*·ta

sometimes иногда i·*nag*·da

son сын ⓜ sihn

song песня ⓕ *pyes*·nya

soon скоро *sko*·ra

sore а болит ba·*lit*

soup суп ⓜ sup

south юг ⓜ yuk

souvenir сувенир ⓜ su·vi·*nir*

souvenir shop сувенирный магазин ⓜ su·vi·*nir*·nih ma·ga·*zin*

Soviet советский sav·*yet*·ski

Soviet Union Советский Союз ⓜ sav·*yet*·ski sa·*yus*

soy milk соевое молоко ⓝ so·i·va·ye ma·la·ko

soy sauce соевый соус ⓜ so·i·vih *so*·us

Spain Испания ⓕ i·*spa*·ni·ya

sparkling wine шампанское ⓝ sham·*pan*·ska·ye

speak говорить ga·va·*rit*'

special особенный a·so·bi·nih

specialist специалист ⓜ spet·sih·a·*list*

speed (velocity) скорость ⓕ *sko*·rast'

speed limit ограничение скорости ⓕ a·gra·ni·*che*·ni·ye *sko*·ras·ti

spider паук ⓜ pa·*uk*

spinach шпинат ⓜ shpi·*nat*

spoiled (food) испорченный is·*por*·chi·nih

spoke спица ⓕ *spit*·sa

spoon ложка ⓕ *losh*·ka

sports store спортивный магазин ⓜ spar·*tiv*·nih ma·ga·*zin*

sportsman спортсмен ⓜ sparts·*myen*

sportswoman спортсменка ⓕ sparts·*myen*·ka

sprain растяжение связок ⓝ rast·ya·*zhe*·ni·ye svya·zak

spring (season) весна ⓕ vis·*na*

square (town) площадь ⓕ *plo*·shat'

stadium стадион ⓜ sta·di·*on*

stairway лестница ⓕ *lyes*·nit·sa

stale чёрствый *chorst*·vih

stamp марка ⓕ *mar*·ka

stand-by ticket стенд-бай ⓜ *styend*·bey

star звёзда ⓕ zvyoz·da

star sign знак ⓜ znak

start начало ⓝ na·*cha*·la

start начинать/начать na·chi·*nat*'/na·*chat*'

station станция ⓕ *stant*·sih·ya

stationer канцелярские товары ⓜ pl kant·sihl·*yar*·ski·ye ta·*va*·rih

statue статуя ⓕ *sta*·tu·ya

stay (hotel) останавливаться/остановиться a·sta·*nav*·li·vat'·sa/a·sta·na·*vit*'·sa

steak бифштекс ⓜ bif·*shteks*

steal красть/украсть krast'/u·*krast*'

steep крутой kru·*toy*

step ступень ⓕ stup·*yen*'

steppe степь ⓕ styep'

stockings чулки ⓜ pl chul·*ki*

stolen краденый *kra*·di·nih

stomach желудок ⓜ zhih·*lu*·dak

stomachache боль в желудке ⓕ bol' v zhih·*lut*·kye

stone камень ⓜ *ka*·min'

stoned (drugs) на колёсах na kal·*yo*·sakh

stop (bus/tram) остановка ⓕ a·sta·*nof*·ka

stop (cease) переставать/перестать pi·ri·sta·*vat*'/pi·ri·*stat*'

stop (prevent) мешать/помешать mi·*shat*'/pa·mi·*shat*'

storm буря ⓕ *bur*·ya

story рассказ ⓜ ras·*kas*

stove печь ⓕ pyech'

straight прямой pri·*moy*

strange странный *stra*·nih

stranger незнакомец/незнакомка ⓜ/ⓕ nyez·na·*ko*·mits/nyez·na·*kom*·ka

strawberry клубника ⓕ klub·*ni*·ka

street улица ① *u·lit·sa*
street market уличный рынок ⑩ *u·lich·nih rih·nak*
strike (work) забастовка ① *za·bas·tof·ka*
string верёвка ① *vir·yof·ka*
stroke (health) удар ⑩ *u·dar*
stroller детская коляска ① *dyet·ska·ya kal·yas·ka*
strong сильный *sil'·nih*
stubborn упрямый *up·rya·mih*
student студент/студентка ⑩/① *stud·yent/stud·yent·ka*
studio студия ① *stu·di·ya*
stupid глупый *glu·pih*
subtitles субтитры ⑩ pl *sub·tit·rih*
suburb пригород ⑩ *pri·ga·rat*
subway (train) метро ⑩ *mi·tro*
sugar сахар ⑩ *sa·khar*
suitcase чемодан ⑩ *chi·ma·dan*
summer лето ⑩ *lye·ta*
sun солнце ⑩ *solnt·se*
sunblock солнцезащитный крем ⑩ *sont·se·za·shit·nih kryem*
sunburn солнечный ожог ⑩ *sol·nich·nih a·zhok*
sunglasses очки от солнца ⑩ pl *ach·ki at solnt·sa*
sunny солнечный *sol·nich·nih*
sunrise заря ① *zar·ya*
sunset закат ⑩ *za·kat*
supermarket универсам ⑩ *u·ni·vir·sam*
superstition суеверие ⑩ *su·iv·ye·ri·ye*
supporter (politics) сторонник/сторонница ⑩/① *sta·ro·nik/sta·ro·nit·sa*
supporter (sport) болельщик/болельщица ⑩/① *bal·yel'·shik/bal·yel'·shit·sa*
surf v заниматься сёрфингом *za·ni·mat'·sa syor·fin·gam*
surface mail обычная почта ① *a·bihch·na·ya poch·ta*
surname фамилия ① *fa·mi·li·ya*

surprise сюрприз ⑩ *syur·pris*
sweater свитер ⑩ *svi·tir*
Sweden Швеция ① *shvyet·sih·ya*
sweet сладкий *slat·ki*
swelling опухоль ① *o·pu·khal'*
swim v плавать *pla·vat'*
swimming (sport) плавание ⑩ *pla·va·ni·ye*
swimming pool бассейн ⑩ *bas·yeyn*
swimsuit купальный костюм ⑩ *ku·pal'·nih kast·yum*
Switzerland Швейцария ① *shveyt·sa·ri·ya*
synagogue синагога ① *si·na·go·ga*
synthetic синтетический *sin·ti·ti·chi·ski*
syringe шприц ⑩ *shprits*

T

table стол ⑩ *stol*
table tennis настольный теннис ⑩ *na·stol'·nih tye·nis*
tablecloth скатерть ① *ska·tirt'*
tail хвост ⑩ *khvost*
tailor портной *part·noy*
take брать/взять *brat'/vzyat'*
take photos снимать/снять *sni·mat'/snyat'*
talk разговаривать *raz·ga·va·ri·vat'*
tall высокий *vih·so·ki*
tampon тампон ⑩ *tam·pon*
tap кран ⑩ *kran*
tap water водопроводная вода ① *va·da·pra·vod·na·ya va·da*
tasty вкусный *fkus·nih*
tax налог ⑩ *na·lok*
taxi rank стоянка такси ① *sta·yan·ka tak·si*
tea чай ⑩ *chey*
teacher учитель/учительница ⑩/① *u·chi·til'/u·chi·til'·nit·sa*
team команда ① *ka·man·da*
teaspoon чайная ложка ① *chey·na·ya losh·ka*
teeth зубы ⑩ pl *zu·bih*

T

telephone телефон ⓜ ti·li·*fon*
telephone звонить/позвонить
zva·*nit'*/paz·va·*nit'*
telephone centre телефонный
центр ⓜ ti·li·*fo*·nih tsentr
television телевизор ⓜ ti·li·*vi*·zar
tell сказать ska·*zat'*
temperature (fever) лихорадка ⓕ
li·kha·*rat*·ka
temperature (weather)
температура ⓕ tim·pi·ra·*tu*·ra
tennis court теннисный корт ⓜ
tye·nis·nih kort
tent палатка ⓕ pa·*lat*·ka
tent peg колышек для палатки ⓜ
ko·lih·shihk dlya pa·*lat*·ki
terrible ужасный u·*zhas*·nih
terrorism терроризм ⓜ ti·ra·*rizm*
thank благодарить/поблагодарить
bla·ga·da·*rit'*/pab·la·ga·da·*rit'*
that (one) то to
theatre театр ⓜ ti·*atr*
their их ikh
there там tam
thermometer термометр ⓜ
tir·*mo*·mitr
they они a·*ni*
thick толстый *tol*·stih
thief вор ⓜ vor
thin тонкий *ton*·ki
think думать *du*·mat'
third а третий *trye*·ti
thirsty (be) хочется пить
kho·chit·sa pit'
this (one) это e·ta
thread нитка ⓕ *nit*·ka
throat горло ⓝ *gor*·la
thrush (health) молочница ⓕ
ma·*loch*·nit·sa
ticket билет ⓜ bil·*yet*
ticket collector кондуктор ⓜ
kan·*duk*·tar
ticket machine кассовый автомат ⓜ
ka·sa·vih af·ta·*mat*
ticket office билетная касса ⓕ
bil·*yet*·na·ya *ka*·sa

ticks (insects) клещи ⓜ pl *klye*·shi
tide (high) прилив ⓜ pri·*lif*
tide (low) отлив ⓜ at·*lif*
tight узкий *us*·ki
time время ⓝ *vryem*·ya
time difference разность
времени ⓕ *raz*·nast' *vrye*·mi·ni
timetable расписание ⓝ
ras·pi·*sa*·ni·ye
tin (can) банка ⓕ *ban*·ka
tin opener консервный нож ⓜ
kans·*yerv*·nih nosh
tiny крошечный *kro*·shich·nih
tip (gratuity) чаевые ⓕ pl
cha·i·*vih*·ye
tired устал u·*stal*
tissues салфетки ⓕ pl salf·*yet*·ki
to в v
toast (bread) гренок ⓜ gri·*nok*
toast (to health) тост ⓜ tost
toaster тостер ⓜ *tos*·tir
tobacco табак ⓜ ta·*bak*
tobogganing санный спорт ⓜ
sa·nih sport
today сегодня si·*vod*·nya
toe палец ⓜ *pa*·lits
together вместе *vmyest*·ye
toilet туалет ⓜ tu·a·*lyet*
toilet paper туалетная бумага ⓕ
tu·a·*lyet*·na·ya bu·*ma*·ga
tomato помидор ⓜ pa·mi·*dor*
tomato sauce кетчуп ⓜ *kyet*·chup
tomorrow завтра *zaf*·tra
tonight сегодня вечером si·*vod*·nya
vye·chi·ram
too (also) тоже *to*·zhih
too (excess) слишком *slish*·kam
tooth зуб ⓜ zup
toothache зубная боль ⓕ zub·*na*·ya
bol'
toothbrush зубная щётка ⓕ
zub·*na*·ya *shot*·ka
toothpaste зубная паста ⓕ
zub·*na*·ya *pa*·sta
torch (flashlight) фонарик ⓜ
fa·*na*·rik

U

touch трогать/тронуть *tro*·gat'/ *tro*·nut'

tour экскурсия ⓕ eks·*kur*·si·ya

tourist турист/туристка ⓜ/ⓕ tu·*rist*/tu·*rist*·ka

tourist office туристическое бюро ⓝ tu·rist·*i*·chi·ska·ye byu·*ro*

towards к k

towel полотенце ⓝ pa·lat·*yent*·se

tower башня ⓕ *bash*·nya

track (path) дорожка ⓕ da·*rosh*·ka

track (sport) трек ⓜ tryek

trade (commerce) торговля ⓕ tar·*gov*·lya

trade (job) профессия ⓕ praf·*ye*·si·ya

tradesperson ремесленник ⓜ rim·*yes*·li·nik

trade union профсоюз ⓜ praf·*sa*·yus

traffic движение ⓝ dvi·*zhe*·ni·ye

traffic light светофор ⓜ svi·ta·*for*

trail тропинка ⓕ tra·*pin*·ka

train поезд ⓜ *po*·ist

train station вокзал ⓜ vag·*zal*

tram трамвай ⓜ tram·*vey*

transit lounge транзитный зал ⓜ *tran*·zit·nih zal

translate переводить/перевести pi·ri·va·*dit'*/pi·ri·vi·*sti*

translation перевод ⓜ pi·ri·*vot*

transport транспорт ⓜ *tran*·spart

travel путешествовать ⓜ pu·ti·*shest*·va·vat'

travel agency бюро путешествий ⓝ byu·*ro* pu·ti·*shest*·vi

travel sickness морская болезнь ⓕ mar·*ska*·ya bal·*yezn'*

travellers cheque дорожный чек ⓜ da·*rozh*·nih chek

tree дерево ⓝ *dye*·ri·va

trip (journey) поездка ⓕ pa·*yest*·ka

trolley тележка ⓕ til·*yesh*·ka

trousers брюки ⓜ pl *bryu*·ki

truck грузовик ⓜ gru·za·*vik*

trust доверять/доверить da·vir·*yat'*/dav·*ye*·rit'

try (attempt) стараться/ постараться sta·*rat'*·sa/pa·sta·*rat'*·sa

try (taste) пробовать/попробовать *pro*·ba·vat'/pa·*pro*·ba·vat'

T-shirt футболка ⓕ fud·*bol*·ka

tube (tyre) камера ⓕ *ka*·mi·ra

tumour опухоль ⓕ *o*·pu·khal'

turkey индейка ⓕ ind·*yey*·ka

turn поворачивать/повернуть pa·va·ra·chi·vat'/pa·vir·*nut'*

TV телевизор ⓜ ti·li·*vi*·zar

tweezers щипчики ⓜ pl *ship*·chi·ki

twice дважды *dvazh*·dih

twin beds adv две односпальные кровати dvye ad·na·*spal'*·nih·ye kra·*va*·ti

twins близнецы ⓜ pl bliz·*nit*·sih

two два/две ⓜ/ⓕ dva/dvye

type тип ⓜ tip

typical типичный ti·*pich*·nih

tyre шина ⓕ *shih*·na

tsar царь ⓜ tsar'

U

Ukraine Украина ⓕ u·kra·*i*·na

ultrasound ультразвук ⓜ ul'·traz·*vuk*

umbrella зонтик ⓜ *zon*·tik

uncomfortable неудобный nye·u·*dob*·nih

understand понимать/понять pa·ni·*mat'*/pan·*yat'*

underwear бельё ⓝ bil·*yo*

unemployed безработный biz·ra·*bot*·nih

unfair несправедливый nye·spra·vid·*li*·vih

uniform форма ⓕ *for*·ma

university университет ⓕ u·ni·vir·sit·*yet*

unleaded очищенный a·*chi*·shi·nih

until до do

unusual необычный nye·a·*bihch*·nih

up вверх vyerkh

uphill в гору v *go*·ru

urgent срочный *sroch*·nih

urinary infection мочевая инфекция ⓕ ma·chi·*va*·ya inf·*yekt*·sih·ya
USA США ⓜ pl es·sha·*a*
useful полезный pal·*yez*·nih

V

vacancy свободный номер ⓜ sva·*bod*·nih no·*mir*
vacation каникулы ⓕ pl ka·*ni*·ku·lih
vaccination прививка ⓕ pri·*vif*·ka
vagina влагалище ⓝ vla·*ga*·li·she
validate утверждать/утвердить ut·virzh·*dat*/ut·*vir*·dit'
valley долина ⓕ da·*li*·na
valuable ценный *tse*·nih
value стоимость ⓕ *sto*·i·mast'
van фургон ⓜ fur·*gon*
veal телятина ⓕ til·*ya*·ti·na
vegetable овощ ⓜ *o*·vash
vegetarian вегетарианец/вегетарианка ⓜ/ⓕ vi·gi·ta·ri·*a*·nits/vi·gi·ta·ri·*an*·ka
vein вена ⓕ *vye*·na
venereal disease венерическая болезнь ⓕ vi·ni·*ri*·chi·ska·ya bal·*yezn'*
venue место концерта ⓝ *mye*·sta kant·*ser*·ta
very очень o·chin'
video recorder видеомагнитофон ⓜ vi·di·o·mag·ni·ta·*fon*
video tape видеокассета ⓕ vi·di·o·kas·*ye*·ta
view вид ⓜ vit
village деревня ⓕ dir·*yev*·nya
vinegar уксус ⓜ *uk*·sus
vineyard виноградник ⓜ vi·na·*grad*·nik
virus вирус ⓜ *vi*·rus
visit визит ⓜ vi·*zit*
visit посещать/посетить pa·si·*shat*'/pa·si·*tit*'
vitamins витамины ⓜ pl vi·ta·*mi*·nih
voice голос ⓜ *go*·las
volleyball (sport) волейбол ⓜ va·li·*bol*

volume (sound) громкость *grom*·kast'
vote голосовать/проголосовать ga·la·sa·*vat*'/pra·ga·la·sa·*vat*'

W

wage зарплата ⓕ zar·*pla*·ta
wait ждать/подождать zhdat'/pa·da·*zhdat*'
waiter официант/официантка ⓜ/ⓕ a·fit·sih·*ant*/a·fit·sih·*ant*·ka
waiting room зал ожидания ⓜ zal a·zhih·*da*·ni·ya
wake (someone) up будить/разбудить bu·*dit*'/raz·bu·*dit*'
walk гулять/погулять gul·*yat*'/pa·gul·*yat*'
want хотеть/захотеть khat·*yet*'/za·khat·*yet*'
war война ⓕ vey·*na*
wardrobe шкаф ⓜ shkaf
warm тёплый *tyop*·lih
warn предупреждать/предупредить pri·du·prizh·*dat*'/pri·du·pri·*dit*'
wash (oneself) умываться/умыться u·mih·*vat*'·sa/u·*miht*'·sa
wash (something) стирать/выстирать sti·*rat*'/*vih*·sti·rat'
wash cloth (flannel) тряпочка для мытья ⓕ *trya*·pach·ka dlya miht·*ya*
washing machine стиральная машина ⓕ sti·*ral*'·na·ya ma·*shih*·na
watch часы ⓜ pl chi·*sih*
watch смотреть smat·*ryet*'
water вода ⓕ va·*da*
water bottle фляшка ⓕ *flyash*·ka
water bottle (hot) грелка ⓕ *gryel*·ka
waterfall водопад ⓜ va·da·*pat*
watermelon арбуз ⓜ ar·*bus*
waterproof непромокаемый nye·pra·ma·*ka*·i·mih
wave волна ⓕ val·*na*
way путь ⓜ put'
we мы mih
weak слабый *sla*·bih

Y

wealthy богатый ba·*ga*·tih
wear носить na·*sit*'
weather погода ① pa·*go*·da
wedding свадьба ① *svad*'·ba
week неделя ① nid·*yel*·ya
weekend выходные ⓜ pl vih·khad·*nih*·ye
weigh взвешивать/взвесить vzvye·*shih*·vat'/vzvye·*sit*'
weight вес ⓜ vyes
weights весы ⓜ pl *vye*·sih
welcome приветствовать priv·*yetst*·va·vat'
welfare социальное обеспечение ⓝ sat·sih·*al*'·na·ye a·bis·pye·*chi*·ni·ye
well здоровый zda·ro·vih
west запад ⓜ *za*·pat
western западный *za*·pad·nih
wet a мокрый *mo*·krih
what что shto
wheel колесо ⓝ ka·li·so
wheelchair инвалидная коляска ① in·va·*lid*·na·ya kal·*yas*·ka
when когда kag·*da*
where где gdye
which какой ka·*koy*
white белый a *bye*·lih
who кто kto
why почему pa·chi·*mu*
wide широкий shih·*ro*·ki
wife жена ① zhih·*na*
win выигрывать/выиграть vih·*i*·gri·vat'/*vih*·i·grat'
wind ветер ⓜ *vye*·tir
window окно ⓝ ak·*no*
windscreen ветровое стекло ⓝ vit·ra·vo·ye sti·*klo*
wine вино ⓝ vi·*no*
winner победитель ⓜ pa·bi·*di*·til'
winter зима ① zi·*ma*
wish желать/пожелать zhih·*lat*'/pa·zhih·*lat*'
with c s
within (time) в течение f ti·*che*·ni·ye
without без byez
woman женщина ① *zhen*·shi·na

wonderful прекрасный pri·*kras*·nih
wood дерево ⓝ *dye*·ri·va
wool шерсть ① sherst'
word слово ⓝ *slo*·va
work ⓝ работа ① ra·*bo*·ta
work v работать ra·*bo*·tat'
work permit разрешение на работу ⓝ raz·ri·*she*·ni·ye na ra·*bo*·tu
world мир ⓜ mir
worms глисты ⓜ pl *gli*·stih
worried обеспокоенный a·bis·pa·*ko*·i·nih
worship поклоняться pak·lan·*yat*'·sa
wrist запястье ⓝ zap·*yast*·ye
write писать/написать pi·*sat*'/na·pi·*sat*'
writer писатель/писательница ⓜ/① pi·*sa*·til'/pi·*sa*·til'·nit·sa
wrong неправильный nye·*pra*·vil'·nih

Y

year (to indicate duration of 1 to 4 years but not age) год ⓜ got
years (to indicate duration of 5 years or longer and age) лет ⓝ pl lyet
yellow жёлтый *zhol*·tih
yes да da
yesterday вчера fchi·*ra*
(not) yet ещё (не) yi·*sho* (nye)
yoga йога ① *yo*·ga
yogurt йогурт ⓜ *yo*·gurt
you sg inf ты tih
you sg pol & pl вы vih
young молодой ma·la·*doy*
your sg inf твой tvoy
your sg pol & pl ваш vash
youth hostel турбаза ① tur·*ba*·za

Z

zip/zipper молния ① *mol*·ni·ya
zodiac зодиак ⓜ zo·di·*ak*
zoo зоопарк ⓜ *za*·park
zucchini кабачок ⓜ ka·ba·*chok*

A

Dictionary
RUSSIAN *to* ENGLISH
русский–английский

Russian nouns in this dictionary have their gender indicated by ⓜ, ⓕ or ⓝ. If it's a plural noun you'll also see pl. When a word that could be either a noun or a verb has no gender indicated, it's a verb. For added clarity, certain words are marked as adjectives a, verbs v or adverbs adv. Adjectives are given in the masculine form only. Nouns and adjectives are given in the nominative case only. Verbs are in the imperfective form only. For more information, refer to the **grammar** chapter. For any food terms, see the **menu decoder**.

This chapter has been ordered according to the Cyrillic alphabet (see **pronunciation**, p13).

А

авария ⓕ a·va·ri·ya accident • emergency
авиапочта ⓕ a·vi·a·*poch*·ta airmail
автобиография ⓕ af·ta·bi·a·*gra*·fi·ya CV • résumé
автовокзал ⓜ af·ta·vag·*zal* bus station
автоприцеп ⓜ af·ta·prit·*sep* caravan
автостоянка ⓕ af·ta·sta·*yan*·ka car park
адвокат ⓜ ad·va·*kat* lawyer
анализ крови ⓜ a·na·lis *kro*·vi blood test
анекдот ⓜ a·nik·*dot* joke
аптека ⓕ apt·*ye*·ka chemist • pharmacy
арендовать a·rin·da·*vat*' rent

арестовывать a·ri·*sto*·vih·vat' arrest
аудио-путеводитель ⓜ au·di·o·pu·ti·va·*di*·til' audio guide

Б

бабушка ⓕ *ba*·bush·ka grandmother
багажная бирка ⓕ ba·*gazh*·na·ya *bir*·ka luggage tag
бальзам ⓜ bal'·*zam* hair conditioner
банка ⓕ *ban*·ka can • jar • tin
банковский счёт ⓜ *ban*·kaf·ski shot bank account
бассейн ⓜ bas·*yeyn* swimming pool
бедность ⓕ *byed*·nast' poverty
бедный *byed*·nih poor
бежать bi·*zhat*' run
без byez without
бездомный biz·*dom*·nih homeless

безопасный biz·a·*pas*·nih safe
безработный biz·ra·*bot*·nih
unemployed
белый *bye*·lih white
белый медведь ⓜ *bye*·lih mid·*vyet'*
polar bear
бельё ⓝ bil·*yo* bedding • laundry
(clothes) • underwear
бензин ⓜ bin·*zin* gas • petrol
берег ⓜ *bye*·rik coast
— моря ⓜ *mor*·ya seaside
беременная bir·ye·mi·na·ya
pregnant
бесплатный bis·*plat*·nih free • gratis
бешенство ⓝ *bye*·shinst·va rabies
билет ⓜ bil·*yet* ticket
билетная касса ⓕ bil·*yet*·na·ya
ka·sa ticket office
бинт ⓜ bint bandage
благодарить bla·ga·da·*rit'* thank
ближайший bli·*zhey*·shi nearest
близкий a *blis*·kih close
близко (от) *blis*·ka (at) near(by)
блокнот ⓜ blak·*not* notebook
блошиный рынок ⓜ bla·*shih*·nih
rih·nak fleamarket
блюдо ⓝ *blyu*·da dish
бог ⓜ bok god (general)
богатый ba·*ga*·tih rich • wealthy
болезненные месячные ⓜ pl
bal·*yez*·ni·nih·ye *mye*·sich·nih·ye
period pain
болезнь ⓕ bal·*yezn'* disease
— сердца ⓕ *syerd*·tsa heart
condition
болен ⓜ *bo*·lin ill • sick
болеть bal·*yet'* hurt
болеутоляющие ⓝ pl
bo·li·u·tal·*ya*·yu·shi·ye painkiller
болит ba·*lit* painful • sore
боль ⓕ bol' pain
— в желудке ⓜ v zhih·*lut*·kye
stomachache
больна ⓕ bal'·*na* ill • sick
больница ⓕ bol'·*nit*·sa hospital
большой bal'·*shoy* big • large

бояться v ba·*yat'*·sa (be) afraid
брак ⓜ brak marriage
брат ⓜ brat brother
брать brat' take
— на время na *vryem*·ya borrow
— напрокат na·pra·*kat* hire
бритва ⓕ *brit*·va razor
бриться *brit'*·sa shave
бросать bra·*sat'* quit
брюки bryu·ki ⓜ pl pants • trousers
будить bu·*dit'* wake (someone) up
будущее ⓝ *bu*·du·shi·ye future
булочная ⓕ *bu*·lach·na·ya bakery
бумага ⓕ bu·*ma*·ga paper
буря ⓕ *bur*·ya storm
быстрый *bihst*·rih fast • quick
быть biht' be
бюро находок ⓝ byu·ro na·*kho*·dak
lost property office
бюро путешествий ⓝ byu·ro
pu·ti·*shest*·vi travel agency

В

в v at • in • per • to
в один конец a v a·*din* kan·*yets*
one-way
важный *vazh*·nih important
ванна ⓕ *va*·na bath
ванная ⓕ *va*·na·ya bathroom
ваш vash your sg pol & pl inf&pol
вверх vyerkh up
велосипед ⓜ vi·la·*sip*·yet bicycle
велосипедист ⓜ vi·la·si·pi·*dist*
cyclist
венерическая болезнь ⓕ
vi·ni·ri·chi·ska·ya bal·*yezn'* venereal
disease
верёвка ⓕ vir·*yof*·ka rope • string
— для белья ⓕ dlya bil·*ya*
clothesline
верховая езда ⓕ vir·kha·*va*·ya
yiz·*da* horse riding
вес ⓜ vyes weight
веселиться vi·si·*lit'*·sa have fun
весело adv *vye*·si·la fun
весна ⓕ vis·*na* spring (season)

Г

ветер ⓜ *vye*·tir wind
ветровое стекло ⓝ vit·ra·*vo*·ye sti·*klo* windscreen
ветрянка ⓕ vit·*ryan*·ka chicken pox
вечер ⓜ *vye*·chir evening
вечеринка ⓕ vi·chi·*rin*·ka party (fiesta)
вечная мерзлота ⓕ *vyech*·na·ya mirz·la·*ta* permafrost
взрослый ⓜ *vzros*·lih adult
взрослая ⓕ *vzros*·la·ya adult
взятка ⓕ *vzyat*·ka bribe
вид ⓜ vit view
видеть *vi*·dit' see
вилка ⓕ *vil*·ka fork • plug (electricity)
вина ⓕ vi·*na* (someone's) fault
ВИЧ ⓜ vich HIV
включая fklyu·*cha*·ya included
вкусный *fkus*·nih tasty
влагалище ⓝ vla·*ga*·li·she vagina
владелец ⓜ vlad·*yel*·its owner
влажный *vlazh*·nih humid
вместе *vmyest*·ye together
ВМС ⓜ ve·em·*se* IUD
вниз vnis down
внук ⓜ vnuk grandson
внутри vnu·*tri* inside
внучка ⓕ *vnuch*·ka granddaughter
во втором классе va fta·*rom* klas·ye second class
вовремя *vov*·ryem·ya on time
вода ⓕ va·*da* water
водительские права ⓝ pl va·*di*·til'·ski·ye pra·*va* drivers licence
водить машину va·dit' ma·*shih*·nu drive
водопад ⓜ va·da·*pat* waterfall
военные ⓜ pl va·ye·*nih*·ye military
возвращаться vaz·vra·*shat*'·sa return (come back)
возвращение денег ⓝ vaz·vra·*she*·ni·ye *dye*·nik refund
воздух ⓜ *voz*·dukh air
возможный *vaz·mozh*·nih possible
возраст ⓜ *voz*·rast age
война ⓕ vey·*na* war

вокзал ⓜ vag·*zal* railway station
вопрос ⓜ va·*pros* question
вор ⓜ vor thief
воскресенье ⓝ vas·kris·*yen*·ye Sunday
восток ⓜ va·*stok* east
вперёд fpir·*yot* ahead
врач ⓜ vrach doctor
время ⓝ *vryem*·ya time
— года ⓝ *go*·da season
все fsye all • everyone
всё fsyo everything
всегда fsig·*da* always
встреча ⓕ *fstre*·cha appointment • date
встречать fstri·*chat*' meet
встречаться с fstri·*chat*'·sa s date v
вторник *ftor*·nik Tuesday
второй fta·*roy* second
вход ⓜ fkhot admission price • entry
входить fkha·*dit*' enter
вчера fchi·*ra* yesterday
вы vih you sg pol & pl inf&pol
выбирать vih·bi·*rat*' choose
выборы ⓜ pl *vih*·ba·rih election
выдача багажа ⓕ *vih*·da·cha ba·*ga*·zha baggage claim
выигрывать vih·*i*·gri·vat' win
выкидыш ⓜ *vih*·ki·dihsh miscarriage
высокий vih·*so*·ki high • tall
высота ⓕ vih·sa·*ta* altitude
выставка ⓕ *vih*·staf·ka exhibition
выход ⓜ *vih*·khat exit
выход на посадку ⓜ *vih*·khat na pa·*sat*·ku airport gate
выходить vih·kha·dit' go out
выходить замуж vih·kha·dit' za·mush marry (for a woman)
выходные ⓜ pl vih·khad·*nih*·ye weekend

Г

газета ⓕ gaz·*ye*·ta newspaper
газетный киоск ⓜ gaz·*yet*·nih ki·*osk* newsagency • newsstand

гастроном ⓜ gast·ra·*nom* delicatessen

где gdye where

гигиеническая салфетка ⓕ gi·gi·i·*ni*·chi·ska·ya salf·*yet*·ka sanitary napkin .

главная дорога ⓕ glav·na·ya da·ro·ga main road

главный glav·nih main

глаз ⓜ glas eye

глисты ⓕ pl gli·*stih* worms

глубокий glu·*bo*·ki deep

глухой glu·*khoy* deaf

говорить ga·va·*rit'* say • speak

год ⓜ got year (1 to 4 years' duration)

голова ⓕ ga·la·*va* head

головная боль ⓕ ga·lav·*na*·ya bol' headache

голоден go·la·din be hungry

голос ⓜ go·las voice

голосовать ga·la·sa·*vat'* vote

голубой ga·lu·*boy* light blue

гора ⓕ ga·*ra* mountain

горло ⓝ *gor*·la throat

горный велосипед ⓜ *gor*·nih vi·la·sip·*yet* mountain bike

город ⓜ go·rat city

горшок ⓜ gar·*shok* pot (ceramics/cooking)

горячая вода ⓕ gar·ya·chi·ya va·da hot water

гостеприимство ⓝ ga·sti·pri·*imst*·va hospitality

гостиница ⓕ ga·*sti*·nit·sa guesthouse • hotel

готов ⓜ ga·*tof* ready

готовить ga·*to*·vit' cook

грабёж ⓜ grab·*yosh* rip-off • robbery

гражданин ⓜ grazh·da·*nin* citizen

гражданка ⓕ grazh·*dan*·ka citizen

гражданство ⓝ grazh·*danst*·va citizenship

граница ⓕ gra·*nit*·sa border

гренок ⓜ gri·*nok* toast (bread)

грипп ⓜ grip influenza

гроза ⓕ gra·*za* thunderstorm

громкий *grom*·ki loud

грудная клетка ⓕ grud·*na*·ya *klyet*·ka chest (body)

грудь ⓕ grud' breast (body)

Грузия ⓕ gru·zi·ya Georgia

грузовик ⓜ gru·za·*vik* truck

группа крови ⓕ *gru*·pa kro·vi blood group

грустный grus·nih sad

грязный gryaz·nih dirty

губы ⓕ pl gu·bih lips

гулять gul·*yat'* walk

Д

давать da·*vat'* bribe • give

далеко da·li·ko far

дата рождения ⓕ *da*·ta razh·*dye*·ni·ya date of birth

дважды dvazh·dih twice

две недели dvye nid·*ye*·li fortnightly

две односпальные кровати adv dvye ad·na·*spal'*·nih·ye kra·va·ti twin beds

дверь ⓕ dvyer' door

двойной dvey·*noy* double

дворец ⓜ dvar·*yets* palace

двуспальная кровать ⓕ dvu·*spal'*·na·ya kra·*vat'* double bed

девочка ⓕ *dye*·vach·ka pre-teen girl

девушка ⓕ *dye*·vush·ka teenage girl

дедушка ⓜ *dye*·dush·ka grandfather

делать *dye*·lat' do • make • share (item)

— **укол** lat'·u·*kol* inject

день ⓜ dyen' day

— **рождения** ⓜ razh·*dye*·ni birthday

деньги ⓕ pl *dyen'*·gi money

деревня ⓕ dir·*yev*·nya village

дерево ⓝ *dye*·ri·va tree • wood

деталь ⓕ di·*tal'* component • part

дети ⓜ pl *dye*·ti children

детская коляска ⓕ *dyet*·ska·ya kal·*yas*·ka pram • pushchair • stroller

E

детское питание ⓝ *dyet*·ska·ye pi·*ta*·ni·ye baby food
дефицит ⓜ di·fit·*siht* shortage
дешёвый di·*sho*·vih cheap
длинный *dli*·nih long
дневник ⓜ dnyev·*nik* diary
дно ⓝ dno bottom (position)
днём dnyom afternoon
до do before • until
добрый *dob*·rih kind • nice
доверять da·vir·*yat'* trust
догадываться da·ga·dih·vat'·sa guess
дождь ⓜ dozht' rain
должен *dol*·zhihn owe
долина ⓕ da·*li*·na valley
дом ⓜ dom home • house
домашние дела ⓝ pl da·*mash*·ni·ye dye·*la* housework
домохозяйка ⓕ do·ma·khaz·*yey*·ka homemaker
дорога ⓕ da·*ro*·ga road
дорогой da·ra·*goy* expensive
дорожка ⓕ da·*rosh*·ka path • track
дорожный чек ⓜ da·*rozh*·nih chek travellers cheque
доставлять da·stav·*lyat'* deliver
достаточно da·*sta*·tach·na enough
дочка ⓕ *doch*·ka daughter
драка ⓕ *dra*·ka fight
древний *dryev*·ni ancient
дрова ⓕ *dra*·va firewood
друг ⓜ druk boyfriend • friend
другой dru·*goy* different • other
дума ⓕ *du*·ma parliament
думать *du*·mat' think
духовка ⓕ du·*khof*·ka oven
душ ⓜ dush shower

Е

еврей ⓜ yiv·*rey* Jewish
еврейка ⓕ yiv·*rey*·ka Jewish
его yi·*vo* his
еда ⓕ yi·*da* food • meal
её yi·*yo* her (possessive)
ежедневный yi·zhih·*dnyev*·nih daily

езда на велосипеде yiz·*da* na vi·la·sip·*yed*·ye cycling
ездить верхом *yez*·dit' vir·*khom* ride (horse)
если *yes*·li if
есть yest' eat
ехать *ye*·khat' go (by vehicle)
ещё (не) yi·*sho* (nye) (not) yet
ещё один/одна ⓜ/ⓕ yi·*sho* a·*din*/ad·*na* another
ещё раз yi·*sho* ras again

Ж

жалоба ⓕ *zha*·la·ba complaint
жаловаться *zha*·la·vat'·sa complain
жаркий *zhar*·ki hot
ждать zhdat' wait (for)
железистая лихорадка ⓕ zhihl·*ye*·zi·sta·ya li·kha·*rat*·ka glandular fever
желудок ⓜ zhih·*lu*·dak stomach
жена ⓕ zhih·*na* wife
женатый zhih·*na*·tih married
жениться zhih·*nit'*·sa marry (for a man)
жених ⓜ zhih·*nikh* fiancé
женский *zhen*·skih female
— монастырь ⓜ ma·na·*stihr* convent
женщина ⓕ *zhen*·shi·na woman
жёлтый *zhol*·tih yellow
живопись ⓕ *zhih*·va·pis' painting (art)
животное ⓝ zhih·*vot*·na·ye animal
жизнь ⓕ zhihzn' life
жить zhiht' live (somewhere)
— в одной (комнате) v ad·*noy* (*kom*·nat·ye) share (room)

З

за za behind
— границей gra·*nit*·sey abroad
забастовка ⓕ za·ba·*stof*·ka strike (work)
заведующий ⓜ zav·*ye*·du·yu·shi manager (general)

завтра *zaf·tra* tomorrow

— вечером *vye·chi·ram* tomorrow evening

— после обеда *pos·li ab·ye·da* tomorrow afternoon

— утром *u·tram* tomorrow morning

завтрак ⓜ *zaf·trak* breakfast

зад ⓜ *zat* bottom (body)

задаток ⓜ *za·da·tak* deposit

задержка ⓕ *zad·yersh·ka* delay

задний *a zad·ni* rear (location)

задняя часть ⓕ *zad·nya·ya chast* back (position)

зажигалка ⓕ *za·zhih·gal·ka* lighter

заказ ⓜ *za·kas* booking • order

заказной *za·kaz·noy* by registered mail

заказывать *za·ka·zih·vat* book • order

закат ⓜ *za·kat* sunset

закон ⓜ *za·kon* law

законный *za·ko·nih* legal

законодательство ⓝ *za·ko·na·da·tilst·va* legislation

закрывать *v za·krih·vat* close

закрытый *za·krih·tih* closed • indoor • shut

закуска ⓕ *za·kus·ka* snack

закусочная ⓕ *za·ku·sach·na·ya* snack bar

зал ожидания ⓜ *zal a·zhih·da·ni·ya* waiting room

замерзать *za·mir·zat* freeze

замок ⓜ *za·mok* lock

замужняя ⓕ *za·muzh·ni·ya* married

занят/занята ⓜ/ⓕ *za·nit/za·ni·ta* busy

занято *zan·ya·ta* engaged (phone)

запад ⓜ *za·pat* west

западный *za·pad·nih* Western

запах ⓜ *za·pakh* smell

запертый *zap·yer·tih* locked

запирать *za·pi·rat* lock

записка ⓕ *za·pis·ka* message

заповедник ⓜ *za·pav·yed·nik* national park

заправочная станция ⓕ *za·pra·vach·na·ye stant·sih·ya* service station

запястье ⓝ *zap·yast·ye* wrist

зарабатывать *za·ra·ba·tih·vat* earn

зарплата ⓕ *zar·pla·ta* salary • wage

заря ⓕ *zar·ya* sunrise

защищать *za·shi·shat* protect

звонить *zva·nit* call • ring • phone

звонок ⓜ *zva·nok* call (phone)

звонок по коллекту ⓜ *zva·nok pa kal·yek·tu* collect call

здание ⓝ *zda·ni·ye* building

здесь *zdyes* here

здоровый *zda·ro·vih* well

здоровье ⓝ *zda·rov·ye* health

зеленщик ⓜ *zi·lin·shik* greengrocer

зелёный *zil·yo·nih* green

земля ⓕ *zim·lya* Earth • land

зеркало ⓝ *zyer·ka·la* mirror

зима ⓕ *zi·ma* winter

знак ⓜ *znak* star sign

знаменитый *zna·mi·ni·tih* famous

знать *znat* know

зубная боль ⓕ *zub·na·ya bol* toothache

зубной врач ⓜ *zub·noy vrach* dentist

зубы ⓜ *pl zu·bih* teeth

И

и *i* and

игла ⓕ *i·gla* needle (sewing)

играть в (домино) *i·grat v (da·mi·no)* play (dominoes)

играть на (гитаре) *i·grat na (gi·tar·ye)* play (guitar)

идти *i·ti* go (on foot)

изнасилование ⓝ *iz·na·si·la·va·ni·ye* rape

или *i·li* or

имя ⓜ *im·ya* given name

инвалид ⓜ *in·va·lit* disabled

иногда *i·nag·da* sometimes

иностранный *i·nast·ra·nih* foreign

искусство ⓝ *is·kust·va* art

K

испорченный is·*por*·chi·nih off • spoiled
их ikh their

К

к k towards
каждый *kazh*·dih each • every
как kak how
какой ka·*koy* which
камера ① *ka*·mi·ra tube (tyre)
камера-автомат ①
ka·mi·ra·af·ta·*mat* luggage lockers
камера хранения ① *ka*·mi·ra
khran·*ye*·ni·ya left-luggage office
каникулы ① pl ka·*ni*·ku·lih vacation
карандаш ⓜ ka·ran·*dash* pencil
карман ⓜ kar·*man* pocket
карманный ножик ⓜ kar·*ma*·nih
no·zhik pocket knife
карта ① *kar*·ta map
— дорог ① da·*rok* road map
катание на коньках ⓝ ka·*ta*·ni·ye
na kan'·*kakh* ice skating
катание на лыжах ⓝ ka·*ta*·ni·ye na
lih·zhakh ski • skiing
кататься на коньках ka·*tat*'·sa na
kan'·*kakh* skate
качество ⓝ *ka*·chist·va quality
кашель ⓜ *ka*·shel' cough
квартира ① kvar·*ti*·ra apartment •
flat
квартирная плата ① kvar·*tir*·na·ya
pla·ta rent (payment)
квитанция ① kvi·*tant*·sih·ya receipt
кислород ⓜ kis·la·*rot* oxygen
Китай ⓜ ki·*tey* China
кладбище ⓝ *klad*·bi·she cemetery
ключ ⓜ klyuch key
книга ① *kni*·ga book
когда kag·*da* when
кожа ① *ko*·zha leather • skin
койка ① *koy*·ka berth (ship)
колготки pl kal·*got*·ki pantyhose
колено ⓝ kal·*ye*·na knee
колесо ⓝ ka·li·*so* wheel

кольцо ⓝ kalt·*so* ring (jewellery)
команда ① ka·*man*·da team
комната ① *kom*·na·ta room (house)
конец ⓜ kan·*yets* end • finish
контора ① kan·*to*·ra office
контрольный пункт ⓜ kan·*trol*'·nih
punkt checkpoint
конфеты ① pl kanf·*ye*·tih candy •
lollies • sweets
кончать kan·*chat*' finish
корабль ⓜ ka·*rabl*' ship
коричневый ka·*rich*·ni·vih brown
коробка ① ka·*rop*·ka box
— передач ① pi·ri·*dach* gearbox
короткий ka·*rot*·ki short (height)
корь ① kor' measles
кость ① kost' bone
кошелёк ⓜ ka·shal·*yok* purse
краденый *kra*·di·nih stolen
кран ⓜ kran tap
красивый kra·*si*·vih beautiful •
handsome
краснуха ① kras·*nu*·kha rubella
красный *kras*·nih red
красть krast' rob • steal
крем ⓜ kryem cream (ointment)
кричать kri·*chat*' shout (yell)
кровать ① kra·*vat*' bed
кровь ① krof' blood
кровяное давление ⓝ kra·vi·*no*·ye
dav·*lye*·ni·ye blood pressure
круглый *krug*·lih round
крутой kru·*toy* steep
кто kto who
кто-то *kto*·ta someone
Кубок мира ⓜ *ku*·bak *mi*·ra World
Cup
кулинария ① ku·li·na·*ri*·ya cooking
купальный костюм ⓜ ku·*pal*'·nih
kast·*yum* swimsuit
купе ⓝ ku·*pe* train compartment
курить ku·*rit*' smoke
куртка ① *kurt*·ka jacket (for men)
кусок ⓜ ku·*sok* piece
кухня ① *kukh*·nya kitchen

Л

латексная салфетка ①
la·tiks·na·ya sal·*fyet*·ka dental dam
левый *lye*·vih left (direction) •
left-wing
лёгкий *lyokh*·kih easy • light (weight)
лёгкое ⑩ *lyokh*·ka·ye lung
лёд ⑩ lyot ice
ледоруб ⑩ lye·da·*rup* ice axe
лезвие ⑩ *lyez*·vi·ye razor blade
лекарство ⑩ li·*karst*·va medication
ленивый li·*ni*·vih lazy
лес ⑩ lyes forest
лестница ① *lyes*·nit·sa stairway
лет ⑩ pl lyet years (to indicate
duration of 5 years or longer and age)
лето ⑩ *lye*·ta summer
лист ⑩ list leaf
лифчик ⑩ *lif*·chik bra
лихорадка ① li·kha·*rat*·ka fever
лицо ⑩ lit·*so* face
лодка ① *lot*·ka boat
лодыжка ① la·*dihsh*·ka ankle
ложка ① *losh*·ka spoon
ломать la·*mat'* break
ломаться la·*mat'*·sa break down
(car)
ломтик ⑩ *lom*·tik slice
луна ① lu·*na* moon
любить lyu·*bit'* like • love
любовник ⑩ lyu·*bov*·nik lover
любовница ① lyu·*bov*·nit·sa lover
любовь ① lyu·*bof'* love
любой lyu·*boy* any
люди ⑩ pl *lyu*·di people

М

магазин ⑩ ma·ga·*zin* shop
— готового платья ⑩ ga·*to*·va·va
plat'·ya clothing store
магазинчик ⑩ ma·ga·*zin*·chik
convenience store
мазок ⑩ ma·*zok* pap smear
маленький *ma*·lin'·ki little • small
мало *ma*·la few

мальчик ⑩ *mal'*·chik boy
марка ① *mar*·ka stamp
маршрут ⑩ marsh·*rut* itinerary
масло ⑩ *mas*·la butter • oil (cooking/
fuel)
мастерская ① ma·*stir*·ska·ya
workshop
мать ① mat' mother
машина ① ma·*shih*·na car •
machine
мебель ① *mye*·bil' furniture
медовый месяц ⑩ mi·*do*·vih
mye·sits honeymoon
медсестра ① mit·sist·*ra* nurse
между *myezh*·du between
международный
mizh·du·na·*rod*·nih international
мелочь ① *mye*·lach' change (coins)
меньше *myen'*·she less • smaller
меня min·*ya* me
менять min·*yat'* exchange
местный *myes*·nih local
место ⑩ *mye*·sta place • seat
— назначения ⑩ naz·na·*che*·ni·ya
destination
— рождения ⑩ razh·*dye*·ni·ya
birthplace
месяц ⑩ *mye*·sits month
мешать mi·*shat'* stop (prevent)
мешок ⑩ mi·*shok* bag
мёртвый *myort*·vih dead
милиционер ⑩ mi·lit·sih·an·*yer*
police officer
милиция ① mi·*lit*·sih·ya police
милый *mi*·lih nice
мир ⑩ mir peace • world
миска ① *mis*·ka bowl
мнение ⑩ *mnye*·ni·ye opinion
много *mno*·ga (a) lot • many
мобильный телефон ⑩ ma·*bil'*·nih
ti·li·*fon* cell phone • mobile phone
может быть *mo*·zhiht biht maybe
можно *mozh*·na can (have
permission)
мой moy my
мокрый a *mo*·krih wet

H

молния ① *mol*·ni·ya zip • zipper
молодой ma·la·*doy* young
молочница ① ma·*loch*·nit·sa thrush (health)
монеты ① pl man·*ye*·tih coins
море ⑩ *mor*·ye sea
мороз ⑩ ma·*ros* frost
морская болезнь ① mar·*ska*·ya bal·*yezn* seasickness • travel sickness
мост ⑩ most bridge
моторная лодка ① ma·*tor*·na·ya *lot*·ka motorboat
мочевая инфекция ① ma·chi·*va*·ya inf·*yekt*·sih·ya urinary infection
мочевой пузырь ⑩ ma·chi·*voy* pu·*zihr* bladder
мочь moch' can (be able)
мошенник ⑩ ma·*she*·nik cheat
муж ⑩ mush husband
мужчина ⑩ mush·*chi*·na man
мусор ⑩ *mu*·sar garbage • rubbish • trash
мы mih we
мыло ⑩ *mih*·la soap
мясник ⑩ mis·*nik* butcher
мяч ⑩ myach ball (sport)

Н

на na on
— борту bar·*tu* aboard
— неполной ставке ni·*pol*·ney *staf*·kye part-time
— полной ставке *pol*·ney *staf*·kye full-time
— себя sib·*ya* self-employed
наводнение ⑩ na·vad·*nye*·ni·ye flood
над nat above
наличные ① pl na·*lich*·nih·ye cash
налог ⑩ na·*lok* tax
— на вылет ⑩ na *vih*·lit airport tax
— на продажу ⑩ na pra·*da*·zhu sales tax
напиток ⑩ na·*pi*·tak drink
наполнять na·paln·*yat*' fill

направление ⑩ na·prav·*lye*·ni·ye direction
насиловать na·si·la·vat' rape
наслаждаться nas·lazh·*dat*'·sa enjoy (oneself)
настоящее ⑩ na·sta·ya·shi·ye present (time)
находить na·kha·*dit*' find
начало ① na·*cha*·la start
начинать na·chi·*nat*' start
наш nash our
— замужем ① *za*·mu·zhim single
невеста ① niv·*ye*·sta fiancée
невиновный nye·vi·*nov*·nih innocent
неделя ① nid·*yel*·ya week
невозможно ni·vaz·*mozh*·na impossible
недавно ni·*dav*·na recently
незнакомец ⑩ nyez·na·*ko*·mits stranger
незнакомка ① nyez·na·*kom*·ka stranger
некурящий ni·kur·*ya*·shi nonsmoking
немецкий ⑩ nim·*yet*·ski German (language)
немного nim·*no*·ga little (not much)
необычный nye·a·*bihch*·nih unusual
неправильный nye·*pra*·vil'·nih wrong
непромокаемый nye·pra·ma·*ka*·i·mih waterproof
несколько *nye*·skal'·ka several • some
нести ni·*sti* carry
нет nyet no
низкий *nis*·ki low
никаких ni·ka·*kikh* none
никогда ni·*kag*·da never
ничего ni·chi·*vo* nothing
но no but
Новогодняя ночь ① na·va·*god*·ni·ya noch' New Year's Eve
новости ① pl *no*·va·sti news
новый *no*·vih new

Новый год ⓜ *no*·vih got New Year's Day

нога ⓕ na·*ga* foot • leg

нож ⓜ nosh knife

номер ⓜ *no*·mir hotel room • number

— комнаты ⓜ *kom*·na·tih room number

— на двоих ⓜ na dva·*ikh* double room

номерной знак ⓜ na·mir·*noy* znak license plate number

норма багажа ⓕ *nor*·ma ba·*ga*·zha baggage allowance

носить na·*sit'* wear

носки ⓜ pl na·*ski* socks

ночь ⓕ noch' night

нуждаться в nuzh·*dat'*·sa v need

нужный *nuzh*·nih necessary

О

оба/обе ⓜ/ⓕ *o*·ba/*ob*·ye both

обед ⓜ ab·*yet* lunch

обедня ⓕ ab·*yed*·nya mass (Catholic)

обеспокоенный a·bis·pa·*ko*·i·nih worried

обещать a·bi·*shat'* promise

обмен ⓜ ab·*myen* exchange

— валюты ⓜ val·*yu*·tih currency exchange

обменивать ab·*mye*·ni·vat' cash a cheque • change money

обменный курс ⓜ ab·*mye*·nih kurs exchange rate

обнимать ab·ni·*mat'* hug

обогремаевый a·ba·gri·*ma*·i·vih heated

оборудование ⓝ a·ba·*ru*·da·va·ni·ye equipment

образование ⓝ a·bra·za·*va*·ni·ye education

обратный a·*brat*·nih return (ticket)

обручение ⓝ ab·ru·*che*·ni·ye engagement

обручённый ab·ru·*cho*·nih engaged (person)

общественный туалет ⓜ ap·*shest*·vi·nih tu·al·*yet* public toilet

обычай ⓜ a·*bih*·chey custom

обычная почта ⓕ a·*bihch*·na·ya *poch*·ta surface mail

огонь ⓜ a·*gon'* fire (heat)

ограничение скорости ⓕ a·gra·ni·*che*·ni·ye sko·*ras*·ti speed limit

одежда ⓕ ad·*yezh*·da clothing

одеяло ⓝ a·di·*ya*·la blanket

один раз a·*din* ras once

один/одна ⓜ/ⓕ a·*din*/ad·*na* alone • one

одноместный номер ⓜ ad·na·*mes*·nih *no*·mir single room

озеро ⓝ *o*·zi·ra lake

океан ⓜ a·ki·*an* ocean

окно ⓝ ak·*no* window

около o·ka·la about

окружающая среда ⓕ a·kru·*zha*·yu·sha·ya sri·*da* environment

он on he

она a·*na* she

они a·*ni* they

оно a·*no* it

опаздывать к a·*paz*·dih·vat' k miss (train)

опасный a·*pas*·nih dangerous • unsafe

оплата ⓕ a·*pla*·ta payment

опухоль ⓕ *o*·pu·khal swelling • tumour

опыт ⓜ *o*·piht experience

осень ⓕ *o*·sin' autumn • fall

особенный a·*so*·bi·nih special

оставаться a·sta·*vat'*·sa stay (in one place)

оставленный багаж ⓜ a·*stav*·li·nih ba·*gash* left luggage

останавливаться a·sta·*nav*·li·vat'·sa stay (at a hotel) • stop (be still)

остановка ⓕ a·sta·*nof*·ka stop (bus/tram)

остров ⓜ *ost*·raf island

П

от ot from
ответ ⓜ at·*vyet* answer
отдельный a ad·*yel*'·nih separate
отдыхать ᴠ a·dih·*khat*' rest
отец ⓜ at·*yets* father
открывать ᴠ at·krih·*vat*' open
открытый a at·*krih*·tih open
отлив ⓜ at·*lif* tide (low)
отличный at·*lich*·nih excellent •
fantastic
отменять at·*min*·*yat*' cancel
отопление ⓝ a·tap·*lye*·ni·ye heating
отправляться at·prav·*lyat*'·sa depart
отпуск ⓜ *ot*·pusk holidays
отъезд ⓜ at·*yest* departure
официант ⓜ a·fit·sih·*ant* waiter
официантка ⓕ a·fit·sih·*ant*·ka
waitress
очень *o*·chin' very
очередь ⓕ *o*·chi·rit' queue
очищенный a·*chi*·shi·nih unleaded
очки ⓝ pl ach·*ki* glasses • goggles
— от солнца at *solnt*·sa sunglasses
ошибка ⓕ a·*shihp*·ka mistake
ошибочный a·*shih*·bach·nih faulty

П

падать *pa*·dat' fall (down)
подруга ⓕ pa·*dru*·ga friend
палатка ⓕ pa·*lat*·ka tent
палец ⓜ *pa*·lits finger • toe
пальто ⓝ pal'·*to* coat • overcoat
пансионат ⓜ pan·si·a·*nat* boarding
house
пара ⓕ *pa*·ra pair (couple)
парикмахер ⓜ pa·rik·*ma*·khir
barber • hairdresser
паром pa·*rom* ferry
партия ⓕ *par*·ti·ya party (politics)
пассажирский класс ⓜ
pa·sa·*zhihr*·ski klas economy class
Пасха ⓕ *pas*·kha Easter
пачка ⓕ *pach*·ka packet (general)
перевес ⓜ pi·riv·*yes* excess
(baggage)
переводить pi·ri·va·*dit*' translate

переводчик ⓜ pi·ri·*vot*·chik
interpreter
перед *pye*·rit in front of
перерабатывать pi·ri·ra·*ba*·tih·vat'
recycle
переставать pi·ri·sta·*vat*' stop
(cease)
перочинный нож ⓜ pi·ra·*chi*·nih
nosh penknife
перчатки ⓕ pl pir·*chat*·ki gloves
песня ⓕ *pyes*·nya song
петь pyet' sing
печень ⓕ *pye*·chin' liver
печь ⓕ pyech' stove
пешеход ⓜ pi·shih·*khot*
pedestrian
пивная ⓕ piv·*na*·ya pub • tavern
пиво ⓝ *pi*·va beer
писатель ⓜ pi·*sa*·til' writer
писательница ⓕ pi·*sa*·til'·nit·sa
writer
писать pi·*sat*' write
письмо ⓝ pis'·*mo* letter (mail)
пить pit' drink
плавать *pla*·vat' swim
плата ⓕ *pla*·ta fare
— за куверт ⓕ za kuv·*yert* cover
charge
— за обслуживание ⓝ za
aps·*lu*·zhih·va·ni·ye service charge
платить pla·*tit*' pay
платье ⓝ *plat*·ye dress
плащ ⓜ plash raincoat
плёнка ⓕ *plyon*·ka film (for camera)
плечо ⓝ pli·*cho* shoulder
плохой pla·*khoy* bad
площадь ⓕ *plo*·shat' town square
пляж ⓜ plyash beach
поворачивать pa·va·ra·chi·*vat*' turn
погода ⓕ pa·*go*·da weather
под pot below
под уклон pad u·*klon* downhill
подарок ⓜ pa·*da*·rak gift • present
подгузник ⓜ pad·*guz*·nik diaper •
nappy
подниматься pad·ni·*mat*'·sa climb ᴠ

261

П

подписывать pat·*pi*·sih·vat' sign (forms)

подпись ① *pot*·pis' signature

подробности ① pl pa·*drob*·na·sti details

подруга ① pa·*dru*·ga girlfriend

подтверждать pat·virzh·*dat*' confirm (booking)

подушка ① pa·*dush*·ka pillow

поезд ⑩ *po*·ist train

поездка ① pa·*yest*·ka ride • trip

пожар ⑩ pa·*zhar* fire (emergency)

поже *po*·zhih later

позавчера pa·zaf·chi·*ra* day before yesterday

поздний *poz*·ni late

показывать pa·*ka*·zih·vat' show

поклоняться pak·lan·*yat*'·sa worship

покупать pa·ku·*pat*' buy

полдень ⑩ *pol*·din' midday • noon

полезный pal·*yez*·nih useful

полёт ⑩ pal·*yot* flight

полицейский участок ⑩ pa·lit·*sey*·ski u·*cha*·stak police station

полка ① *pol*·ka berth (train) • shelf

полночь ① *pol*·noch' midnight

полный *pol*·nih full

половина ① pa·la·*vi*·na half

полотенце ⑩ pa·lat·*yent*·se towel

получать pa·lu·*chat*' get

помещение ⑩ pa·mi·*she*·ni·ye accommodation

помогать pa·ma·*gat*' help

помощь ① *po*·mash' help

понедельник ⑩ pa·nid·*yel*'·nik Monday

понимать pa·ni·*mat*' understand

понос ⑩ pa·*nos* diarrhoea

портфель ⑩ part·*fyel*' briefcase

посадочный талон ⑩ pa·*sa*·dach·nih ta·*lon* boarding pass

посещать pa·si·*shat*' visit

после *pos*·lye after

послезавтра pas·li·*zaf*·tra day after tomorrow

посол ⑩ pa·*sol* ambassador

посольство ⑩ pa·*solst*·va embassy

постельное бельё ⑩ past·*yel*'·na·ye bil'·*yo* bedding

посылать pa·sih·*lat*' send

посылка ① pa·*sihl*·ka package • parcel

поток ⑩ pa·*tok* stream

потому что pa·ta·*mu* shta because

поход ⑩ pa·*khot* hiking

похожий pa·*kho*·zhih similar

похороны ⑩ pl po·kha·ra·nih funeral

поцелуй ⑩ pat·sih·*luy* kiss

почему pa·chi·*mu* why

почка ① *poch*·ka kidney

почта ① *poch*·ta mail • post office

почти pach·*ti* almost

почтовые расходы ⑩ pl pach·*to*·vih·ye ras·*kho*·dih postage

почтовый индекс ⑩ pach·*to*·vih *in*·diks post code

почтовый ящик ⑩ pach·*to*·vih *ya*·shik mailbox

правило ⑩ *pra*·vi·la rule

правильный *pra*·vil'·nih right (correct)

правительство ⑩ pra·*vi*·til'·stva government

православная церковь ① pra·vas·*lav*·na·ya *tser*·kaf' Orthodox Church

православный pra·vas·*lav*·nih Orthodox

правый *pra*·vih right (direction) • right-wing

праздник ⑩ *praz*·nik celebration • holiday

прачечная ① *pra*·chich·na·ya laundry

предпочитать prit·pa·chi·*tat*' prefer

предупреждать pri·du·prizh·*dat*' warn

презерватив ⑩ pri·zir·va·*tif* condom

прекрасный pri·*kras*·nih perfect • wonderful

RUSSIAN *to* ENGLISH

P

прибытие ⓝ pri·*bih*·ti·ye arrivals

приветствовать priv·*yetst*·va·vat' welcome

прививка ⓕ pri·*vif*·ka vaccination

приглашать pri·gla·*shat'* invite

пригород ⓜ *pri*·ga·rat suburb

приготавливать pri·ga·*tav*·li·vat' prepare

приезжать pri·i·*zhat'* arrive

прилив ⓜ pri·*lif* high tide

примерочная ⓕ prim·ye·*rach*·na·ya changing room

приносить pri·na·*sit'* bring

природа ⓕ pri·*ro*·da nature

присматривать pris·*mat*·ri·vat' look for

присмотр за детьми ⓜ pris·*motr* za dit'·mi childminding

приходить pri·kha·*dit'* come

приходящая няня ⓕ pri·khad·*ya*·sha·yan yan·ya babysitter

причина ⓕ pri·*chi*·na reason

пробовать pro·ba·vat' try (taste)

проверять pra·vir·*yat'* check

проводник ⓜ pra·vad·*nik* carriage attendant

продавать pra·da·*vat'* sell

продление ⓝ prad·*lye*·ni·ye extension

продовольствие ⓝ pra·da·*volst*·vi·ye food supplies

прозвище ⓝ *proz*·vi·she nickname

прокат автомобилей ⓜ pra·*kat* af·ta·ma·*bil*'·yey car hire

промышленность ⓕ pra·*mihsh*·li·nast' industry

пропавший pra·*paf*·shih lost

просить pra·*sit'* ask (for something)

проспект ⓜ prasp·*yekt* avenue

простой pra·*stoy* simple

простуда ⓕ pra·*stu*·da cold

простужаться pra·stu·*zhat'*·sa have a cold

простыня ⓕ pra·*stihn*·ya sheet (bed)

противозачаточная таблетка ⓕ pra·ti·va·za·*cha*·tach·na·ya tab·*lyet*·ka the Pill

противозачаточные средства ⓝ pl pra·ti·va·za·cha·tach·nih·ye *sryetst*·va contraceptives

профессия ⓕ praf·*ye*·si·ya trade (job)

профсоюз ⓜ praf·sa·*yus* trade union

проход ⓜ pra·*khot* aisle (on transport)

проходить pra·kha·*dit'* pass

прошлое ⓝ *prosh*·la·ye past

прошлый *prosh*·lih last (previous)

прямой pri·*moy* direct • straight

прямым набором номера pri·*mihm* na·*bo*·ram *no*·mi·ra direct-dial (by)

публичный сад ⓜ pub·*lich*·nih sat public gardens

пустой pu·*stoy* empty

пустыня ⓕ pu·*stihn*·ya desert

путеводитель ⓜ pu·ti·va·*di*·til' entertainment guide • guidebook

путешествие ⓝ pu·ti·*shest*·vi·ye journey

путешествовать pu·ti·*shest*·va·vat' travel

— автостопом af·ta·*sto*·pam hitchhike

путь ⓜ put' route • way

пьяный *pya*·nih drunk

пятница ⓕ *pyat*·nit·sa Friday

Р

работа ⓕ ra·*bo*·ta job • work

работать ra·*bo*·tat' work

работодатель ⓜ ra·bo·ta·*dat*·yel' employer

рабочая ⓕ ra·*bo*·cha·ya manual worker

рабочий ⓜ ra·*bo*·chi manual worker

разведённый raz·vid·*yo*·nih divorced

разговаривать raz·ga·va·ri·vat' talk

разговорник ⓜ raz·ga·*vor*·nik phrasebook

размер ⓜ raz·*myer* size (general)

разность времени ① *raz·nast' vrye·mi·ni* time difference
разрешение ⑩ *raz·ri·she·ni·ye* permission • permit
— на работу ⑩ *na ra·bo·tu* work permit
рак ⑩ *rak* cancer
ранний *ra·ni* early
расписание ⑩ *ras·pi·sa·ni·ye* timetable
располагаться *ras·pa·la·gat'·sa* camp
распродажа ① *ras·pra·da·zha* sale
распроданы *ras·pro·da·nih* booked out
рассвет ⑩ *ras·vyet* dawn
рассказ ⑩ *ras·kas* story
расслабляться *ras·lab·lyat'·sa* relax
растение ⑩ *rast·ye·ni·ye* plant
расти *ra·sti* grow
растяжение связок ⑩ *rast·ya·zhe·ni·ye svya·zak* sprain
расчёска ① *ras·chos·ka* comb
ребёнок ⑩ *rib·yo·nak* baby • child
ребро ⑩ *ri·bro* rib
ревнивый *riv·ni·vih* jealous
резать *rye·zat'* cut
река ① *ri·ka* river
ремень ⑩ *rim·yen'* seatbelt
ремёсла ⑩ pl *rim·yos·la* crafts
ремесленник ⑩ *rim·yes·li·nik* tradesperson
рецензия ① *rit·sen·zi·ya* review
рецепт ⑩ *rit·sept* prescription
решать *ri·shat'* decide
ритмизатор сердца ⑩ *rit·mi·za·tar syert·sa* pacemaker
родители ⑩ pl *ra·di·ti·li* parents
Рождество ⑩ *razh·dist·vo* Christmas (Day)
розовый *ro·za·vih* pink
роскошь ① *ros·kash'* luxury
рот ⑩ *rot* mouth
рубашка ① *ru·bash·ka* shirt
ружьё ⑩ *ruzh·yo* gun
рука ① *ru·ka* arm • hand

руководитель ⑩ *ru·ka·va·dit'·yel'* leader
ручка ① *ruch·ka* pen
рыболовство ⑩ *rih·ba·lofst·va* fishing
рынок ⑩ *rih·nak* market
ряд ⑩ *ryat* row (theatre)
рядом с *rya·dam s* beside • next to

С

с s since • with
сад ⑩ *sat* garden
садиться *sa·dit'·sa* board (plane/ship)
садовод ⑩ *sa·da·vot* gardener
салфетка ① *salf·yet·ka* napkin • serviette
салфетки ⑩ pl *salf·yet·ki* tissues
самолёт ⑩ *sa·mal·yot* plane
санитарная сумка ① *sa·ni·tar·na·ya sum·ka* first-aid kit
санный спорт ⑩ *sa·nih sport* tobogganing
сапоги ⑩ pl *sa·pa·gi* boots
свадьба ① *svad'·ba* wedding
свежемороженый *svi·zhi·ma·ro·zhih·nih* frozen
свежий *svye·zhih* fresh
свёкор ⑩ *svyo·kar* father-in-law (wife's father)
свекровь ① *svi·krof'* mother-in-law (husband's mother)
свет ⑩ *svyet* light
светлый *svyet·lih* light (colour)
светофор ⑩ *svi·ta·for* traffic light
свидетельство ⑩ *svid·ye·tilst·va* certificate
— о владении автомобилем ⑩ *a vlad·ye·ni af·ta·ma·bil·yem* car owner's title
— о рождении ⑩ *a razh·dye·ni* birth certificate
свинка ① *svin·ka* mumps
свободный *sva·bod·nih* available • not bound
связи ① *svya·zi* connection (transport)

C

связь ⓕ svyas' relationship
святой ⓜ svi·*toy* saint
священник ⓜ svya·*she*·nik priest
север ⓜ *sye*·vir north
сегодня si·*vod*·nya today
— **вечером** *vye*·chi·ram tonight
сейчас si·*chas* now
сельское хозяйство ⓝ *syel*'·ska·ye khaz·*yeyst*·va agriculture
семейное положение ⓝ sim·*yey*·na·ye pa·la·*zhe*·ni·ye marital status
семья ⓕ sim·*ya* family
сердечный приступ ⓜ sird·*yech*·nih *pri*·stup cardiac arrest • heart attack
сердитый sir·*di*·tih angry
сердце ⓝ *syerd*·tsih heart
серп и молот ⓜ syerp i *mo*·lat hammer and sickle
серый *sye*·rih grey
сеть ⓕ syet' net
сидеть sid·*yet*' sit
сильный *sil*'·nih strong
синий *si*·ni dark blue
сказать ska·*zat*' tell
скидка ⓕ *skit*·ka discount
сколько *skol*'·ka how much
скорая помощь ⓕ *sko*·ra·ya *po*·mash ambulance
скоро *sko*·ra soon
скорость ⓕ *sko*·rast' speed (velocity)
— **протяжки плёнки** ⓕ prat·*yash*·ki *plyon*·ki film speed
слабительное ⓝ sla·*bi*·til'·na·ye laxative
слабый *sla*·bih loose • weak
сладкий *slat*·ki sweet
следовать *slye*·da·vat' follow
слепой sli·*poy* blind
слишком *slish*·kam too (excess)
словарь ⓜ sla·*var*' dictionary
слово ⓝ *slo*·va word
сломанный *slo*·ma·nih broken (down)

служащая/служащий ⓜ/ⓕ *slu*·zha·shi/*slu*·zha·sha·ya (office) employee
слушать *slu*·shat' listen
слышать *slih*·shat' hear
смазка ⓕ *smas*·ka lubricant
смешной smish·*noy* funny
смеяться smi·*yat*'·sa laugh
смотреть smat·*ryet*' look (after) • watch
смущённый smu·*sho*·nih embarrassed
снег ⓜ snyek snow
снимать sni·*mat*' take a photo
снимок ⓜ *sni*·mak photo
собор ⓜ sa·*bor* cathedral
собрание ⓝ sa·*bra*·ni·ye meeting
совет ⓜ sav·*yet* advice
Советский Союз ⓜ sav·*yet*·ski sa·*yus* Soviet Union
современный sa·*vrim*·ye·nih modern
соглашаться sa·gla·*shat*'·sa agree
солнце ⓝ *solnt*·se sun
сон ⓜ son dream
соска ⓕ *sos*·ka dummy • pacifier
сотрясение мозга ⓝ sat·ris·*ye*·ni·ye *moz*·ga concussion
Сочельник ⓜ sa·*chel*'·nik Christmas Eve
спальное место ⓝ *spal*'·na·ye *mye*·sta sleeping berth
спальный вагон ⓜ *spal*'·nih va·*gon* sleeping car
спальный мешок ⓜ *spal*'·nih mi·*shok* sleeping bag
спасательный жилет ⓜ spa·sa·*til*'·nih zhil·*yet* life jacket
спать spat' sleep
СПИД ⓜ spit AIDS
спина ⓕ spi·*na* back (body)
спиртной напиток ⓜ spirt·*noy* na·*pi*·tak drink (alcoholic)
спички ⓕ pl *spich*·ki matches
спорить *spo*·rit' argue
спортзал ⓜ spart·*zal* gym (place)

спрашивать *spra·shih·vat'* ask (a question)

среда ① *sri·da* Wednesday

средняя школа ① *sryed·ni·ya shko·la* high school

срочный *sroch·nih* urgent

ставить *sta·vit'* put

— машину *ma·shih·nu* park a car

стараться *sta·rat'·sa* try (attempt)

старый *sta·rih* old

стена ① *sti·na* wall

стирать *sti·rat'* wash (something)

стоимость ① *sto·i·mast'* value

стоить v *sto·it'* cost

стол ⓜ *stol* table

столовая ① *sta·lo·va·ya* canteen

страна ① *stra·na* country

страница ① *stra·nit·sa* page

страхование ⓝ *stra·kha·va·ni·ye* insurance

стрелять *stril·yat'* shoot

строить *stro·it'* build

суббота ① *su·bo·ta* Saturday

суд ⓜ *sut* court (legal)

судья ⓜ *sud·ya* judge

суеверие ⓝ *su·iv·ye·ri·ye* superstition

сумочка ① *su·mach·ka* handbag

сушить *su·shiht'* dry (general)

сходить *skha·dit'* get off (a train, etc)

сцепление ⓝ *stsep·lye·ni·ye* clutch (car)

счастливый *shis·li·vih* happy • lucky

счастье ⓝ *shast·ye* luck

счёт ⓜ *shot* bank account • bill • check

считать *shi·tat'* count

США ⓜ pl *es·sha·a* USA

сын ⓜ *sihn* son

Т

там *tam* there

таможенная декларация ① *ta·mo·zhih·na·ya di·kla·rat·sih·ya* customs declaration

таможня ① *ta·mozh·nya* customs

танцевать *tant·sih·vat'* dance

танцы ⓜ pl *tant·sih* dancing

тарелка ① *tar·yel·ka* plate

твёрдый *tvyor·dih* hard (not soft)

твой *tvoy* your sg inf

телефон-автомат ⓜ *ti·li·fon·af·ta·mat* pay phone

телефонная будка ① *ti·li·fo·na·ya but·ka* phone box

тело ⓝ *tye·la* body

тёмный *tyom·nih* dark

тень ① *tyen'* shade • shadow

тёплый *tyop·lih* warm

терять *tir·yat'* lose

тест на беременность ⓜ *tyest na bir·ye·mi·nast'* pregnancy test kit

тесть ⓜ *tyest'* father-in-law (husband's father)

тётя ① *tyot·ya* aunt

техникум ⓜ *tyekh·ni·kum* college

тёща ① *tyo·sha* mother-in-law (wife's mother)

тихий *ti·khi* quiet

ткань ① *tkan'* fabric

то *to* that (one)

тоже *to·zhih* also • too

ток ⓜ *tok* current (electricity)

толстый *tol·stih* fat • thick

только *tol'·ka* only

тому назад *ta·mu na·zat* ago

тонкий *ton·ki* thin

торговля ① *tar·gov·lya* trade (commerce)

торговый центр ⓜ *tar·go·vih tsentr* shopping centre

тормоза ⓜ pl *tar·ma·za* brakes

тосковать по *ta·ska·vat'* pa miss (person)

тост ⓜ *tost* toast (to health)

тот же самый *tod zhe sa·mih* same

точно *toch·na* exactly

тошнота ① *tash·na·ta* nausea

трава ① *tra·va* grass • herb

травма ① *trav·ma* injury

травяной *trav·ya·noy* herbal

трогать *tro·gat'* feel • touch

T

у

тропинка ① tra·*pin*·ka path • trail
тротуар ⑩ tra·tu·*ar* footpath
трудный *trud*·nih difficult
тряпочка для мытья ①
trya·*pach*·ka dlya miht·*ya* wash cloth
туалетная бумага ① tu·al·*yet*·na·ya
bu·*ma*·ga toilet paper
турбаза ① tur·*ba*·za tourbase •
youth hostel
турецкий tu·*rets*·ki Turkish
туфли pl *tuf*·li shoes
ты tih you sg inf
тюрьма ① tyur'·*ma* jail • prison
тяжёлый tya·*zho*·lih heavy

У

у ... есть u ... yest' have
убийство ⑩ u·*bist*·va murder
уборка ① u·*bor*·ka cleaning
увлажняющий крем ⑩
uv·lazh·*nya*·yu·shi kryem moisturiser
угол ⑩ u·gal corner
удар ⑩ u·*dar* stroke (health)
удобный u·*dob*·nih comfortable
ужасный u·*zhas*·nih awful • terrible
уже u·*zhe* already
ужин ⑩ u·*zhihn* dinner
указывать u·*ka*·zih·vat' point
укус ⑩ u·*kus* bite (dog/insect)
улица ① u·*lit*·sa street
уличный рынок ⑩ u·*lich*·nih
rih·nak street market
улыбаться u·lih·*bat*'·sa smile
ультразвук ⑩ ul'·traz·*vuk* ultrasound
умереть u·mir·*yet*' die
умываться u·mih·*vat*'·sa wash
(oneself)
универмаг ⑩ u·ni·vir·*mak*
department store
универсам ⑩ u·ni·vir·*sam*
supermarket
услуга ① us·*lu*·ga service
устал u·*stal* tired
установление личности ⑩
u·sta·nav·*lye*·ni·ye *lich*·na·sti
identification

утверждать ut·virzh·*dat*' validate
утро ⑩ u·tra morning
ухаживать за u·*kha*·zhih·vat' za
care for
ухо ⑩ u·kha ear
учитель ⑩ u·*chi*·til' teacher
учительница ① u·*chi*·til'·nit·sa
teacher
учить u·*chit*' learn

Ф

фабрика ① *fa*·bri·ka factory
фамилия ① fa·*mi*·li·ya surname
фары pl *fa*·rih headlights
фонарик ⑩ fa·*na*·rik flashlight • torch
фунт ⑩ funt pound (money/weight)
фургон ⑩ fur·*gon* van
футболка ① fud·*bol*·ka T-shirt

Х

хвост ⑩ khvost tail
хлопок ⑩ *khlo*·pak cotton
ходить пешком kha·*dit*' pish·*kom*
hike
ходить по магазинам kha·*dit*' pa
ma·ga·*zi*·nam go shopping • shop
хозяин ⑩ khaz·*ya*·in landlord
хозяйка ① khaz·*yey*·ka landlady
холм ⑩ kholm hill
холодильник ⑩ kha·la·*dil*'·nik
refrigerator
холодный kha·*lod*·nih cold
холост ⑩ *kho*·last single (man)
хорошенький kha·ro·*shihn*'·ki pretty
хороший kha·ro·*shih* fine • good
хотеть khat·*yet*' want
хочется пить *kho*·chit·sa pit' thirsty
хрупкий *khrup*·ki fragile
художник ⑩ khu·*dozh*·nik artist
художница ① khu·*dozh*·nit·sa artist

Ц

цвет ⑩ tsvyet colour
цветок ⑩ tsvi·*tok* flower
целовать tsih·la·*vat*' kiss

цена ① tse·*na* price
ценный *tse*·nih valuable
центр города ⓜ tsentr go·ra·da city centre
церковь ① *tser*·kaf' church

Ч

чаевые ① pl cha·i·*vih*·ye tip (gratuity)
час ⓜ chas hour
частный *chas*·nih private
часто *cha*·sta often
часы ① pl chi·*sih* clock • watch
часы работы ⓜ pl chi·*sih* ra·bo·tih opening hours
чашка ① *chash*·ka cup
чек ⓜ chek check • cheque
человек ⓜ chi·lav·*yek* person
челюсть ① *chel*·yust' jaw
чемодан ⓜ chi·ma·*dan* suitcase
через *che*·ris across
череп ⓜ *che*·rip skull
чёрно-белый chor·nab·ye·*lih* B&W (film)
Чёрное море ⓝ chor·na·ye *mor*·ye Black Sea
чёрный *chor*·nih black
— рынок ⓜ *rih*·nak black market
четверг ⓜ chit·*vyerk* Thursday
четверть ① *chet*·virt' quarter
чинить chi·*nit'* repair
число ⓝ chis·*lo* date (day)
чистить a chi·*stit'* clean
чистый *chi*·stih clean • pure
читать chi·*tat'* read
чтение ⓝ *chtye*·ni·ye reading
что shto what
что-то *shto*·ta something
чувства ⓝ pl *chust*·va feelings

Ш

шапка ① *shap*·ka hat
шахматы ⓜ pl *shakh*·ma·tih (chess) set

Швейцария ① shveyt·*sa*·ri·ya Switzerland
Швеция ① *shvyet*·sih·ya Sweden
шерсть ① sherst' wool
шея ① *she*·ya neck
шина ① *shih*·na tire • tyre
широкий shih·*ro*·ki wide
шить shiht' sew
шкаф ⓜ shkaf cupboard • wardrobe
школа ① *shko*·la school
шоссе ⓝ sha·*se* highway • motorway
шприц ⓜ shprits needle • syringe
штраф ⓜ shtraf fine (penalty)
шумный *shum*·nih noisy

Э

этаж ⓜ e·*tash* floor (storey)
это *e*·ta this (one)

Ю

юбка ① *yup*·ka skirt
юг ⓜ yuk south
юриспруденция ① yu·ris·prud·*yent*·sih·ya law (study, profession)

Я

я ya I
ядовитый ya·da·*vi*·tih poisonous
язык ⓜ yi·*zihk* language
яичник ⓜ yi·*ich*·nik ovary
яичниковая киста ① yi·*ich*·ni·ko·va·ya kis·*ta* ovarian cyst
янтарь ⓜ yin·*tar'* amber
ясли ⓜ pl *yas*·li crèche

Index

For topics that are covered in several sections of this book, we've indicated the most relevant page number in bold.

10 Ways to Start a Sentence

When's (the next bus)?	Когда (будет следующий автобус)?	kag·*da* (*bu*·dit *slye*·du·yu·shi af·*to*·bus)
Where's (the station)?	Где (станция)?	gdye (*stan*·tsih·ya)
I'm looking for (a hotel).	Я ищу (гостиницу).	ya ish·*yu* (ga·*sti*·ni·tsu)
Do you have (a map)?	Здесь есть (карте)?	zdyes' yest' (*kart*·ye)
I'd like (the menu).	Я бы хотел/ хотела (меню). **m/f**	ya bih khat·*yel*/ khat·*ye*·la (min·*yu*)
I'd like to (hire a car).	Я бы хотел/ хотела (взять машину). **m/f**	ya bih khat·*yel*/ khat·*ye*·la (vzyat' ma·*shih*·nu)
Can I (come in)?	Можно (войти)?	*mozh*·na (vey·*ti*)
Please (write it down).	(Запишите), пожалуйста.	(za·pi·*shiht*·ye) pa·*zhal*·sta
Do I need (a visa)?	Нужна ли (виза)?	*nuzh*·na li (*vi*·za)
I need (assistance).	Мне нужна (помощь).	mnye *nuzh*·na (*po*·mash)